Hobbes, Locke, and Confusion's Masterpiece

In *Hobbes, Locke, and Confusion's Masterpiece*, an important new study of the foundations of modern political theory, Ross Harrison, the eminent political philosopher, analyzes the work of Hobbes, Locke, and their contemporaries. He provides a detailed account of the turbulent historical background that shaped the political, intellectual, and religious content of political theory as it evolved in seventeenth-century England.

Harrison explores such questions as the limits of political authority and the relationship between the legitimacy of government and the will of the people in a non-technical style that will appeal to professionals and students in philosophy, politics, theology, and history.

Ross Harrison is Reader in Philosophy at the University of Cambridge.

Hobbes, Locke, and Confusion's Masterpiece

An Examination of Seventeenth-Century Political Philosophy

ROSS HARRISON

University of Cambridge

CAMBRIDGE UNIVERSITY PRESS

CAMBRIDGE UNIVERSITY PRESS
Cambridge, New York, Melbourne, Madrid, Cape Town, Singapore,
São Paulo, Delhi, Dubai, Tokyo

Cambridge University Press
The Edinburgh Building, Cambridge CB2 8RU, UK

Published in the United States of America by Cambridge University Press, New York

www.cambridge.org
Information on this title: www.cambridge.org/9780521017190

First published 2003

A catalogue record for this publication is available from the British Library

Library of Congress Cataloguing in Publication data
Harrison, Ross.
Hobbes, Locke, and confusion's masterpiece / T.R. Harrison.
p.   cm.
Includes bibliographical references and index.
ISBN 0-521-81700-5 (hardback) – ISBN 0-521-01719-X (pbk.)
1. Hobbes, Thomas, 1588–1679 – Contributions in political science.
2. Locke, John, 1632–1704 – Contributions in political science.
3. Political science – History – 17th century.   I. Title.
JC153.H66 H37   2002
320′.01–dc21   2002022279

ISBN 978-0-521-81700-4 Hardback
ISBN 978-0-521-01719-0 Paperback

Transferred to digital printing 2010

Contents

Introduction

In this work, I explore some of the greatest and most important political philosophy ever written. I discuss masterpieces, but, as I shall show, these masterpieces appeared against a background of confusion. They were written in the seventeenth century, a conflicted, contested, multiply confused period. So, no doubt, were other centuries. However, in this case, the confusion brought forth masterpieces, and it is these masterpieces, in particular the great works of Hobbes and Locke, that I chiefly consider.

I take my title, *Confusion's Masterpiece*, from Shakespeare's *Macbeth*, a work that was written near the start of the century being examined. In Shakespeare's play, just after discovery of the murdered King Duncan, comes the following speech:

Confusion now have made his masterpiece!
Most sacrilegious murder have broke ope
The Lord's anointed temple, and stole thence
The life o' the building!

The speaker is Macduff, the good man in the play, and foil to its eponymous, villainous hero. Eventually he restores the moral order by killing the villain, the king's murderer. For Macduff, as he shows here by his speech, the murder of a king destroys the established and understood order embodied in the king. Hence for Macduff (and hence also for well-thinking, proper opinion), murder of a king is the ultimate damaging act against order. It is, as he puts it, the masterpiece of confusion.

At this time in history, such order was generally taken to be established by God. So the king is here said by Macduff to be 'the Lord's anointed temple'. Therefore the villainous act is not just a fundamental breach of order in the political sphere, but also in the moral and religious sphere. It is sacrilege, defiling the temple of the Lord God. It is, as Macduff says, 'sacrilegious murder'.

Shakespeare was a member of the King's Players, the king's own theatre company. The king for whom Shakespeare was writing the play, King James (VI of Scotland, I of England), was associated with the doctrine that kings ruled by divine right. As King James frequently pointed out, God himself called kings gods. Speaking to his parliament (in 1610, four years after *Macbeth* was first performed), James told them that 'the state of monarchy is the supremest thing upon earth'. So they knew where they stood. He added that 'Kings are justly called Gods, for that they exercise a manner or resemblance of divine power upon earth'. They had heard that before. Even before James came to England, he had written a book, *The True Law of Free Monarchies* (1598). In it, he had already warmed to his favourite theme, writing that 'Kings are called Gods by the prophetical King David'. So that was how God told him. He spoke, in the Bible, through the mouth of the great King David. David calls kings 'the Lord's anointed', and even the great King David knows that he must not kill the Lord's anointed. Kings are anointed, the Lord's anointed temple. Reading the Bible tells us that killing a king is sacrilege.

So much might be clear to Macduff and to King James (and probably also to Shakespeare, who no doubt wrote what actors call 'The Scottish Play' to honour his new Scottish king). However, as Shakespeare himself observed in another play, there are many sad stories of the death of kings. Indeed, in England later that century, a king was executed. This was James's own son, King Charles I. Conflict, civil strife, confusion, confusion's masterpiece. In this case, kingly order was eventually restored. One way to see how right-thinking opinion attempted to make sense of these terrible events is by reading the church service written for the annual celebration of the Restoration. In it, the people promise 'all loyal and dutiful allegiance to thy Anointed Servant now set over us'. So we have a new king, but we still have allegiance to the anointed, God's holy temple. The people pray to be saved from 'the unnatural rebellion, usurpation, and tyranny of ungodly and cruel men, and from the sad confusions and ruin thereupon ensuing'. So once we have violence against the Lord's anointed, we have 'confusions and ruin'.

With rebellion, we also have something said to be 'unnatural'. Earlier, King James was eager to stress that his untramelled authority (above parliament and law) came not only from God but also from Nature. For him, the king was father to his people. Fathers naturally care for their children; children naturally respect their fathers. Rebellion was unnatural. Murder of the king, like murder inside the family, would be an 'unnatural' murder. (Shakespeare, in *Hamlet*, describes murder by a brother as 'most foul, bloody, and unnatural'.) Go against nature in this way and things become confused. Order is subverted. Consider God's law as laid down in the official translation of the day (the Authorised, or King James, version of the Bible, which appeared five years after *Macbeth*). This law forbids sexual relations between humans and animals. As the King James Bible translates the injunction, 'it is confusion' [*Leviticus* 18.23].

So much for the preservation of right order and the prevention of confusion. So much for the opinions of the right-thinking Macduffs of the time. Yet these so-called confused things actually happened. As we have seen, King James's own son was made confusion's masterpiece. Indeed, it almost happened to King James himself. In the year before *Macbeth* was performed, an attempt was made to blow him up together with his complete parliament (the 'Gunpowder Plot' – Guy Fawkes, 5 November 1605). Four days later, King James made another attempt to address his parliament, and this time he succeeded. He explained that 'kings are in the word of God himself called gods'. (Business as usual.) People heard about the divine power of kings, but clearly not everyone saw it that way; and if other views were possible, then more than mere assertion of authority was needed to decide who was right. James took God to be on his side, but his opponents, the plotters who attempted to blow him up, took God to be on their side. They also thought that they were fulfilling the work and wishes of God. They were Roman Catholics, a different version of the Christian religion, and they thought that God wanted another religious order in the country. They thought that God was in favour of their removal of heretical kings to bring this about. In spite of the divinity that for James shaped the ends of kings, they had other ideas, and if there are diverse ideas and authorities, thought and argument are needed to work out who is right.

Just before Macduff enters and discovers the murdered Duncan, the porter of the castle listens to his knocking and pretends, with terrible unconscious irony, to be the porter of hell's gate. He describes people seeking admission to hell. Among them is 'an equivocator, that . . . committed treason enough for God's sake, yet could not equivocate to heaven'. These equivocators, these Jesuits, dissembled in their arguments, committed treason. They were the Gunpowder Plotters. For the porter, and for Shakespeare's audience, they went to hell. Yet they were there, and account had to be taken of their views. They might equivocate, juggle justifications two ways, but they were in the news.

The fictional murder of *Macbeth* is a work of the night. The murderer, Macbeth, consorts with witches; it is devil's work, fit only for hell. The real plotters against James also hid by night. It might be thought that the good thoughts of day, just as the good thoughts of Macduff, would be clearly against it. However, when King James's son came to be killed, it was done by public execution in the centre of London in the middle of the day. It followed publicly presented arguments and legal process. Again, religious differences were partly responsible. But here it was argued and fought out in the full light of day. Rebellion, civil war, England torn apart. Yet it was during this masterpiece of political confusion that Hobbes wrote his masterpiece about political confusion, *Leviathan*.

So we start the century with an idea of hierarchical order controlled by absolute kings, established and upheld by God. Religion runs for it, religion runs against it, religion gives other sources of validity and authority by means of which particular political arrangements can be questioned or defended. This raises questions of justification, and also of the possibility of alternative political arrangements. As well as the backing of God, there is the backing of Nature. Yet, in both cases, it can be questioned what real backing this gives. Other bases of justification can be produced, and so we are involved in political philosophy. The political philosophy was produced as a cure for the confusions of the time, but it is still read with great respect and care today.

This duality of appeal – both to its own time and to our own time – has difficulties and advantages. What we see in the thought of these great philosophers is inevitably the view from here (where we have fewer kings and where religion is less called on for ultimate validation). How the hills look from here explains the landscape I intend to explore. Yet one aim of this work is to show how these distant impressions change once we get among the hills themselves. The historical writings that we now refer to for our own contemporary purposes were originally responses to quite different theoretical and practical situations, and (inevitably) formed by reaction to what came before them, rather than after. So, as well as discussing questions raised by such major thinkers as Hobbes, Locke, and Grotius in the abstract, I also wish to make more sense of these questions by showing how they arose in particular intellectual and historical contexts. Their philosophies have the advantage for us of being driven by high theory, which travels beyond ancient troubles and can be translated into contemporary concerns. The fundamental problems and solutions they raise and discuss are ones that we still can discuss, use, or criticise today. However, their philosophies also have the advantage of originating from real and pressing problems of political order on their own historical ground.

If philosophy starts with scepticism – the questioning of established ideas – these philosophies of the seventeenth century start with a very real form of scepticism, the questioning of established order implied by its destruction and confusion. The philosophers wrote amidst confusion, and so faced the real and pressing question of why and how there could be order. This is the historical reality, but more abstractly a fundamental question of political philosophy is the grounds and scope of political obligation. Before we decide what the state ought to do, we have to decide whether there should be a state at all. So the sceptical position with which political philosophy works is anarchism – the idea that no political claims are taken to have validity. Another fundamental, sceptical position is amoralism, so that no normative claims are allowed validity. Any answer to such scepticisms provides foundations. The extreme view would be to suppose that all that exists, or is of importance, are individual people, and that the only claims of reason on these people are the claims of individual self-interest. This is, in effect, to put the problem the way it was originally proposed by Hobbes. We start with individuals, and all reasons are in terms of individual interest. Any polity that can be argued for, or emerge, with so slim presuppositions will be dialectically robust.

The central problems here are the relation between individuals and their political communities – relations of power, of authority, of decision-making, of judgement. These are all discussed, first concentrating on Hobbes, later on Locke, although other major thinkers, including Grotius and Pufendorf, also appear. The problem is to find a normative foundation, and then apply these norms to discovering the right answers about government. I start the main treatment with Hobbes. However, history does not start with Hobbes. I attempt to remedy this to some extent in the first chapter, which aims to give some sense of the intellectually problematic world into which Hobbes and Locke were born. Yet much has inevitably been left out, and as well as omitting the classical and medieval foundations of modern political philosophy, I have not even brought out how much the Biblically influenced seventeenth century on which I concentrate was also a great consumer of Greek and Latin classics. Even in terms of political thought, the seventeenth century has natural and important predecessors I barely mention – Machiavelli, More, Bodin. The foundations of modern political thought (to take the title of a famous work by Quentin Skinner) lie further back (Skinner's two volumes stop before this century starts). However, I still hope that starting with the seventeenth century makes good intrinsic sense for the reasons I have indicated. What I aim to tell is not the whole story. It never could be. However, I hope that it is of interest as well as of importance.

1

The Word

In the beginning was the word. The word was the word of God. The same was in the beginning with God. The same is in the beginning of this story, which starts its main action in the seventeenth century, the century of the great philosophers Hobbes and Locke. This period is known as 'Early Modern', and the century of Hobbes and Locke is also the century of Galileo and Newton – science, it would seem, rather than religion, the start of the thrusting, modern, scientific world. However, if we look at Hobbes and Locke, we find among their own words extensive use of the word of God, extensive use, that is, of the Christian Bible. Locke wrote a *Paraphrase of the Epistles of St Paul*, an account of part of the Bible. He wrote a work, *The Reasonableness of Christianity*, whose whole argument is composed of quotations from the Bible. His battle in political philosophy with Robert Filmer is a battle of biblical texts. Hobbes, by contrast, was notorious in his day as an unbeliever, or heretic. Yet in the famous frontispiece of Hobbes's *Leviathan*, behind the figure of the sovereign ruler made up of many little people, stands the word of God. Running on each side of the ruler's crown are words from the Bible. Leviathan is licensed by the word, and the original leviathan was a ferocious biblical beast.

'Early Modern' is a retrospective term. At the time, the people thought that they were late rather than early, and people always think that they are modern. Similarly with the preceding Medieval Period, the 'Middle Ages'. In some sense, everyone always thinks that they are living in the middle of time, occupying a brief present between the past behind and the future before. However, the people of the Middle Ages did not realise that they were in any special way in the middle of time. The Middle Ages also has been classified subsequently, and, by implication, degraded. Retrospectively, it is a period that ends with a Renaissance, or re-birth. It is thought to be a dark period between the bright joys of the Ancient world and its subsequent rediscovery. Alternatively, it is sandwiched between the Ancient world, interesting in its own way, and the Modern world, interesting in our way – a static, non-progressive interlude.

In fact, the period we now call the Middle Ages was shot through with tension, conflict, and difficulty, much as any other period in which people have tried to live together in cooperation and competition. However, beginning as I do with the centuries after the Middle Ages, I shall stay with some of the semi-mythic picture of it as a period of religious and intellectual unity. For this highlights the even more obvious conflicts of the period that immediately follows. There were heretics in the Middle Ages, and battles against heretics. There was religious war, crusades against heathen peoples. There was schism in the church, whereby the Western church, centred on Rome, parted company with the Eastern church, centred on Constantinople. However, in the Latin-based culture of Western Europe, there was a single church with a nominal single head, the Pope. Disputes were argued inside this framework. There was also, over much of it, a nominal single secular overlord, the Emperor. All this was what was altered in a profoundly new way in the early sixteenth century with Martin Luther and the Reformation. Now there was political, religious, and cultural conflict in the heart of Latin-based Western Europe. In this early modern world, the Protestants (as the followers of Luther, Calvin, and other reformers came to be called) fought with the Catholics (as we can call those who remained loyal to the Pope and the old supposedly universal church). The Catholics had the authority of their church and its transmitted tradition. The Protestants had the authority of the Bible, which they took to be the direct word of God, unmediated by Pope or priest. In the beginning of the Reformation was the word of God, and the word was carried into war. The Early Modern is a period of profound conflict – of religious war, of political upheaval on behalf of the word of God.

In this chapter, I describe the religious, political, and intellectual world of this Early Modern period, the world into which the great seventeenth-century philosophers were born. Hobbes and Locke are great philosophers because they seem to have, or at least to propose, solutions to perennial intellectual problems. They are great philosophers because they thought differently and better than their contemporaries. However, to understand them, we have to understand the possibilities available to them and the problems before them. We have to see what was common before analysing the special; we have to make sense of the problems before understanding the solutions. In trying to understand these possibilities and problems, I shall look in this chapter not only at their own seventeenth century but also at the century before it, when the first religious reformers wrote and when the religious wars started. For these conflicts are still the conflicts of the age of Hobbes and Locke. I shall illustrate them from some more commonplace work than that of the great philosophers. Then, in the next chapter, I move to the discussion of one of the greatest works of political philosophy ever written, Hobbes's *Leviathan*.

Religion and War

Leviathan was published exactly in the middle of the seventeenth century (at the start of 1651). A quarter of a century earlier there appeared another famous work, which I shall also discuss later, the monumental treatment of the laws of war and peace (*De Jure Belli ac Pacis*) by the Dutch thinker, Hugo Grotius. For Hobbes and Grotius, and for the world they inhabited, the chief problem was war. Hence the title of Grotius's book, which in fact deals much more with war than with peace. Grotius was from Holland, a country that had just resumed its war of liberation from its one-time Spanish masters. This conflict was merely on the edge of the series of inter-linked conflicts that we know as the Thirty Years War, in which Germany (as we now call it) tore itself to pieces with dreadful suffering to its people. When Grotius's work was published, he was in fact in exile – he was in Paris. He had to escape both prison and Holland after the execution of his political leader, Oldenbarnevelt. There had been civil conflict, dissension.

When *Leviathan* was published, Hobbes, an Englishman, was also in exile – also in Paris. He had escaped England as the cause he had espoused – the supremacy of the King – had come under criticism. While Hobbes was in Paris, the conflict in England developed into a series of bitter civil wars. Brother fought brother; the king was executed; constitutions and fundamental political questions had to be invented. Nothing was safe or certain. Even in Paris, while Hobbes was writing *Leviathan,* France itself lapsed into a period of civil war. Such was the difficulty of the times. So also was the difficulty of knowing what to do about it. Yet it is in response to such difficulties that these profound works appeared, and it is the necessarily fundamental nature of their treatment that still makes them important. For these wars and conflicts were not just examples of political organisations unwinding in predictable and persistent ways. They were wars fought where the intellectual world was also uncertain. Ignorant armies clashed by night. It was not just states that deconstructed, but also the supposed knowledge that was meant to explain and control them.

First, and central, were the problems caused by religion. In the simple temporal typology with which I started, the Medieval world may seem like an age of faith, a religious wedge between the pagan Ancient world and the secular, scientific world of the modern. However, although Hobbes may have met Galileo, and although he was in close contact in Paris with the leading scientific group in Europe, this was still a fully religious world. Indeed, the problem was not that there was too little religion, but rather too much. There were too many religions, and they did not agree. All the conflicts just described were in part religious conflicts. Grotius had to flee Holland because of a conflict between Protestants, between parties that could be called Arminian and strict Calvinist (there known as Remonstrant and Counter-Remonstrant). One strand of the English civil wars was a loosely similar conflict. The wars in Germany were generally between Protestants and Catholics, renewing the conflicts that had broken out the previous century after the Reformation. The civil conflicts disturbing Paris while Hobbes was writing were not religious in the same way, but France was still under the shadow of a very bitter series of religious civil wars at the end of the previous century.

Too many religions (for, as we have seen, it was not just Protestants and Catholics; the Protestants could also disagree and destroy each other). This not only led to war between parties, but also to other ways in which political structures were destabilised. The Pope, as head of the Catholic church, thought that he had the power (which he used) to depose secular rulers. He could excommunicate Protestant kings and relieve their subjects from their vows of obligation. There was no way that religion and politics could be kept separate or religion regarded as a merely private matter. Everyone agreed that in a single state, there should be a single church. In the middle of the sixteenth century, at the end of the first round of religious wars in Germany, peace was established on the principle *cuius regio eius religio* – that is, the religion of any territory was to be the religion of its ruler. This recognised that there were several (Christian) religions, but it also recognised that in each area there was to be uniformity – a Catholic ruler meant a Catholic people, a Lutheran ruler a Lutheran people, and so on. There were always some arguments for toleration, particularly where (as in France) the price of attempting to enforce religious uniformity proved very high. By 1689, when Locke wrote his letter on toleration that promoted pluralism of religion in a single territory, this was beginning to be acceptable. But even so, Locke wrote only four years after the French King finally managed to impose (Catholic) religious uniformity on France. Conversely, even Locke was only promoting a Protestant pluralism; Catholics and atheists were to be excluded from toleration.

This world of enforced religious uniformity and passionate doctrinal and physical religious conflict is today in the West unfamiliar, even though it can still be experienced in that peculiar time capsule located in Northern Ireland. Yet it is the context of Hobbes and Locke, of the famous founding works of modern political philosophy. Indeed, it partly explains their fame. For needing starting points, needing authority from which to write, it was no longer sufficient simply to reach for the obvious truths of religion. God no longer talked directly to men. On this, nearly everyone was agreed (and those that didn't were disposed of as mad rather than divinely inspired). So even though the thoughts of God were, of course, absolutely and unquestionably true, there was still the question of how to get hold of these thoughts. Perhaps the divinely appointed Pope and the teaching magisterium of the church could authoritatively explain it. However, that would not work for Protestants, many of whom in this period thought that the Pope was in fact the anti-Christ. Perhaps the answers could be read in the Bible. But this would not work for Catholics, who had to let their Pope and priests read it for them; and, indeed, when Protestants read it for themselves, they did not seem all to read the same things. Perhaps the answer was inspiration, the direct communication of God's Holy

Spirit to the individual soul. However, again different individual souls seemed to be differently inspired. This world was a world dominated by religion, but it was also a world dominated by conflicting religious ideas. And specifically because of this, religion could not automatically produce an answer to political and other problems. So these philosophers had to produce their own.

A Sixteenth-Century Example

Before the answers, the problems. As an example of the strains and political problems posed by religion, I shall now describe aspects of a work written in the middle of the sixteenth century, a work published in 1556, a year after the *cuius regio eius religio* peace of Augsburg. I take this example, not because it is a particularly great work, but because it illustrates central problems and possible answers available at that time. It is also written in English, and so the problems of translation are less severe (although the problems of translation between different periods in the same language should not be underestimated). In quoting from it (as also in the quotations in the next few chapters), I modernise spelling, emphasis, and occasionally punctuation, but I leave the words and word order untouched. Although written by an Englishman, it is in fact yet another work written in exile. So, in this aspect, it joins the greater works of the following seventeenth century. I noted that the chief works of Hobbes and Grotius were written in exile; this was also true of Locke's chief work of political philosophy. It reveals the turbulent and dangerous political conditions in which these authors were stimulated to philosophise about politics. Problems are also more sharply perceived by people fleeing for their lives, and exile may give opportunity for reflection.

My example is an English bishop, a man called John Ponet. Ponet was the Bishop of Winchester at the end of the Protestant regime of the boy king Edward VI. Winchester is one of the greatest English bishoprics, and Ponet moved with, and was favoured by, political power. Then there was a reversal. The Protestant boy king died and was replaced by a Roman Catholic queen, Mary. Ponet became associated with a rebellion against her, and fled abroad. Even without any seditious activities, being a Protestant bishop in itself was potentially fatal. The ones who stayed were burned at the stake. In the year Ponet wrote, Thomas Cranmer, formerly Archbishop of Canterbury, Ponet's old master and whose chaplain he had once been, was burned as a heretic in Oxford. Even being abroad was not safe. Ponet's student friend, the great Greek scholar and tutor to the boy king Edward, John Cheke, was captured in Brussels, tied into a cart, and taken back to captivity in England (where fear of death made him renounce Protestantism). Such were the circumstances in which John Ponet, in exile in Strasbourg, published his *Short Treatise of Politic Power.*

These few facts about Ponet are sufficient to show the question that arises naturally out of his situation, the question of political obedience. You have a loyalty to both God and country. Yet the lawful governor of the country tells you, by the law of the country, to do those things that you think are against the laws of your God. So what should you do, and is it lawful for anyone to resist? Ponet writes a work that seeks to prove that it is legitimate to resist government, that it is sometimes legitimate to remove kings, that tyrants may be killed. So here is a question, here an answer. The question is the most fundamental one in political philosophy, the limits of political obligation. It opens up into a closely connected series of questions. Before we know the limits of political obligation, we need to know its value. We need to know its basis. We need to be able to understand the nature of the entities to which it is supposed we are obliged. In asking whether authorities have authority, we need to ask what authority is. So we have a whole set of fundamental questions here. What are states, kings, governors? What is a citizen? What, if anything, is special about them? What, if anything, is the difference between the public and the private, between relations that involve political societies and relations merely between individuals? Is there a set of norms controlling and correcting our appropriate behaviour with respect to these strange entities? May the authorities take our lives by way of judicial punishment or by forcing us to fight in wars? May they do it in ways in which private individuals may not? May they take our property from us in ways that private individuals may not? These are the first and fundamental questions of political philosophy, which all relate to the question of the nature and limits of political obligation.

Someone might argue that the question of the limits of political obligation is misconceived because it is a mistake to think that we are ever politically obliged. All political authority is evil and has no claim on our allegiance. Then, in a case like Ponet's, the problems of resisting Queen Mary would be merely practical. However, Ponet does not argue like this. For Ponet, there not only are, but there also ought to be, kings and other authorities. His explanation of this is the orthodox Protestant one of the time. Because of the wickedness of man, political authority has been set up by God. In this orthodox treatment, politics results from the fall of man, from Adam's original sin. So Ponet has to guard this flank, noting that 'some there be that will have too little obedience, as the Anabaptists' who 'would have all politic power taken away' [p. 47]. Their mistake is in 'thinking that people may live without sin, and forget the fall of man' [48]. So, as with Luther and Calvin before him, there has to be obedience to political authority. People are not safe to be alone, and Ponet follows Luther and Calvin in wishing to distance himself firmly from the revolutionary 'Anabaptists'. However, although there has to be obedience, for Ponet there are also limits to obedience. It is on this flank that he chiefly concentrates. The 'English papists' who 'want the civil power obeyed in all things' [47] are mistaken. As well as 'too little' there can be 'too much' obedience. Not everything the king says should be done. Perhaps this seems obvious. However, it is not the only answer that can be given; it needs argument. It is not, as we shall see, the answer argued for by Hobbes. It is not, as we shall see, the answer given by many of Ponet's Protestant contemporaries. However, for Ponet himself, it follows relatively straightforwardly from his claim that 'men ought to have more respect to their country than to their prince: to the commonwealth than to any one person' [61]. The prince is only one person, and so sometimes we should disobey the prince for the sake of the country.

'Prince' is a term of art in all these writers, meaning whoever is first in power, whether king, queen, or other official. To say 'my country before my queen' sounds fine, but we would like to know what a 'country' is and on what basis Ponet can claim that 'next unto God men ought to love their country' [61]. Much later he winds himself into his final peroration with visions of the possible paradise to come if his 'good country men and true English hearts' repent of their sins and so 'may avoid the eternal pains of hell prepared for sinners'. What these English hearts have to do is to 'cleave to the sincere word of God'. Well, of course; God comes first, and no one wants to go to hell. But what we need to know is why this involves the English hearts getting rid of, or indeed possibly killing, their queen. Then, says Ponet, you will 'no longer hate your country, but be true and faithful to it' [181]. The problem is what counts as hating the country, and why loving the queen is hating the country. There is also an ontology at work here that again will only properly be approached with Hobbes. An ontology and an epistemology. How can we know what a 'country' requires from us (such as, for example, that it requires us not to have Roman Catholic religious services)? Asking the representative of the country, the queen who, as Hobbes later put it, 'bears the person' of the country, will not get the answer Ponet wants. What the queen would say is that loyalty to the country is loyalty to her. In any case, whatever the 'country' is, it is not just an area of land. When Ponet wrote, England and Scotland were separate countries, but England and Wales were not; division between physical features alone would never get this result.

Indeed, the terms used by Ponet (writing, as I said, in English) show the various possibilities of the objects of political obligation. There is the 'prince'. There is the 'country'. As we have just seen, there is also the 'common wealth' (always two words for Ponet). He talks of 'the people', which at one point [153] he explains as 'the politic body'. He also talks of 'states' ('states, bodies politic, and common wealths' [22]). So, if I am loyal, to whom or what am I loyal? Being English, to England perhaps. But is England the sovereign of England, she who holds supreme power in England, Queen Mary? Not as we have seen for Ponet. So is it the fields and heaths of Ponet's county of Kent? Friend of the 'country', Ponet is not like a modern friend of the earth, defending the countryside against state-inspired motorway ravage. Ponet is not defying Queen Mary merely to protect a piece of earth. So perhaps it is the 'people', but what are they? This is one to watch as we approach Hobbes and Locke.

We can identify the prince, but is it possible to identify the people on behalf of whom we might resist the prince? They are just a crowd (often called at this time, after the Latin, a 'multitude') and the problem is to reduce them to a unity. Perhaps this can be done by representation, so that they can be represented by someone with a single will. As the great Medieval philosopher Thomas Aquinas puts it, someone has responsibility for the people and 'bears its person' (*eius personam gerit* [ST 1a2ae. 57 art 2]. But this bearer of the people's 'person' is, for Aquinas, the prince (*princeps*). So, again, this would not work for

Ponet. If Queen Mary is England, then England cannot be defended against Queen Mary. Similarly, if Queen Mary is the people of England (or bears their person), then these people can not disagree with Queen Mary.

It is not plausible (at least as we think of it) that Queen Mary is either the country or the people of England. However, lacking as yet a theory, we cannot yet say why this is wrong, or on what basis Queen Mary might properly be resisted. We have not yet specified an alternative object of political obligation to the living queen. Ponet has mentioned several alternatives, and we have been circling round the centre. It is not just pieces of land, it is not just groups of people. It is something organised, people organised in a particular political way and in (political) control of an area of land. It is Ponet's 'body politic' – that is a body, a unit, something incorporated (embodied). It is a 'commonwealth'. It is a 'state'. These are the terms of Ponet on which to concentrate. Of these, 'state' is the word we would most naturally use today. However, Ponet is writing just at the point at which 'state' first acquires this modern use. Perhaps he could have talked about resisting Queen Mary for the sake of the state, but this is not what he does. Over a century later, the King of France famously declared that he was the state. In Ponet's time, the 'state' was just emerging from being something the prince had, or was in. In the earlier sense, it was a position, an estate. Queen Mary was someone of high state, and any prince of sense wanted to maintain their state. When Ponet is describing what a wicked prince does, he says he kills people 'to be sure of his state' [99] – that is, to keep his position. An official exhortation promoting 'obedience to rulers' was issued by Ponet's fellow bishops in the previous reign, when, as it says, 'God hath sent us his high gift, our most dear sovereign lord King Edward the Sixth'. It talks of the necessity of 'kings, princes, rulers, magistrates, judges, and such states of God's order'. This was in 1547. These people were, we might still say, 'stately'. However, when the homily was reissued in 1574, 'states' here was changed to 'estates'; its use to mean a high position was obviously starting to sound strange.

Just as in modern use, 'state' for Ponet sometimes merely refers to the condition of the country – that is, the state of the realm. However 'state' could also be used more specifically to mean its political condition (its political state). Thus Ponet criticises Queen Mary for 'the subversion of the policy and state of the realm' [149]. That is, there is a political way it ought to be and this has been subverted. Hence he 'liketh not the state in England' [141]. These are Medieval uses, the *status publicus* of the community; its public state. As such they are not really yet the state we could defend against its queen. There are however also signs of an alternative entity emerging that could be set against the flesh and blood real entity of the queen. Notice, for example, in the last quoted remark, Ponet says 'the state in England', not 'the state of England'. Yet even this is not yet an abstract, independent, personified entity. We move still closer when Ponet mentions 'the body or state of the realm or commonwealth' [105]. This sounds like a transitional use. It could be merely the state (condition) of the realm but it seems, rather, to be its particular, political 'body' – that is, its political state thought of as a kind of separately embodied entity. On the same page, we have 'the body of every state', the state itself now has a 'body', and we are starting to reach the modern state.

In any case the usual term at this time for the principal object of political philosophy is not 'state' but, rather, 'commonwealth'. Even a hundred years later, in a much greater work of political philosophy written in English, Hobbes's *Leviathan*, the state does not make much of an appearance; even though, as we would now say, the state is what it is all about. Its title page is 'Leviathan, or the matter, form, and power of a commonwealth, ecclesiastical and civil'. It is about a 'commonwealth'. The 'state' gets mentioned, particularly in a prominent position in the first paragraph of the *Introduction*, where Hobbes talks of 'that great LEVIATHAN called a COMMON-WEALTH, or STATE, (in Latin CIVITAS)'. Yet even here, the first mention is of 'commonwealth'. Part II of the work is called 'Of Commonwealth'. In it, Hobbes has chapters discussing the causes of a commonwealth, the kinds of commonwealth, and so on. At the crucial moment of generation of his monster, he calls it 'a COMMONWEALTH, in Latin CIVITAS', without any mention of the state.

Earlier, Hobbes had written a work in Latin, *De Cive* (that is, *On the Citizen*). The citizen is someone who lives in a *civitas*. So what Hobbes is searching for is a word to translate *civitas*. The literal translation is 'city' (and *polis*, the Greek word for 'city', is what gives politics its name). But 'city' will no longer do; politics is no longer something that principally happens in a *polis*. Ancient city states (as we now call them) and medieval North Italian republics were units of territory dominated by a city (Athens, Florence). However, someone like Ponet could not think of himself as born in and bound to a city. This is not just because he happened to come from an area of the countryside uncontrolled by a city. Even if he had been born in London, he would not have been a Londoner in the same way as Machiavelli and Dante were Florentines or Plato an Athenian. The appropriate territorial units were much larger; Ponet's 'country' is the nearest. However, as I said, the 'country' is not just land; it is not just town and countryside. It is a territory organised in a particular way. It is a territory in which things are common or public. The city has common spaces, public monuments, public organisation, and common goods. Common wealth. The word they use is 'commonwealth'. The modern citizen is a citizen of a commonwealth rather than a city; 'commonwealth' translates *'civitas'* even though in its literal meaning it is closer to the Latin behind 'republic' (*Res publica*, common or public things).

Bisecting the distance between Ponet and Hobbes is another English writer, Richard Hooker. Hooker wants to show that church and state are not two separate things for a Christian people. What he actually says is 'church and commonwealth'. The commonwealth of England and the church of England is the same thing, a thing with one head. Hooker is writing in the reign after Ponet's Queen Mary. He is writing under Queen Elizabeth, with the church and state safely restored to Protestantism under its one head (or 'governor'). Elizabeth restored the position of her (and Queen Mary's) father, King Henry VIII, who took both secular and ecclesiastic jurisdiction into his single firm hands, hence dismissing the authority of the Pope. The preamble to the crucial act of parliament in which Henry disallowed appeals to the Pope in Rome sets out the justificatory position. As the preamble puts it, 'this realm of England is an empire' – that is, its governor has no legal superior, its king has imperial authority. As the preamble puts it, the king has 'plenary, whole and entire power'. The English here echoes the Latin, the idea of *plena potestas*, full power. This standardly gets translated as 'sovereignty'. Later in the century, the French thinker Bodin argued that in any regime there had to be a single sovereign. Even if this is not analytically correct, it was becoming more and more true as a matter of fact in the new regimes of Europe. Henry abolished the Pope (as a judicial authority in his country) and hence gave himself plenary power, full sovereignty. In the Middle Ages, there were two swords, Pope and Emperor. With Henry they became one.

However, if we have this full power, this unification of authority in a single person, we are back with Ponet's problem. For the revolution of kings may, as it did, bring in a prince who favours the Pope. It may bring in Queen Mary. Then the parliament that passed the acts abolishing papal jurisdiction undoes all the acts of King Henry. They beg that they 'may as children repentant be received into the bosom and unity of Christ's church'. The one-time Bishop of Winchester, Ponet, flees to Strasbourg. The one-time Archbishop of Canterbury stays behind and is burned at the stake. What is Ponet to do or say? In Henry's act, just referred to, it says that the 'body politic' owes the king a 'natural and humble obedience'. So it would seem that whatever the king says goes. There is no room for resistance. If the king says Protestant, then Protestant; if the queen says Catholic, then Catholic. *Cuius regio eius religio.* And, indeed, many quite obvious Protestants (such as William Cecil, who later ran the state for the Protestant Queen Elizabeth) stayed behind, went to the Catholic mass, performed political services for Queen Mary, and generally behaved in exactly the way in which Henry's act implies and of which Hobbes would later approve. There would seem no other (conceptual) place left for Ponet to go. With the advent of Mary, the Bishop of Winchester should be passing the rosary beads through his hands and, on royal instructions, making his peace with the Pope.

Conscience and King

However, Henry's act does not in fact say only what I have just reported. It actually says that with respect to Henry, everyone 'be bounden and owe and bear next to God a natural and humble obedience'. God is first, the king comes next. So the question is whether the word of the king can be trumped by the word of God. We have the king, uniting everything with his single sword. But we also have the Bible. Hence we would seem to have another source of authority as well as the king. We can read the Bible and discover when and whether we should obey the king. In the beginning was the word. However, this will not work for King Henry, at least in his own eyes. Bibles need interpretation, and Henry took himself to be the ultimate arbiter of such interpretation in England. He had, after all, taken over from the Pope. Although not a priest, he had all the magisterial, doctrinal, and jurisdictional power of the Pope with respect to England. If the Catholics were required to let their church read their Bibles for them, so also Henry warned people not to try interpretation at home. He did allow the Bible to be translated and so read, but 'be not judges yourselves' is what he told them to do with it (this is from a 1545 speech to parliament). Any problems about the Bible or doctrine were to be referred to him. Again, more than a hundred years later, Hobbes echoes Henry's sentiments. In his history of the English Civil War, Hobbes places prominently among its causes the fact that 'after the Bible was translated into English, every man, nay, every boy and wench, that could read English, thought they spoke with God almighty, and understood what he said' [*Behemoth*, p. 21]. Neither Hobbes nor Henry was having any of that nonsense. Apart from anything else, it led to sedition.

Yet sedition in the case of Ponet was precisely what he was promoting (and indeed what he had already attempted). He was a Protestant, a God-fearing man. That is, God was to be feared more than princes. The Bible is the word of God. Of course, the Bible says many things. Hence the caution of Hobbes and Henry. However, one thing it does say is that we should obey God rather than man. This (*Acts* 5.29) is one of the frequently cited texts in the religiously founded political polemic of the period. For Ponet, God is the 'power of powers' [52], and he can cite many other authorities on obeying God rather than man. Even in that formidable man, King Henry, we have just seen that obedience to him is 'next to God'. Even for Henry, God is first. God is the ultimate, superior authority; God trumps everything else. But, given this, the argument for the limits of political obligation to princes would seem to be simple. For if God is the superior authority, then, where there is a conflict between him and a lesser authority, we should clearly follow the superior authority. The analogy is dealing with someone's agent or deputy. If the deputy is not doing what his principal requires, then we should respect the wishes of the principal rather than the agent. As Ponet puts it, 'the king or governor is but God's minister or steward, ordained not to misuse the servants, that is, the people' [95].

Hence, in such circumstances, we should not obey the prince. That the prince is a mere minister of God shows that the prince is there for a purpose, and need not be obeyed if not fulfilling that purpose. The purpose of kings, at least for Ponet and other Protestant thinkers of the time, is to enforce the law of God. This law (at least as they saw it) forbids idolatry, and (again as they saw it) Roman Catholicism is idolatry. As Ponet puts it, Queen Mary had brought 'the devilish power of the Romist antichrist into England again with his miserable mass and popish slavery' [139]. This is a sin. It is against the law (of God). Hence it deserves punishment. The point of the prince is to uphold the law (of God), and so a prince breaking this law, just like anyone else, is properly punished. Ponet runs through a series of examples to show that the prince is not above the law. A prince who sleeps with a man's wife commits adultery, a prince who takes his subject's goods without consent commits theft, and so on. These actions are wrong and ought to be punished. So also (for Ponet) is introducing the miserable Mass.

This (apart from the Mass) might again just seem straightforward, but again we need only to wait for Hobbes to have a very different view about the legitimate powers of princes. This is so even though Hobbes also subscribes to the view that obedience to the prince's commands stops when they are clearly against the will of God. One reason Hobbes can do this, as we have already seen, is that his prince controls interpretation of the Bible. The prince, of course, must not do anything against the law of God, but for Hobbes (and Henry) it is for the prince to say what is the law of God. In both centuries, people believed that political power had been instituted by God. It both centuries, they believed that its purpose was, as Ponet puts it, 'to maintain justice' [22]. So it was uncontentious that princes should be just. Where the problems start is with the question of who, if anyone, is entitled to judge whether princes are just, and what, if anything, anyone is entitled to do if it seems that they are not just. In Ponet's time, the furthest that even advanced Protestant thought tended to get was that 'inferior magistrates' might resist an unjust overlord. So, for example, the Protestant princes in Germany might resist the Emperor; the United Provinces (that is, the Northern Netherlands) might under their prince resist the Spanish king. But even in Ponet's seemingly radical contemporary John Knox, there was reluctance to go further. Ponet, however, does. Every individual person may do it. Indeed, since we are talking here of religious duties rather than individual rights, every individual person ought to do it. It is not surprising that people did not normally go that far. If every private individual who thinks that his political governors are mistaken is thereby licensed to punish, kill, or otherwise remove them, this seems to license anarchy. If anarchy follows, then we no longer have that political power that was ordained by God for the promotion of justice. In trying to improve it, we destroy it.

So it is a long step from the claim that political power is instituted by God for a purpose to the claim that therefore people may resist and remove it if they judge that it is not fulfilling the purpose. The first claim does indeed give a basis for criticism. However, even if it seems worthy of criticism, action does not necessarily follow. Indeed the original orthodox Protestant view, as held by Luther and his followers at the start of the Reformation, was that nobody was entitled to do anything at all. Political power was indeed instituted by God. Because of human sinfulness, we have to be forced to behave rightly, and political power is the method God uses. However, the essence of this method is that we have to obey. We are not entitled to resist; indeed we are forbidden to do so. This might be taken to follow from the nature of the power, but the biblically minded original reformers chiefly based it on the words of the Bible.

The key passage here is the beginning of Chapter 13 of Paul's *Epistle to the Romans*, where Paul writes (as the later King James translation puts it), 'let every soul be subject to the higher powers. For there is no power but of God: the powers that be are ordained of God'. (In Tyndale's English translation, produced before Ponet became a bishop, it also declares that 'the powers that be, are ordained of God'.) Therefore, as Paul writes, whoever 'resisteth the power, resisteth the ordinance of God: and they that resist shall receive to themselves damnation'. If we resist political power, we are damned, condemned to everlasting torment in hell. A little later, Paul says that we should obey not just to avoid this 'wrath, but also for conscience sake'. So it is clear, or at least would seem to be so, that all political power is from God and so has to be obeyed, whether it is right or wrong, Protestant or Catholic, Christian or heathen. It is not for individuals, or indeed any other body, to try and second guess it or presume to call the shots. However heathen, mad, unjust, or wrong, we merely have to suffer. Paul's words to the Romans were endlessly used. Luther cited it; so did Calvin (why should God have given us an unrighteous prince? Answer – for our sins, the explanation of human as well as natural disasters).

Of course, a little play can be made with the texts. It was, for example, noticed that it refers to 'powers', in the plural (*potestatibus* in the Latin vulgate, which was the main version they used). So perhaps it did allow some other powers in as well as the prince. Perhaps 'inferior magistrates' have a role. But, even so, this would not allow any action by individuals. The individual just has to obey whatever powers there are. In any case, the point of shiny new modern states (or common-wealths) like that produced by King Henry is to reduce the plurality of powers. All jurisdiction is with the king, and everyone else is equally subject. Ploughman, Duke, Archbishop, they all get their marching orders from a single power, a single powerful king. The prince is the 'minister' of God (as the King James translation puts it here; it is also *minister* in the Latin). But even though he is merely God's minister we cannot reach beyond him. Back in the biblical ages of prophecy, people might have gotten special messages from God telling them to dispense with kings. Armed by such special commissions directly from the Almighty, they might resist the king in the name of God. However (and this is the orthodox Protestant position), the age of prophecy is now over. The days when you could gain special esteem from God by driving tent pegs through the heads of political superiors sleeping in your tent have departed. In the modern world, the will of God is that we must obey. We must obey because we know that it is right on the basis of our 'conscience' (*propter conscientiam*). 'And make no mistake', says Calvin in his *Institutes*, 'it is impossible to resist the magistrate with-out also resisting God' [IV.20.23]. Rulers may be cruel and wicked but 'it is not for us to remedy such evils' [29].

So, given this passage in *Romans* and given that Ponet, like a good Protestant bishop, has to give the Bible ultimate authority as the word of God, that would seem to be the end of the question. For conscience sake, he should do what Mary says. The *Exhortation* by his fellow bishops that I quoted from earlier said that 'we must in such case patiently suffer all wrongs and injuries; referring the judgement of our cause only to God'. Just like Calvin, it quotes *Romans*, 'the powers that be, be ordained of God'. So at the very least, one would expect Ponet to pass over this damaging passage in silence. However, in fact, he does not avoid mentioning *Romans* 13. Indeed, he takes it in his stride. For him, it merely supports his overall theme that political power was instituted for the sake of justice. So it fits into the argument: since

God has a purpose in appointing the powers that be, the ones that do not fulfil this purpose are no longer the object of the command to obey. He also has another obvious but nevertheless powerful dialectical move available. Since this purpose is the point of princes, anyone who does not fulfil it is not really a prince at all. If Mary does not behave like a queen (as the word of God explains what it is to be a queen), then she is not really a queen. And, of course, if not a queen, she can be resisted, punished, or otherwise eliminated. The Bible only tells us to obey the powers that be, but her actions have made Mary merely one of the powers that were. The argument Ponet is using here was formerly used, as he is quite explicit, by some of his opponents, the Catholics. They claimed that the church might dispense with a Pope that had, for example, become a heretic. As Ponet puts it, 'it is lawful ... to remove him from his office, for he is no bishop or pope that abuseth his popedom and bishopric' [103].

I shall come back later to Ponet's use of Catholic material. However, staying for the moment with Protestantism, the seeming ease with which Ponet turns aside the most central text against him shows the perils of biblical interpretation. This can be illustrated by another biblical passage on kings also frequently referred to at this time. *The Epistle to the Romans* is at least a New Testament, Christian text. But this next fought-over passage is from the depths of the Old Testament, a work that might be thought merely to contain instructions for a distant Jewish people and lack relevance for modern, Christian Europe. However, the whole Bible is the word of God and, as such, it was pressed into service. Therefore much was made of some remarks the prophet Samuel made while attempting to dissuade people from having a king. You want a king, Samuel said, but here is what kings will do: they will take your children, the best of your fields, a tenth of your sheep, and so on. A fairly straightforward warning, it would seem. Or perhaps not. In this period, it gets quoted as remarks about the 'rights' of kings. So here we have a message of God himself about the rights of kings: kings have a right to take your daughters, the best of your fields, a tenth of your sheep, and so on.

One of Ponet's chapter headings is 'whether all the subject's goods be the kaiser's and king's own' [79]. He says not: private property is independent of kings and 'kaisers'. Hence taking it is theft; it is not allowed even for kings. However, someone picking up this passage of

Samuel can read, as the direct word of God by way of his prophet, that kings have a right to their subjects' fields and flocks. Naturally Ponet resists such a reading ('this was spoken of the prophet Samuel to fear the people . . .' [87]). You have your view, and with the view you sort out the interpretation. Neither view is just absurd, and anyone who thinks that it is just absurd to think that kings are entitled to take what they want at whim should wait for Hobbes. But Hobbes not only has the view (on other grounds than biblical interpretation); elsewhere he cites this text itself. In his citation [*Leviathan*, 20.16, p. 105], Hobbes says 'God himself by the mouth of Samuel saith, *This shall be the right of the kings ..*'. Notice how Hobbes calls it a 'right'. So, much earlier, did Calvin (in the Latin edition of the *Institutes*). They are probably helped by the Latin Bible, the Vulgate, where it reads, *Hoc erit jus regis*; it is a *jus*, a right, what is just. On the other hand, someone wanting to attack Hobbes, such as George Lawson, who wrote *An Examination of the Political Part of Mr. Hobbs his Leviathan*, wants to show that 'the translation . . . is perverted'. For Lawson, it should be 'this is the manner of the king'.

So they went at it. It does not matter to them that these are merely the supposed words of a long dead shadowy figure. It does not matter to them that this was an obscure quarrel of a distant people. They do not see problems in reportage, textual transmission, and translation. The context makes these the direct words of God (of his Holy Ghost, speaking by the mouth of the prophet). Another example from the time of Hobbes is the poet John Milton. Once the king was executed in England, the Royalist party contracted a leading continental scholar, Salmasius, to write an attack on the barbarity. Salmasius quoted this part of the Bible on the rights of kings to take their subject's property (royal taxation without parliamentary consent being at the centre of the English arguments). The English regicides hired Milton to defend them. He waded into Salmasius and, being Milton, went deep into the Hebrew. Samuel was not talking of what kings ought to do, but of what they wanted to do. An earlier example is Bodin, at the start of his chapter on sovereignty. Again discussion of the Hebrew. This time, Luther's follower, Melanchthon, gets criticised for thinking that Samuel talked of the rights of kings. And so it went on. The King James version of the Bible, and more modern translations, do not talk here of rights. So if God spoke in Hebrew rather than Latin, then Lawson, Milton, and Bodin were right, and Hobbes, Melanchthon, and Calvin were wrong. But this is not the main point. The main point is that the Bible is a very flexible direct word of God.

At the first flood of Reformation enthusiasm, it might be thought that all that was needed was to open up the Bible (duly translated into the vernacular) and find what to do. The Old Testament, regarded by more circumspect interpreters as God's instructions to a particular people, the Jews, is taken to lay religious duties on all people. John Knox read there that the greatest sin was idolatry, and that a people who permitted idolatry (as the ancient Jewish people are frequently represented as doing) was heading for damnation. Particularly if they had covenanted to obey God, they had a religious duty (as well as the natural self-interest of avoiding everlasting damnation) in extirpating idolatry. Hence, in Scotland, they had a religious duty to remove the Catholic Queen. She went, eventually adding her name to the sad, romantic, executed queens of history. The oratory of Knox was such that when people left church after one of his sermons, they tore apart the idolatrous building that was across the road (and presumably not just because they were relieved to get out of the church). So the power to tear kingdoms was there. But there was also the fact that this power could be used in many directions. Something else had to be found to provide justification and authority.

The Law of Nature

In fact, even Protestant Ponet, writing at almost the same time as Knox was preaching from the Bible against Catholic idolatry, uses, as I showed, arguments drawn from Catholic sources. There are wider and longer rational traditions on which he could draw than the bitterly contested interpretation of a single authoritative text. The seemingly seamless Middle Ages, on which Protestants supposed that they had made a great advance, had had its own political problems. With highly educated clerics, but clerics on different sides and also working for the secular powers, these problems led to intellectual argument, and political theory is pressed into political service. Emperor fought with Pope; Pope with Emperor. In each of these realms, inferiors worried about superior power. The Italian cities wanted an intellectual position that freed them from the Emperor; they would be princes for themselves, much as King Henry later declared England to be an empire.

The bishops had problems with the Pope. Indeed, anyone would be bound to have some sort of conceptual problems with the Pope at a time when there were first two and then eventually three Popes, all claiming supreme, full, single authority. This was at the high point of the so-called conciliarist movement, the idea held by some prominent churchmen that church councils were superior to Popes, that the body of the church was superior to any one member, even its head. The Pope was held to be greater than any single lesser person or power, but less than the whole. Hence the outlines of a constitutional position of limited monarchy were constructed in the Middle Ages, just as the outlines of self-governing republican liberty.

The arguments were there. This is why Ponet, the Protestant bishop, when he is pushed, can start using Catholic arguments. He can note 'at one clap, in the council held at Constance in Germany, in the year of our Lord 1415, were three popes popped out of their places' [103]. So Popes went; 'it is no new thing to depose evil kings and governors'. (He also claims that a later council had 'Pope Eugenius served with that sauce'; however he fails to note that this time the sauce serving was unsuccessful and indeed, once Constance had restored a single Pope, the days of popping Popes were over.) Under pressure, Ponet uses and explicitly recognises these Catholic precedents. He says that the 'reason that moved them' is 'honest and just, and mete to be received and executed among reasonable creatures', calling it 'this law of nature to depose and punish wicked governors' [102–3]. The key here is this so-called 'law of nature'; the additional arguments on which Ponet can rely are those of natural law. Shortly after mentioning the popping of Popes, he says of 'the law of nature' that it 'testifieth to every man's conscience, that it is natural to cut away an incurable member, which (being suffered) would destroy the whole body', noting that while kings 'are the heads of a politic body, yet they are not the whole body' [108]. Hence we may proceed to the cashiering of kings.

So it is not just what some Catholics happen to have done. This would not be persuasive for a Protestant bishop. It is, rather, their appeal to the law of nature, a law that can be appealed to by Catholics and Protestants alike, indeed by Christians and non-Christians. The point of the law of nature is that it is universal. Ponet describes it in a completely standard way, but it will be useful to look at his standard description to understand its possibilities. For this so-called law will be our constant companion and problem through the next few chapters. In his work (which, it will be remembered, I am merely using to place problems on the stage), Ponet says that the law of nature 'is no private law to a few or certain people, but common to all : not written in books, but graved in the hearts of men : not made of man, but ordained of God : which we have not learned, received, or read, but have taken, sucked, and drawn it out of nature' [107]. The sentence continues, but this is enough to give us the first flavour of the possibilities and problems of the 'law of nature'.

This law is a law in the same sense as the positive laws of particular countries with which it is here contrasted. That is, it prescribes what people ought to do. We might wonder, therefore, how it can be 'natural', thinking perhaps that laws are norms (oughts, prescriptions), whereas natural things are facts (*is* rather than *ought*). Alternatively, we might think that there is no law but positive law, laws that are instituted by particular law-makers. However, Ponet says here that it is not a law for 'a few or certain people', such as the positive laws constructed by particular law-makers. The whole point is that instead it is 'common to all', universal rather than particular. It is therefore the law on which all countries and people agree rather than the laws separately instituted by each. In fact, as I said, Ponet's thought is absolutely standard both for the time and also for the preceding centuries. This is what 'natural law' or 'the law of nature' then meant. The modern idea that a 'natural law' is a scientific law that describes the blind, factual, operations of nature dates from after Ponet.

Universality and nature go together. This starts with the classical Greek contrast between those things that are true by nature and those things that are true by convention. *Phusis* against *nomos*. From these Greek words, we might expect the former to turn into physics and the latter to turn into prescriptive norms. However, if we take Aristotle as an example, he says that 'there is in nature (*phusei*) a common principle of the just and unjust that all people in some way divine, even if they have no association or commerce with each other' [*Rhetoric* 1373b]. That is, it is common or universal, rather than being local or conventional. It is true by the nature of things rather than particular human agreements. Yet it is still law in the prescriptive sense; it delineates what is just. Aristotle here quotes from Sophocles' *Antigone*, a play in which Antigone appeals to a justice outside the conventions or norms of a single city, of her own city. So it is the same move as Ponet much later makes, reaching to something outside the conventions of a particular country to criticise what is happening at home. In other words, there is more to what we ought to do than be merely citizens of our own country (city). Our ethical life is constructed by more than our own particular communities. According to the Latin writer Cicero, when Socrates was asked to where he belonged, he replied 'the world' [*Tusc Disp* V 37]. In Cicero's *Laws*, he claims that the mind can realise that it is not shut in as the resident of a particular spot 'but is a citizen of the whole world (*civem totius mundi*), as it were of a single city' [*De Leg.* I 23]. We are citizens of the world; the city that frames our ethical life is universal; our home is wider than our first home. Right things will not just be right in Rome or Jerusalem but right everywhere.

If there is such a law, such universal justice, then its truths obviously cannot come from the particular actions of particular peoples in particular places. It has to come from nature ('sucked out of nature' as Ponet put it in the long sentence quoted earlier). So it cannot just depend on where we happen to have been educated or on what we happen to have read (hence Ponet's claim that it is 'not learned, received, or read'). Hence our knowledge of it has to depend upon our (universal) human nature. It has to be innate in us, or at least accessible on the basis of our innate, natural qualities. It is, as Ponet puts it here, 'graved in the hearts of men'.

This would seem to be merely problematic or impossible, but we can add another element that also goes back to its classical origins. This is the idea of reason. People are, by nature, rational animals. They, universally, are reasonable creatures, able to use reason in the discovery of truth. So if we can use reason (natural reason) in the discovery of justice, then we can discover what is just by nature; discover what is just independent of human conventions. So, for example, Cicero says that 'true law is right reason in agreement with nature (*recta ratio naturae congruens*)' [*Republic* III, 22]. Aristotle and Cicero are non-Christian, pagan authors; what Ponet calls the 'ethics'. However, when we turn to Christianity, although Augustine thought that Christians should be pilgrims (aliens) in this world and that our real city was the heavenly city of God, in the high Middle Ages Thomas Aquinas can say that 'natural law is nothing other than the sharing in the eternal law by rational creatures (*rationali creatura*)' [ST 1a2ae. 91 art2rep]. We have

now added the Christian God (although there are also theological elements in Cicero's account), a god that supports the 'eternal' law. Yet
this eternal law is the law of a rational God and, as such, recognisable
by human creatures. So, just as the 'ethnics' used reason, we also, by
the use of 'right reason', may discover the universal 'law of nature'.

God, of course, also appeared in the long sentence I quoted earlier
of Ponet, the Protestant bishop (where he said that the law of nature
is 'not made of man, but ordained of God'). Elsewhere he talks of
'God's laws (by which name also the laws of nature be comprehended)'
[22–3]. The world is ordered by God. The truth about what should be
done, like every other part of proper order, must come from God.
Indeed, its creation by God helps to explain how the law of nature can
contain true, independent, universal principles of justice. Not for one
city, but for the whole world, since the whole world is God's; as God's
rational creature I am citizen of the world. Creation by God also helps
to solve the problem of the prescriptive quality of the law – that is, how
it is meant to bear on the will and motivate people into action. For if
natural law is the will of God, then it is applied as will to human wills,
spurring them into action.

So far, perhaps, so good. With God, we have argumentative resources lacked by the 'ethnics'. However, when we bring in God and
the will of God we still have a problem. This is the problem of the
relation between the will of God and the truth of this universal natural
law. Is the law of nature good because God wills it, or does God will
it because it is good? That is, are there indeed rational truths about
goodness that form an independent, rationally discoverable natural
law, a law that we can know that God wills because both God and the
law are rational? Or is it that, by contrast, there is nothing good or bad
in itself, but God just makes things good or bad for us by his pure will
and power?

On the former option, there is scope for reason, something in
which, albeit imperfectly, created people can copy God. We can use
our natural reason to find out the natural law; to find out what we
ought to do. Hence the pagans (the 'ethnics') can discover it. On the
latter option, there is merely the inscrutable will and power of God.
Reason is then of no help to us, and we can only find out what to
do by discovering what God wants. Then it seems that only Christians
should be able to tell. We need revelation. We need to read the Bible,

the word of God, to discover his commands. However, if we are back to the Bible, then we seem to have lost natural law as a resource with which we can criticise the actions of Popes and kings. We are back again to the contentious interpretation of particular texts. We have also lost a resource that can be applied in any kind of argument with any kind of person, be they Protestant or Catholic, Christian or non-Christian. There is no reason why such people should take note of the deliverances of this particular text (as opposed to the deliverances of reason itself), even worse if the text indicates that the much of the will of God is inscrutable.

In the high Middle Ages, the world could be supposed to be a rational world, constructed by a rational God according to laws comprehensible in part by rational creatures. Optimism about human powers meant optimism about the possibility of our discovering some of the content of natural law by reason alone. Old, pagan, classical philosophers were pressed into service. Aristotle was synthesised with Christianity. Yet long before the conciliarists were popping Popes, late Medieval thinkers were exhibiting a lack of confidence in our ability to have or know a purely rational law of nature. In William of Ockham, for example, reason is not able to reveal the real essences of things, and law is only what is commanded. God happens (as we can read in the Bible) to have commanded us not to kill, but he might as easily have made murder a virtue. We can make no inferences based on reason alone into the nature of the good. This late Medieval lack of confidence was taken further by the Protestant Reformers. They were deeply pessimistic. Human beings are flawed, fallen creatures. Original sin has destroyed our independent possibility of goodness, both with respect to knowledge and also with respect to motivation. We may only wait for undeserved grace, unable by any act to ensure salvation. Particularly with Calvin, we get a hidden, terrifying God, whose mere arbitrary will determined before the origin of the world who was to be saved and who damned. The divine mysteries of his regal power are not to be penetrated. Rationality is of no use. We have merely faith, hope, and submission. This divine power could be copied by the new divine-right kings, whose mysteries of state were also not to be penetrated and whose terrible, apparently arbitrary, will we also merely had to obey.

Mystery, faith, obedience. In this context, we might perhaps hope to get beyond the terrible, arbitrary will of the king to the even more terrible, arbitrary will of God. Neither of these wills would be more obviously rational than the other, and so it would be pointless to criticise either from the standpoint of rationality. However, the bigger battalions are on the side of God. The risk of the king's dungeons and executioners are outweighed by the risk of the everlasting fires of hell. Of course, if absolutely everything is predestined by mysterious almighty power, and if our appearance in heaven or hell is purely arbitrarily attached to anything we attempt to do, we cannot rise even to this purely prudential rationality. Nothing is left but prayer. However, we might be slightly more optimistic, thinking that we have some scope to exercise common prudence. Then, as people like Ponet illustrate, we may read the word of God to discover what he wills us to do with the king.

What Hooker Knew

This is a pessimism about knowledge. Yet, on any account, knowledge of natural law is liable to be problematic, and this problem frames much of the story that follows. For even if it is no longer possible to recapture the confidence of the high Middle Ages, what has to be recaptured is something that fills the argumentative space occupied by traditional natural law. Just as the religious armies fought themselves into stalemate on the battlefields of Europe, so also with the war over the religious texts. The word of God is disputed. We cannot just read off the answer. We need something else to guide our interpretation. We need another way of finding out what is right. As rational creatures, we need to be able to use our rationality. So, somehow, rationality has to be recovered. As we approach the great seventeenth-century political philosophers, we may think of them in different ways applying rationality to politics, as giving different descriptions of natural law. This is not merely a recovery of high Medieval rational confidence. It is a new natural law. However, as I just put it, it occupies the space of the old natural law. It aims to give considerations of reason that can be applied universally, and that therefore can be used in arguments between Protestants and Catholics in a deeply divided Europe, and in arguments between Christians and others in a world in which it has been discovered that most of its inhabitants are not Christians guided by the Bible.

Of course, some, particularly Catholic, thinkers of the time continued in the Medieval manner, and Protestants like Richard Hooker (whom Locke several times quotes favourably) specifically wished to redeploy Medieval natural law as a way of resisting the Bible-based views of the more extreme Protestants who wished to reconstruct his church. Hooker can in fact be used as an example of the possible resources of traditional natural law to contrast with the new constructions to come. He is half-way in time between Ponet and Hobbes, and like them, conveniently for our purposes, writes in English. I shall use him here as a quick example by drawing on only one chapter of his main work, *Of the Laws of Ecclesiastical Polity* (which he published in 1593). This is Chapter 8 of Book I, and is entitled 'Of the natural way of finding out laws by reason to guide the will unto that which is good'. In other words, Hooker intends here to deal with all the central elements already mentioned of natural law: it is a prescriptive law influencing the will, it is a law of reason, and it comes from, or is about, nature. The obvious problem with natural law is also suggested in this chapter heading. This is the problem of how it can be found out, or known. Hooker's claim in the chapter is that there is a 'law rational... which men commonly use to call the law of nature, meaning thereby the law which human nature knoweth itself in reason universally bound unto'. So we have nature, we have reason, and we have binding force. We have a claim to knowledge. However, how we might acquire such knowledge has still to be explained.

On the face of it, there are two ways we could discover these truths of practical reason. We might investigate reason itself or we might investigate reason's effects on people's beliefs and behaviour. Hooker in fact tries both. He says that 'the most certain token of evident goodness is if the general persuasion of all men do so account it'. General agreement is to be the chief test of the truth of natural law. This is a coherent strategy. As we have seen, the truths of natural law are universally true, true for all times and all peoples. Therefore we may hope to discover these truths by finding their effects on the widely varying peoples for which they are true. If these peoples who vary in so many other ways all nevertheless agree in believing them, this provides substantive evidence for their truth. Another Protestant divine, if not quite a bishop like Ponet, Hooker here brings God into the explanation. He says that 'the general and perpetual voice of men is as the sentence of

God himself'. God has made natural law true for all people. Therefore what all people recognise as true can be taken to be the voice of God because 'that which all men have at all times learned, nature herself must needs have taught; and God being the author of nature, her voice is but his instrument'. So this is one method, a plausible a posteriori proof procedure but obviously depending on the truth of its empirical claims. It will only work if there are as a matter of fact things about which all people agree.

The other method, an a priori method, is to look at reason itself. Since, or so Hooker claims, there cannot be an infinite regress of reasons, the 'main principles of reason are in themselves apparent', or self-evident. There have to be what he calls 'axioms' that are 'so manifest that they need no further proof'. Hooker gives examples of such axioms, such as 'the greater good is to be chosen before the less'. If anything is self-evident, this would indeed seem to have a good claim. (Situations can be constructed where the greater good can only be gotten by first choosing the less, but what Hooker clearly means is that faced with an exclusive choice between a greater and a lesser good, it is rational to choose the greater.) However, the problem with this method is that we are just expected to know, or see, that certain proposed truths are self-evident. Either we just introspect our own intuitions, or else this method collapses into the first method of discovering whether there are universal practical intuitions, shared by all peoples. Some other of Hooker's proposed 'axioms', such as *God to be worshipped* or *parents to be honoured*, are much less obviously axiomatic than his first example. They are less obviously axiomatic because they seem more obviously culturally relative. They have a smell of Biblical instructions, and so seem to come from Hooker's own Protestant culture. Other cultures may manage to get by without a god; family relations work differently in different places. Yet these two proposed 'axioms' are both highly prominent in the Christian Bible. Revelation, which puts Hooker in a privileged position, may here be providing an alternative track to discovery of the will of God, even though the point of Hooker's chapter is that these 'laws are investigable by reason without the help of revelation'.

Of course, different methods may give the same result, and we can see the conciliance of Hooker's methods in another of his examples. This is the so-called 'golden rule' (although not here so called by him), the claim that we should treat others as we would like them to treat us. This can be found in the Bible (both Old and New Testaments). It is one of Hooker's proposed 'axioms'. It is something that he says 'all men acknowledge to be good'. Therefore for him it has universal agreement (the voice of God) behind it. Indeed, in the next century people did manage to provide impressive empirical evidence of just how widespread and disconnected were the cultures in which the golden rule was held. So we could use different methods. We could use Biblical revelation, we could rely on the axioms of practical reason, or we could engage in empirical observation of agreement in belief between widely varying cultures. Whichever method we use, we will still come up with the golden rule. So it might seem that we could set it down as a proper part of the natural law, understood as it was at this time as part of the will of God.

Indeed, Hooker says even more about this example than this. For in this case, he does not merely cite it as an 'axiom' but also provides some rational grounding for its truth (or at least for the truth of the closely related instruction that we should love others as ourselves, also prominent in the Bible). He argues that my desire to be loved by others imposes on me a 'natural duty' of bearing the same affection to them. The assumptions here are a basic equality and that we have to act, or feel, for reasons. Given this, there is no reason why I should have something that does not equally provide a reason for others to have it as well. I cannot claim that I should be loved without being rationally committed to the claim that so also should others. This is a familiar argument, or, more accurately, later became familiar. Nevertheless, it reminds us of the resources of pure practical reason.

So, as we approach the new (seventeenth) century and, in the next chapter, the more seriously argumentative start of this book, Hooker suggests resources as to how we can know natural law; how, that is, we might reach objective truths about practical reason and justice with which we might construct a political philosophy. However, Hooker's 'most certain token' is that there is universal agreement on some of these principles, and the general persuasiveness of his claims centrally depends upon this assumption. Yet, as we shall discover shortly, it is just this presupposition that at this period particularly comes under threat.

This is a serious, potentially devastating, threat. Without universal agreement, no axioms; without axioms, no knowledge; without knowledge, no available natural law. It might perhaps be replied that many truths elude knowledge, and natural law just happens to be one of these. However, we can here deploy an argument that shows that if there is natural law at all, then it is something of which we should have knowledge. This argument can be introduced by considering a question raised by Aquinas, which is whether promulgation is essential to law [ST 1a2ae. 90, 4]. At first, it seems not because natural law, which Aquinas affirms here is 'law in the fullest sense of the word', does not need promulgation. Natural law, that is, being truths of reason, just seems to be there, and so is not promulgated by particular people. On the other hand, as Aquinas observes from the law of the church, it is a principle that a law only has effect when it is promulgated. This he defends because a law has to be 'applied' (*applicatur*) to have force, and promulgation is its application. He could have concluded from this that natural law is therefore not, after all, law in the fullest sense. However, since he holds to the assumption that it is law, he reaches the conclusion that natural law must, contrary to first appearances, have been promulgated. As he puts it, 'natural law is promulgated by God's so inserting it into men's minds (*mentibus*) that they can know it by nature'. In other words, we get an argument for the claim (as made, for example, by Ponet) that natural law is engraved on the minds (or hearts) of people. There is no valid law without promulgation; hence we must in some way be able to know natural law if we are to be judged by it. Hence there must be a way in which we can know natural law. Hence it must be inscribed in our hearts, written in our minds, or some such thing. What seemed to be an unwritten law, by contrast with the written laws of particular countries, turns out also to be in some way written (engraved, inscribed). Indeed, some people thought that this was not a metaphor, and that the law of nature was literally a part of written law. It was another bit of the written word of God. This word of God that we have to follow was taken to be written in two ways, both written in the Bible and also written in the hearts of men. Reading either, we discover that we are not to kill, that we must love others as ourselves, and so on.

This is effectively a bootstrap argument as it relies on a truth of natural law – namely, that it is unjust for people to be judged and condemned by a law that they could not possibly know. So promulgation becomes a matter of natural justice, or as it has been put more recently, it is part of the 'inner morality' of the law. The premiss of the argument is a (supposed) truth of natural law; therefore if there are no truths of natural law (or none known), the argument cannot start. However, if we are allowed to suppose that there is no valid law without promulgation (as, in fact, is supposed by most people), then if there is valid natural law, there clearly has to be promulgation. Christians have the Bible, and they may assume that promulgation for them is via the Bible. Then they presuppose that the will of God is such that the truths of revelation coincide with the truths of reason. However, these truths of reason are also meant to apply to people who do not have the Bible. If these pagan people are also supposed to be bound by these truths, obliged to keep the same universal natural law, then the truths must also have been promulgated to them. Hence, as well as being in the Bible, they have to be written on the hearts of all people. Or, if this is just thought to be a metaphor, natural human reason must be sufficient to be able to discover the truth about what we ought to do or be.

Universal Doubt

If there is such universal inscription, we should be able to gather wide-ranging evidence for its truth. If the fundamental truths of justice are intuitively knowable by everyone, then we would expect widespread cross-cultural agreement on these fundamental truths. However, as I said, it is just this that at this period comes under threat. We can see this in a later defender and user of natural law, John Locke, whose political philosophy will be considered later. When a young man, Locke lectured at Oxford (in Latin) on the law of nature. Part of his argument is that there is indeed such a law of nature. However, his third lecture is devoted to arguing that it is not 'inscribed in the minds of men' (*hominum animis inscribatur*). The argument here is that it is not known by the young, the foolish, and so on. Even more devastating is the fifth lecture, which is devoted to establishing that the law of nature cannot be known from 'the general consent of men' (*ex hominum consensu*). For this is directly rejecting what Hooker and all the others before him thought.

Locke was a great collector of traveller's tales. As more peoples were discovered, more variety in human behaviour was realised. Locke uses some of this material in arguing in Book I, Chapter 3 of his *Essay Concerning Human Understanding* that there are 'no innate practical principles'. Cicero had held that what had unanimous consent was innate (*innatus*); here Locke claims that 'it is impossible to establish a universal consent'. Once people look 'abroad beyond the smoke of their own chimneys', they then find that 'the Caribs were wont to geld their children on purpose to fat and eat them' and so on, and on. Even the 'great principle of morality' that was used earlier as illustration is dispatched, for, claims Locke, '*to do as one would be done to, is more commended, than practised*'. This last objection, however, only works as an argument if (as Locke in fact also holds) behaviour may be taken as the best evidence for belief. The argument used is about universal agreement about principles, not about whether these principles are universally put into practice.

This is a much later snapshot of the problem of universal agreement, even though it is from someone who nevertheless claims to believe that there is a law of nature. The problem of universal agreement (by rational creatures on the law of reason) was already severe at the time that Hooker was writing. It forms the intellectual world into which Hobbes and Grotius were born. It forms the final piece of the background to their difficulties in constructing a new natural law. Part of the reason why the results of these philosophers is so interesting is because their work was so hard. The times were not propitious for optimism about rational construction. It was a deeply sceptical age. It is not just that people were thought to be sinful and flawed, threatened by a hidden and terrifying god. It was not just that all the accepted Medieval religious beliefs and practices had been disrupted and put into question. So also was its complete, Aristotelian-based, science. As Hobbes's contemporary John Donne put it, 'the new philosophy calls all in doubt; the element of fire is quite put out'. In Hobbes's and Donne's day, all was still in doubt because the old science had been lost, but the new replacement science was yet to be formed. These sceptical problems relate to knowledge of natural bodies, the science of the physical world. However, things were, if anything, even worse with respect to knowledge of the moral or human world (and, no doubt, have been so ever since). Religion leads to conflict, and conflict leads to doubt. New worlds are discovered with people behaving differently, people knowing not God. There are different religions, beliefs, customs, and laws. Ancient scepticism is rediscovered. The world is a world of appearances. Things can be said for and against each question, but the truth is undiscoverable, indeed may not exist. There is much talk about what ought to happen, but these *oughts* compete. People ought to obey their princes without question, people ought to obey God rather than man and pop their princes, and so on. But these are just competing appearances.

Indeed, to the disillusioned, cynical eye, these moral appearances can all be stripped off to reveal the underlying naked play of interest. We can, perhaps, have a human science, a science of politics, but this is a purely descriptive activity, showing how people are driven by their interests. We can analyse what people actually do; we can make no coherent sense of what they ought to do. Machiavelli can be read as instructions about how to survive in a brutal and hostile world; Tacitus was in fashion. However, it might seem that nothing can be coherently said in the subject we now think of as political philosophy – that is, the rational consideration of normative ideas applied to political action. We can describe people competing and killing, but we can no longer discuss how people ought to live together in a city.

In the next chapter, I shall start to examine Hobbes's radical response to moral and political scepticism. However, first let me finish this chapter by outlining some of the challenge Hobbes had to meet. Hobbes first became aware of the force of the problem of scepticism and started formulating his answers while on an earlier stay in Paris than his civil war exile there. This was in the 1630s, when he first became acquainted with the circle of leading thinkers around Marin Mersenne. All these thinkers were interested in trying to answer scepticism. Nowadays, the best known member is Descartes (and Hobbes wrote one of the *Objections* that Mersenne collected and published to Descartes' *Meditations*). Descartes is today a staple of undergraduates starting philosophy with the problem of scepticism, even though he tends to be more used as a way of putting the problem rather than for his own answers. In any case, Descartes' answers are to metaphysical scepticism, proving first himself then the good God who does not deceive us. As regards the moral and political scepticism that Hobbes was trying to resist, Descartes does not get very far. The best he can do (in his *Discourse on the Method* of 1637) is to outline a 'temporary house', which he proposes to inhabit until the problem is resolved.

The first principle of Descartes' 'temporary house' is to 'obey the laws and customs of my country'. This response, to keep the law and follow custom, is the response of the sceptics themselves. The Mersenne circle was reacting to the French sceptics of the previous generation, principally Montaigne and Charron. Montaigne notoriously carved on the beams of his room the question, 'what do I know?' Charron turned it into a statement, carving on the front of his house, 'I know nothing' (with not even the saving Socratic, 'except that I know nothing'). Both recorded with delight the great variety of morals and conflicting ways in which different people live. Just as with ancient scepticism, it was this variety (the variety of the appearances of the good) that is the source of their scepticism. Different countries have different customs. There is no way of saying which is right. Therefore, according to them, we should just live according to the customs of our country. 'Now the advice which I have to give to him that would be wise', says Charron in his long book *On Wisdom*, 'is to keep and observe both in word and deed the laws and customs he findeth established in the country where he is' (II.8.7).

This is a suitable sceptical response. Follow the apparent flow of life. However, it undercuts truth. As Charron puts it in the same section, 'laws and customs are maintained in credit, not because they are just and good, but because they are laws and customs: this is the mystical foundation of their authority, they have no other'. Yet if this is all there is to justice, then as Montaigne notes, justice changes when we cross a river or a mountain range. Montaigne himself objects to this that 'truth ought to have one face, always and everywhere the same. If a man's justice and equity had any substance and real existence, he would not let it be bound by the conditions of this country or that' (*Apology for Raimond Sebond*). So the relation between universal agreement and objective truth about justice is turned the other way round: because there is no agreement, we have to conclude that there is no justice.

It might be thought that this does not matter in the sceptical strategy, since this strategy is precisely to follow the appearances and bracket out all claims to truth. We can still carry on the practical business of life, in our temporary houses, following the appearances. This might perhaps be a practical answer to certain kinds of metaphysical scepticism (perhaps the demon deceives me as to whether it really is an apple, but appearing to eat the apparent apple gets me by). However, it will not work in precisely the areas with which Montaigne and Charron were most concerned, politics and religion. The sceptical writings of Montaigne were meant to promote fideism in religion (I follow the religious appearances of my society) and political passivity and obedience (I accept what appears to be justice on my side of the mountain). We just follow the local customs; in a later way of putting it, we play the language games of the world into which we are born. However, in neither politics nor religion will this work if there is a conflict of customs, a discordant clatter of competing language games. Yet when Montaigne was writing, France was destroying itself in the wars of religion. In such conditions, there are no agreed local customs about either politics or religion. So following custom and appearance may not even be a temporarily habitable house. With civil war, or other internal political turmoil, custom can no longer be taken even as a practical guide.

Therefore some attempt has to be made, made by reason, to outline some more universal and objective truth. This truth can then be used to adjudicate and persuade in a discordant world, a world rent by civil and international war. This truth, this truth of reason, will be universal and international. It will not be derived from differing customs or from contested texts. It will not just be a description of how people actually behave. Instead, we will have a defensible method of making value claims that can be applied to the stuff of politics. These value claims will be independent of the Bible, with its competing local customs of interpretation, they will be independent of individual prophetic enthusiasms, and they will be independent of church traditions.

So this is what we need. This is the profound problem (a problem still with us) to which the philosophers discussed in the next chapters supply answers. In doing so, as I said, they can be thought of as supplying new constructions of natural law. This natural law, or law of right reason, can then be used against the scepticism that erodes the possibility of objective moral truth. The escape from scepticism starts before Hobbes, with Grotius. In the *Prolegomena* to Grotius's great work on the laws of war and peace, he takes on Carneades, the ancient sceptic. Carneades here is standing in for the modern sceptics. Grotius produces a new natural law to justify right action in war and peace. It is used to establish the rights of warring nations, to adjudicate arguments between Protestants and Catholics. Reason speaks, independently of contentious texts. Grotius's great work was published in 1625. However, I shall defer discussion of him until a later chapter. Instead I shall start with Hobbes who, partly influenced by Grotius, also constructed new rational foundations. I start with Hobbes because what he creates from an absolutely fundamental starting point is still one of the most radical and challenging political philosophical constructions ever. It was viciously attacked in his lifetime, and has ever since been a favourite target. More disagreed with than followed, Hobbes is still someone whom nearly all subsequent thinkers have had to find their way through, or round.

2

The Great Beast Leviathan

Hobbes wrote two books named after biblical beasts. One was *Behemoth*, his history of the English civil war. This, like the beast Behemoth himself, is still little known. The other was *Leviathan*. Both it, and its name, are much more familiar. After giving the work its title, the great beast first appears in the text itself in the chapter that explains the origin and nature of what we now normally call the state. A unity has to be produced from a multitude of people, and when this is done we have 'a common-wealth, in Latin *civitas*. This is the generation of that great Leviathan, or rather (to speak more reverently) of that Mortal God, to which we owe under the Immortal God, our peace and defence' [17.13, p. 87]. So Leviathan is what we now normally call the state, what Hobbes normally calls the commonwealth, and what he says should be thought of as a 'mortal god'.

This is the first entry of the beast who gives his name to Hobbes's great work. One reason for the work's greatness is that it shows how a political philosophy could be constructed by the use of reason alone. Or so I claimed in the last chapter: Hobbes gives authority to reason at a time when there was not only deep conflicts that blunted the power of biblical or church authority, but also serious scepticism about the power of reason itself. We shall come later to the problem of scepticism about reason. However, even on the brief evidence cited so far, there seems to be a prior problem about whether Hobbes is really relying on rational rather than biblical authority. Leviathan is, after all, a biblical beast, and even if for Hobbes he is a mortal god, he is still subject to the immortal god – that is, God himself. Also, as I noted in the last chapter, on the frontispiece of *Leviathan* we get a biblical quotation. So it is the Bible that Hobbes chooses to deliver the most succinct statement of what the work is about. It seems therefore that it is the Bible that lends it its authority. Later in the work, Hobbes explains how he has 'set forth the nature of man together with the great power of his governor, whom I compared to Leviathan'. He gives the biblical reference, saying that he took 'the comparison out of the two last verses of the one and fortieth of *Job*, where God, having set forth the great power of Leviathan, calleth him king of the proud' [28.27, p. 166]. (The Book of Job is one of the books that constitute the Old Testament, the part of the Christian Bible that is in common with the Hebrew scripture.) Then he quotes from *Job*, including the passage on the title page (there it is in Latin, here in English; typically he quotes there from memory and here he gives his own translation). So there is no doubt what particular point Hobbes intends by using the mysterious term 'Leviathan'. Although Leviathan, a gigantic, powerful sea monster, appears in the Book of Psalms, and although he is God's enemy, Satan himself, in the Book of Isaiah, it is clear that Hobbes wants to use him as he is used in the Book of Job.

So, to understand the beast, it seems that after all we have to understand the Bible. *Job* is a work of justification. It tries to resolve the old problem of why the good frequently seem to suffer and the bad seem to do well. Job is a good man who does everything right, and yet has the most appalling sufferings. He demands an explanation. Various friends attempt to justify the ways of God to man. They do not do very well. Eventually God himself appears. Here we might expect a superior piece of moral philosophy, or reasoning, resolving the problem of pain and showing why Job's sufferings fit into God's just world. This is not, however, what we get. Instead, God, out of the whirlwind, shows just how much of nature is completely out of Job's control. Then, in Chapter 41, he gives a long description of Leviathan. 'Canst thou draw out Leviathan with a hook?', God asks. No, continues God, the beast is far too great to be caught. Job could not put a hook in his nose, play with him like a bird, and so on. All this would be pointless in the face of such power: 'out of his mouth go burning lamps, and sparks of fire leap out. Out of his nostrils goeth smoke, as out of a seething pot'. Arrows, darts, and such like are hopeless against him; 'he laugheth at the shaking of a spear'. So we have here a lengthy description of a creature of enormous power. Nothing can frighten him, and it is pointless trying to threaten, or attempt to capture or kill him, let alone try to bargain with him ('will he make a covenant with thee?'). So, in the face of such power, we do not try to bargain or ask for justice; the only rationality is the rationality of prudence. Faced with a beast who 'esteemeth iron as straw and brass as rotten wood' we need to be fearful, respectful, and silent. Our attempt should merely be to preserve ourselves. As the Bible sums it up, in the King James version from which I have been quoting, 'upon earth there is not his like who is made without fear'. This is the verse (in Latin) in the frontispiece of Hobbes's *Leviathan*. In this Latin version, the word 'power' is inserted. There is no power on earth, it says, that can be compared to him.

So power is what it is all about. Power is what the famous title of Hobbes's book represents. We ask for justification, and the answer we get is power. This is the answer for the biblical Leviathan, described as 'king over all the children of pride'. His power gives us reason, however proud we are. This is the answer for Hobbes's own Leviathan, his 'governor', the sovereign. These 'mortal gods' are also properly kings over the proud by virtue of their power. They are terrifying monsters, not to be covenanted with but merely feared and obeyed. It is the same for the immortal god – that is, God himself. Job asked for justification, and the answer he got was a revelation of power. As Hobbes himself puts it, in a later reference to Job in *Leviathan*, the question of why the good suffer 'is decided by God himself, not by arguments derived from Job's sin, but his own power' [31.6, p. 188]. God is far too powerful to need to explain himself. Leviathan, by contrast, is a mere creature of God. Indeed, as he appears in the *Psalms*, he shows the power of God, because God can master even the Leviathan. However, no one else can. From our point of view, Leviathan also does not need to explain himself. He also relies upon sheer, stupendous power. So also with that other creation, the mortal god, the state. It also is less than God himself. It also, no doubt, can be controlled and mastered by God. However, from our point of view, the state does not need to justify itself. The power of its argument is again power itself. In the chapter of *Leviathan* on power, Hobbes calls it 'the greatest of human powers' [10.3, p. 41]. It is the king of all the proud, and (as the frontispiece puts it, winding the quotation behind the sovereign with the sword) there is not its like on earth.

So that is Leviathan, at least as represented by Hobbes. He is a biblical creature, God's answer to Job. However, although Leviathan is a biblical creature, Hobbes's description nevertheless also gives a first clue as to how we might reconstruct political philosophy for a sceptical age. The reasons that God gives to Job are in a sacred text, but their validity does not depend upon the text's being sacred. They do not depend upon any accepted written authority. Instead, they are reasons that can be universally understood. What both God and Hobbes do with the beast Leviathan can be appreciated even when all else is argument, civil strife, and confusion. We may lack all authority for argument, but we can use the argument of power. As the Mafia might put it, after placing the horse's head in the bed, it is an argument that cannot be refused. The horse's head threatens death to the person whose bed it is, and thereby gives him a reason to act. We may not like or approve of it; we may even think that it is a reason he might after all refuse, but we all understand how he has been given a reason. So, whatever we think of the Bible or whatever our competing views of moral authority, we all understand the motivational force that can be applied by superior power. For Hobbes, irresistible might is irresistible right. As he puts it, 'to those therefore whose power is irresistible, the dominion of all men adhereth naturally by their excellence of power' [*Lev* 31.5, p. 187].

This is a first clue to how we can take something that seems to be based on biblical quotation and find instead lurking in it universal content, a universal reason for action. This reason works for the biblical scholars, for those thinking themselves subject to almighty God. They have reason to do what God says that derives from his almighty power. However, it also works for everyone else. It works for those subject to the mighty Mafia or the mighty Leviathan. They also have reason, the same reason, to do what they are told; they also are subject to mighty power. So although in Hobbes we get the words of God, if we ask why we should bother about the words of God, Hobbes's answer here is that 'the right... whereby God reigneth over men... is to be derived... from his *irresistible power*'. Power endorses God, so perhaps we can dispense with the biblical texts in which (at least as read by Hobbes)

God endorses power. It is power that gives the primary reason; the reason based on sacred text is merely circumstantial.

So once we shake the core out of its quaint biblical clothing, we seem to find a prudential respect for power as the central, motivating reason for action; and, indeed, I shall later try to show that something like this is analytically correct as to the deep structure of Hobbes's argument. However, to pull this plum out from under the biblically scarred surface of the text is deeply problematic. Hobbes not only lived in the religiously saturated world described in the last chapter, but also seems to be just as concerned as the people described there to swap biblical quotations and appeal to biblical authority. Indeed, he was cited there as a participant in a long-running argument about how to interpret the biblical Book of Samuel on the rights of kings. The entire body of Hobbes's text is clothed with biblical quotation. So reading Hobbes without the religion may merely be an anachronistic adaptation for our own modern interests, a Hobbes for heretics. No doubt, parts of what Hobbes says can be fitted into models of universal reason, just as can parts of the religious thinkers discussed in the last chapter. However, the question is whether in the end Hobbes is really any different from Ponet and Hooker, as they were described there. With both, we have bits of universal reason, called natural law, but also large doses of biblical quotation. *Leviathan* is composed of four parts, and the last two parts (little read, but half of the work) are all about religion and the state. They are called 'Of a Christian Commonwealth' and 'Of the heart of Darkness'. When, late in life, Hobbes published a Latin translation of *Leviathan*, he added a new appendix designed to clear up problems. We might expect to find here Hobbes's own response to the tricky political objections that have been made to his work since its first appearance. Not so. What Hobbes wants to put right are, as he sees it, theological misunderstandings to what he had said. The first chapter of the appendix, for example, is on the Nicene Creed. The second is about heresy. The third is explicitly called 'On certain objections against *Leviathan*'. Here we might expect to get something similar to Descartes' *Replies* to contemporary objections – that is, Hobbes's response to what we now take to be the heart of the work, the political theory. However, what Hobbes's replies are in fact about is the Holy Trinity and the Kingdom of God.

That is one problem I shall pick up later: if we need to use the Bible to decode the thought (as I have just attempted to do in understanding the biblical beast Leviathan), we cannot just separate the thought from the Bible, or think that it does not depend upon biblical authority. But, as was seen in the last chapter, if it does depend upon biblical authority, then it will not only be deeply contested, but also, even if it succeeds, speak to no more than a sect. Yet what Hobbes wants and needs to do, placed in a sceptical age amid deep conflicts of all kinds, is to find a new natural law, based on universal reason. This reason has to appeal to Bible readers and non-Bible readers, Protestants and Catholics, Christians and pagans. This leads to the next problem. For if Hobbes's new reasons, which are meant to do this, are Mafia head-in-the-bed reasons, mere considerations of personal prudence, it is doubtful whether they can fill the space of natural law, as traditionally conceived. It is doubtful whether they will have the content, and do the job of, the 'right reason' of Cicero or Aquinas. Yet Hobbes also thinks he can provide much of this content, such as keeping agreements, or having neutral arbiters (it being universally agreed to be against natural justice for the judge to have a personal interest). Having such content helps him to call it, as he does, the 'law of nature'; but the problem then is how this content can be constructed from reasons of mere self-interested prudence.

Hobbes Himself

So these are two methodological problems to pick up before we examine Hobbes's construction of his new so-called natural law, and his subsequent explanation and justification of both states and the justice that, he thinks, only states can provide. However, before doing this, let us learn a little more about the man and his works so we can better place them amid his age and his problems. I have been talking as if *Leviathan* were all there was to Hobbes. However, *Leviathan*, although it is Hobbes's best known work, is neither his first, nor even his second, treatment of his political philosophy. In fact, it was written when he was over sixty. So before continuing the pursuit of the great sea monster, and before solving the two methodological problems I have just listed, we need to gain a better and a fuller sense of what was going on when Hobbes wrote both it and its predecessors.

Hobbes was born in 1588. *Leviathan*, one of the founding texts of modern political philosophy, appeared in 1651; so, as noted, its author was already in his sixties when it was written. The year of Hobbes's birth, 1588, was the year of the Spanish Armada, the great invasion fleet that was sent by Catholic King Philip of Spain to topple Protestant Queen Elizabeth from her throne. Hobbes said that he was born as a twin with fear, the story being that the news of the Armada caused his mother to go prematurely into labour. Born with this twin, Hobbes lived with fear. Fear led him into to exile in France early in the conflicts between king and parliament (1640). Fear is also the driving theme of his philosophy. We have seen that the whole point of the beast Leviathan is that he is so terrifying. *Leviathan* says that the 'passion to be reckoned upon is fear' [14.31, p. 70]. So if power is (perhaps) one clue to Hobbes's philosophy, fear, its obverse, is another. Power gives reason to command and fear gives reason to obey. Indeed, if the whole of Hobbes's philosophy were to be summed up in a sentence, it might be that we would have so much to fear from each other without a state, that it is rational for us to have a state that we fear even more. Put thus baldly, this does not sound wholly rational; yet rationality driven by fear is the work's central motif.

Hobbes was not just fearful. He had reason to fear. Although people near power were personally somewhat safer than in the century described in the last chapter, it was still a dangerous age for people who were in the wrong place at the wrong time. In the sixteenth century, as described in the last chapter, an Archbishop of Canterbury was burned for heresy. In the seventeenth century, while Hobbes was in fearful exile, an Archbishop of Canterbury was executed for being too good a servant of his king. Earlier, shortly after Hobbes left, the king's chief servant, Strafford, was executed. Later, the king himself (who naturally had also been on the side of the king) was executed. So, death for those prominently on the side of the king. Hobbes, who during this period was firmly on the side of the king, had some reason to be fearful. Then parliament took over, there was an interregnum in England, and Hobbes started to have things to fear in France. He returned to England. After some years, the monarchy was restored, and Hobbes now had other things to fear. He was denounced as a heretic. It was thought that the 1666 Great Fire of London might be divine punishment for harbouring Hobbes. Parliamentary proceedings were started against him. He could not be sure that the days of burning heretics were over. He worked on the law of heresy to show that it could not (legally) happen to him. The nearest in fact he came to the flames was when, after his death, his books were burned by the public hangman at Oxford.

So, a fearful world, danger, things falling apart, and Hobbes is right in the centre of civil conflict. This, incidentally, reveals yet another problem in taking the message of *Leviathan* to be just that the sea monster state is so terrifying that we should cease argument and simply obey without further thought. For Hobbes is writing in the midst of a succession of civil wars (and of arguments about who was to govern and how they should govern). This shows that whatever else people feared, they were not in fact so fearful of the existing state or government that it was quite unthinkable for them to ask questions or oppose it. Of course, everyone who took up arms thought that he was defending the state, as he understood it, rather than attacking it. But this is not the kind of mistake anyone would make about the Leviathan described by God in the Book of Job; therefore the Leviathan described by Hobbes in the book of *Leviathan* seems to be limping somewhat behind. His first shot at the problem of conflict and obedience (at least in terms of writing a full, connected treatment) was during the first arguments between King Charles and his parliament in 1640. Hobbes was at the time engaged in writing a comprehensive study of all useful knowledge. However, the conflict, or emergency, led him to advance the more political part of the work. So in that year he circulated a manuscript draft to his friends of the work he called *The Elements of Law*. The *Elements*, written in English, contains a clear, fluent, treatment of Hobbes's political philosophy, which did not change greatly in his two later treatments. It is in two parts, *Human Nature* and *De Corpore Politico* ('The Political Body'), which were turned in 1650 into two published books, seemingly without Hobbes's knowledge or approval (my quotations here are not from these books but from a modern edition of the manuscript). Hobbes left for exile in the year he wrote the *Elements*, and in 1642, now in Paris, had another treatment of his political philosophy printed and circulated to friends for comment. This time he wrote in Latin, and called the work *De Cive* ('On the citizen'). Again, and more specifically so, this was only part of his overall project, which was to be a work in three parts that would give, successively, the true knowledge first of matter, then of human nature, and last of political reality. Eventually something of this shape did appear in three Latin works, the first part as a book on body in 1655 (*De Corpore*) and the second part as a book on man in 1658 (*De Homine*). However, again, or so Hobbes claimed, the political emergencies of the time forced him to advance the third, political, part of his work, so that it appeared well before the others. The 1642 version, (which, being given to friends for their criticism, was a printed, but not strictly a published, edition) was rewritten by him and then published by the famous Dutch publisher Elzevir in 1647. It was the work that first made Hobbes's international reputation. In Latin, still the language of international intellectual exchange, it was the main work used by later continental admirers of Hobbes (such as, for example, Pufendorf).

De Cive is divided into three parts, 'Liberty', 'Government', and 'Religion'. Hobbes begins the Preface by saying that 'this book sets out men's duties (*officia*), first as men, then as citizens and lastly as Christians'. So the citizen part is sandwiched between a consideration of natural duty (natural law – the duties we have as human beings) and material more specifically about Christianity. *De Cive* rivals *Leviathan* in having a revealing frontispiece. This time, the picture is divided into three parts, corresponding to the three parts of the work. In the part captioned 'Liberty' (*Libertas*), we see skimpily dressed people with bows and arrows either hunting animals or each other. This represents the first part of *De Cive*, 'liberty' – that is people without government. The picture is taken from contemporary pictures of native Americans, who were thought to be in such a condition. (Later, in *Leviathan*, Hobbes replies to the charge that there is no experience of people without government by citing 'the savage people in many places of *America*' [13.11, p. 63].) By contrast, in the picture of 'Government' (*Imperium*), we have prosperously dressed people engaged in agriculture. (As it might be, England before the civil wars.) At the top of the picture, 'Religion' (*Religio*), we see a portrayal of the last judgement with people heading for heaven or hell.

This top part of the picture is the part occupied in *Leviathan* by the mighty sovereign with his sword (and the Latin quotation from the Book of Job). As an educated scholar, writing in Paris and appealing to other educated Europeans, Hobbes had written *De Cive* in Latin. However this next work, *Leviathan*, is written in English. Hobbes clearly

therefore had an English audience in mind, and, indeed, within a year
of its publication, he returned to England. By now the king, whom
Hobbes had supported, had been executed, and England was being
run by the regicides. It might be thought (and this was alleged by his
enemies) that Hobbes wrote *Leviathan* to smooth his path of return to
the successor regime, and some remarks at its end do indeed seem to
be pitched towards the contemporary English situation. However, he
was still in exile in Paris when he wrote it; he was not only in contact
with the exiled court, but had been acting as mathematical tutor to
the old king's son, the crown prince in waiting. Hobbes dedicated a
specially inscribed manuscript copy of the work to the prince. Rather
than trying to pave the way for return with his work, it is more likely
that he had to return because of the offence its religious opinions gave
to the exiled court.

In Hobbes's theory actual power is important. Old royalist as he was
(and late tutor to the crown prince in waiting), he nevertheless felt
he could make his peace with the new regime. They were the ones
who actually had the power. This may have looked like a good bet in
1651, but, as mentioned above, by 1660 the exiled prince had been
restored. Power had shifted, and Hobbes looked as if he had backed
the wrong side, as well as having attracted the odium natural to people
who change sides (at least from those who do not). The Restoration,
as it was called, sought to restore all the old powers of church and
king and pretend that the distressing interlude had not happened.
This was when Hobbes, who looked to be a threat both to state and
church, came under pressure as a supposed heretic. All the people
he had offended had now returned to London. His old mathematical
pupil, the newly restored King Charles, called Hobbes 'the bear'. King
Charles enjoyed watching Hobbes being baited at court. They went for
the beast. Hobbes was hunted; *Leviathan* was hunted. The religious
professionals did not like the suggestion involved in Hobbes's biblical
beast that only enormous power counts. They objected. The bishop
of Derry, Bramhall, wrote a work called *The Catching of Leviathan, or
The Great Whale*. The bishop, like God, would master the great sea
creature. George Lawson, a Shropshire pastor, wrote the *Examination*
of Hobbes, which was quoted from in the last chapter. For him, 'civil
government derives its being from heaven'. He objects that a community 'is a multitude of reasonable men, not a leviathan, which is

an irrational brute'. However, for Hobbes, the power of the irrational
brute gives reasons to reasonable men.

In this period of suspicion of him, Hobbes was not allowed to re-
publish the hunted and hated *Leviathan* (its first publication had benefited from the lack of censorship in England during the interregnum).
However, it appeared abroad in 1668 in a Latin version, translated and
altered by Hobbes himself, making a fourth instalment of his political
philosophy (this is the one with the appendix noted above). Hobbes
also wrote some other works with political relevance in this last period of his life (although, again, he was not allowed to publish them),
such as his history of the civil war, *Behemoth*, and his *Dialogue Between a
Philosopher and a Student of the Law*. So, with a very long and active life,
we have several works of Hobbes to use as a basis of the study of his
thought. However, even though we can see the effects of changes in
the political environment, and even though Hobbes responds to crit-
icisms, the central core of his political thought is remarkably stable.
In what follows, I shall use all three treatments as evidence (although
my references to them will enable anyone more suspicious or sensi-
tive than I am to see from which stratum a particular remark comes).
The only thing that needs to be remembered is that the *Elements* and
Leviathan are written in English and that *De Cive* is written in Latin, so
I am quoting a (modern) translation (it used to be thought that
Hobbes himself had produced the translation that appeared in his
lifetime, but since this is not the current received opinion, I am not
using it).

Biblical Authority

With these biographical and bibliographical details in place, it is time
to return to the problems. The first (the natural and deepest philosophical question) is the source of Hobbes's authority. By what right
does he speak?, and why should anyone bother about what he says?
More specifically, we now have to establish how fairly Hobbes may be
disentangled from the biblical quotations that fill his text, and from
the corresponding claim that he relies on Biblical authority. Of course,
like Ponet and Hooker described in the last chapter, he wants to lay out
natural law. But what is the authority of this law, and how can Hobbes
know it? The answers to these two questions for the people studied in

the last chapter was God (God created it and gave it authority; also, one way or the other, by Bible or reason, God enables us to know it). So the problem is whether Hobbes's answer is any different.

It is not contested that Hobbes had a good knowledge of and made extensive use of the Bible. *Leviathan* alone refers to more than fifty books of the Bible. Nor shall I discuss, or contest, the claim that Hobbes was a Protestant believer. His contemporaries argued over Hobbes's real beliefs, and debate is just as divided today. Hobbes lived at a time in which it was politic to hide one's real views about religion, so he, like others, was liable to be misunderstood. Even in modern commentary on Hobbes, we see him placed as everything from an atheist to an orthodox Protestant thinker who believes that the Bible is the basis of our knowledge of God's law of nature. It is pointless to try and achieve any speedy or conclusive resolution of this question. However, luckily, this is not the question that needs to be answered. What, instead, has to be decided is how much of a load-bearing role God has to play in Hobbes's political philosophy, and my claim will be that he does not. I think, and will attempt to show, that the premises, argument, and conclusions would all still stand even if we were to remove God from the thought. Hobbes believed in God (or at least said he did), just like virtually all his contemporaries. However, if the religious elements in his thought were to be removed or refuted, this would not lead to the inevitable collapse of the rest.

This is the important question in deciding how or whether Hobbes's thoughts can travel into our contemporary agnostic age. Of course, we have to be methodologically careful. This particular rational reconstruction, this Hobbes for heretics, is just what we would expect. Just because this is our modern point of view, this is the way we naturally tend to read Hobbes. So we have to be careful. Our reconstruction is liable to put the opposite pressure on Hobbes's central thought to the pressure that operated at his own time. We try to squeeze out the religion, hence may be disposed to eliminate it more rapidly than we properly should. The pressure on Hobbes himself was to keep in the religion so that the readers of his work could navigate between familiar landmarks. It is all a question of balance. It would be as absurd on the one side to think that Hobbes was really only writing modern games theory as it would be absurd on the other to think that he was no more than another minor player in the battle of biblical texts described in the last chapter. The crucial question is, as I put it, whether the religion is load-bearing in the doctrine, hence to what extent a rational reconstruction may properly be attempted. It is important for us to see what ideas we can get from Hobbes with the religion stripped off. If God is not load-bearing in the system, then we may legitimately do this. However, it seems that this is also fair to Hobbes himself (and is connected with his unsavoury, heretical reputation).

This unsavoury reputation was of course connected with more direct theological views such as his treatment of the Trinity (where, as we have seen, Hobbes was still defending and modifying his views in his eighties). However, he also uses the Bible in his more political work, so the bishops who attacked him had a basis. It is not just the biblical creature, Leviathan itself, that needs biblical knowledge in order to decode. It is also that in both the *Elements* and in *De Cive*, Hobbes has a whole chapter in which he quite explicitly shows that his new natural law can be supported by the Bible. In the last chapter, we saw Ponet in exile using the Bible and preaching sedition, the removal of the tyrant queen. Hobbes, by contrast, in his exile wished to support kingly power and argue in favour of the established order. He is against sedition. In the preface to *De Cive*, he says that any preacher who says that it is consistent with the word of God (*verbo Dei*) that a sovereign may rightly be killed or citizens may rightly take part in any rebellion is not to be believed [21]. So preachers like Ponet are to be rejected; the word of God is rightly to be read in a different way. Yet, while rejecting sedition, Hobbes also uses Biblical authority. As we saw, the word of God on submission to lawful authority was read in many different ways. As Hobbes reads it, the word of God will not license sedition; in this, he returns to the views of the original Reformers. Like them, he uses the *Romans* text described in the last chapter about being subject to the powers that be. So far, this could be merely Bible against Bible, just as was there described, the intellectual arm of the religious wrangling that led to dissension and war. Some preachers preach sedition, others (with Hobbes) preach obedience, both refer to the word of God, and both denounce the other in the name of God. All of this makes Hobbes sound exactly like the people described in the last chapter, makes it natural for the bishops to attack him, and was familiar in their biblically saturated world. Nevertheless, my aim is to show that in spite of these biblical appearances, the Bible is not in fact for Hobbes a fundamental resource in the way that it is with Ponet (or Luther or Calvin or Hooker, or even Locke). Indeed, given the conflicts over biblical interpretation, it couldn't be: once all depends upon the Bible, people read the Bible in different ways, and we have civil strife and sedition. Hence, if we wish to avoid this (avoid the disaster of a civil war partially caused by conflicting interpretations of the true religion), we should neither rely on, nor let people engage in, their own biblical interpretation.

The interpretative aim is ultimately to elude the Bible, but this has to be made compatible with the Bible's being read into the fine texture of the text. Here is another example. In the chapter of *Leviathan* called 'Of Civil Laws', Hobbes says that 'heaven and earth shall pass; but not one tittle of the law of nature shall pass, for it is the eternal law of God' [26.24, p. 144]. This explicitly tells us something about the 'law of nature', just as in the last chapter it is held to be an unalterable constant (universal and immutable). However, again as in the last chapter, it is claimed that this is because it is the law of (the universal, immutable) God. So the doctrine itself seems to bring in God, in what I called a load-bearing way. It is because it is the eternal law of God that we have the law of nature. However, the connection with the law of God is not only explicitly claimed here by Hobbes, but is also more subtly suggested by the way he phrases his text. For it closely echoes the Bible, God's sacred text, and hence acquires additional authority. Any of Hobbes's contemporaries reading his claim that 'heaven and earth shall pass; but not one tittle of the law of nature shall pass' would naturally think of the biblical remark that 'it is easier for heaven and earth to pass, than one tittle of the law to fail'. This is as in the King James translation, the authorised translation of Hobbes's day (the unusual word 'tittle' appears not only here [*Luke* 16.17] and in the similar *Matthew* 5.18, but also at both places in Tyndale's earlier translation). Not a tittle shall pass says the Bible; not a tittle shall pass says Hobbes. So it would seem that Hobbes says what he says because the Bible says what it says; that the Bible is not just convenient clothing but also the authoritative basis of the thought.

Nevertheless I aim to show that neither God nor the Bible is ultimately load-bearing in the core of the thought, and in so doing, I have to discover on which other authority (or authorities) Hobbes relies. At that time, if book-based authority did not come from the Bible, it came from the recovered books of the classical world. So the answer might be that Hobbes turned back the gnarled darkness of the Bible by flooding it with the bright lights of classical Greece and Rome. This idea also seems to fit well with his biography. Hobbes was not only biblically learned; he was also a good scholar of the Greek and Latin classics. In his eighties, he translated the whole of Homer from Greek into English just to fill up his time. His first main published work was also a lengthy translation, this time of the Greek historian Thucydides. It was as a classical scholar that he was recommended to a noble family on graduating from Oxford, and for the rest of his life his employment was as a servant to this and other families, working as a secretary and tutor to the children. His knowledge of the Greek and Latin classics was the key; such humanist education was prized and major families wished to give it to their children. If Hobbes makes a new start, therefore, after the biblically inspired disputes described in the last chapter, it might be expected that he does it by bringing to bear the bright pagan lights of the classics. However this is not how in fact it happens. Hobbes could indeed see religion causing sedition and wars, and wishes to try and curb this capacity of religion. Yet he also thinks that sedition and wars are also caused by classical knowledge. A major cause, he thought, of the civil wars in England was people's reading of the Greek and Latin classics. As he puts it in *Leviathan*, 'by reading of these Greek and Latin authors men from their childhood have gotten a habit (under a false show of liberty) of favouring tumults and of licentious controlling the actions of their sovereigns' [21.9, p. 111]. He thought, as he puts it in a later chapter, that 'men have undertaken to kill their kings because the Greek and Latin writers in their books and discourses of policy make it lawful and laudable' [29.14, p. 170]. So also in his explicit history of the English civil war, *Behemoth*, where he says that people 'became acquainted with the democratical principles of Aristotle and Cicero, and from love of their eloquence fell in love with their politics' [43]. That way sedition lies as well, and Hobbes' argument is against sedition and in favour of strong sovereigns. So the authority on which he relies is neither the Bible nor Cicero. Classical humanist and biblical scholar though he was, there is no point in trying to draw out his Leviathan with a hook baited with either Biblical texts or classical quotation.

So if not the Bible or the Greek and Roman classics, what else have we got? In fact, the most revealing way to look at Hobbes is not as a textual scholar or as a religious polemicist but, instead, as a scientist. He is best thought of as a participant in the modern scientific revolution. His laws of nature (understood in the traditional sense of the rules of right conduct) were for him similar to what we now more normally call the laws of nature (meaning descriptions of the regular behaviour of the universe). Hobbes applied what he called science to morals and politics. He says that the 'science' of the 'laws of nature' 'is the true and only moral philosophy' [*Lev* 15.40, p. 79]. In his own mind, he was not only the scientific innovator in this particular area but also a master of the whole scientific field.

In the dedicatory epistle at the start of *De Cive*, Hobbes outlines the parts of 'philosophy' (*philosophia*). He says that 'in treating of figures it is called geometry, of motion physics, of natural law (*de jure naturale*) morals, but it is all philosophy'. Here we get an extended sense of 'philosophy' so that it includes what we would now call 'science', or such subjects as physics and geometry. But notice that by 'natural law' Hobbes does not mean such physical (or geometrical) scientific laws but, rather, what is properly the subject matter of 'morals' (*moralis*). So natural laws are the universal, objective principles of right action, as discussed in the last chapter. On the other hand, the study of these is part of an overall subject area ('philosophy' or 'science'), which includes as well physics and geometry. All the first parts of *De Homine* are about optics, with diagrams, discussions of microscopes, refraction, parabolas, ellipses, and so on. Both the *Elements* and *Leviathan* start by discussing perception. *De Corpore* is stuffed with geometry. So (to use our later language), Hobbes was a scientist who discussed with scientists; it was as if Galileo or Newton had ventured into political philosophy.

Science was not mere dispassionate knowledge. It had a practical point. Hobbes, who had worked briefly for Bacon, believed like him that knowledge was power. Power gives reasons and reasons give power. At the start of *De Cive* he explains the point of his political philosophy (his civil science, *scientiam civilem*). The geometers, he notes, have managed to produce strong defence works and marvellous machines. 'If the moral philosophers', he says, 'had done their job with equal success I do not know what greater contribution human industry could have made to human happiness' [Ep. Ded. 6]. Since Hobbes has not yet acted, this is yet to come. However, its point for him is clear. It is the knowledge we need in order to achieve better practice. As he asks in a string of rhetorical questions in the Preface, 'how many men have been killed by the erroneous doctrine that sovereign kings are not masters but servants of society?' [5]. It is like medicine: we make scientific advances which we can then apply to the saving of lives. It is like geometry: we start from agreed definitions and then prove 'theorems'. Looking back in *Leviathan*, he reflects that 'neither Plato nor any other philosopher hitherto have put in order and sufficiently proved all the theorems of moral doctrine' [31.41, p. 193]. Theorems are what we are after. However, once we have the theorems (thanks to the proofs of the great moral scientist Hobbes), we then put them to use. For, as he also says here, 'the science of natural justice is the only science necessary for sovereigns'. Sovereigns act, and the science on the basis of which they act is Hobbesian civil science.

With this emphasis on natural civil science in mind, let us return to the problem of the relation between Hobbes's natural law and his use of God and the Bible. The question here, as I put it before, is whether God has a load-bearing role in Hobbes's use of natural law and in the political philosophy that he uses it to construct. The crucial point is the following. If God is to feature as an intrinsic and essential part of the science of politics that Hobbes develops, then the important thing is not whether God exists but whether he is a fit subject for science. Natural science must be based on natural knowledge, and so the important question is whether God's attributes can be known. Yet Hobbes claims that our belief in God (and particularly our beliefs about his nature) is a matter of faith, not of knowledge. Thus, in *De Cive*, he says that 'there should be no arguing about the nature of God' because we cannot understand the nature of God by reason alone [15.15]; or, in the corresponding place in *Leviathan*, after making the same point, he adds 'in the attributes which we give to God we are not to consider the signification of philosophical truth but the signification of pious intention' [31.33, p. 191]. In other words, it is a matter of faith and piety, not of what he here calls 'natural science'; hence it can not be the basis of political science.

In Hobbes' own list of the sciences, such as the large chart of them that he draws up in the ninth chapter of *Leviathan*, theology does not appear. Once the queen of the sciences, it has now been shunted off into a quite different area. Writing after Hobbes, the German philosopher Pufendorf makes this particularly clear in his account of the law of nature. He starts by distinguishing it from theology on the one side and civil law on the other: there are lawyers; there are theologians; he is doing something different. So was Hobbes before him. A particular example of the importance of this is our knowledge about survival after death. If God is to be conceived of as a normal law-maker, then he has to be able to punish us for non-performance of his laws. The orthodox account of God's punishment is that this happens at the last judgement, when after death everyone is divided into sheep or goats for dispatching to heaven or hell. So if this divine law is to have a scientific, law-like role, it has to guide our actions through knowledge of God's intentions both as to what we ought to do and also as to what will happen to us if we don't do it. We might be able to acquire the former knowledge naturally; this is the problem of promulgation of the law of nature as discussed in the last chapter. However, without using faith or the Bible we would seem to be completely stuck on acquisition of knowledge of the last judgement (of the punishment for non-performance). Hobbes claims that 'there is no natural knowledge of man's estate after death' [*Lev* 15.8, p. 74], so the crucial piece of knowledge is not available to us naturally. Therefore in our scientific construction of natural law, we have to do without knowledge of God's intentions for us in the afterlife. These may be perhaps be available by use of the Bible. However, it is not given naturally, and hence cannot be part of natural political philosophy. We may in fact have these beliefs in what God does, and they may indeed be consistent with the constructed system; however, they cannot play a load-bearing role in the construction.

Hobbes's central consideration is natural law, and this is what we are attempting to reconstruct and see whether it can be used in our sceptical age. For Hobbes, the science of natural law is part of natural science. Hence it cannot contain, or depend upon, anything supernatural. Yet, as we have just seen, God himself, God's attributes, God's actions such as at the last judgement, are all supernatural for Hobbes. So they cannot be in the core of his philosophy. Nor can we get them indirectly, by naturally validating the sources of revelation. For, as Hobbes puts it, 'no man can infallibly know by natural reason that another has had a supernatural revelation of God's will' [*Lev* 26.40, p. 149]. We cannot use our science to prove that the Bible is a sacred book, which contains revealed truths. As Hobbes puts it in the *Elements*, 'the knowledge we have that the Scriptures are the word of God is only faith' [11.8]. So as well as not being able naturally to know these things directly, we are not even able naturally to know that they are indirectly available by means of revelation.

This is the answer. No load-bearing role. But why then all the use of biblical quotation? Partly it is because Hobbes did not limit himself to politics. Instead, he wanted to study, know, and tell people about everything that could be known, whether it was matter, geometry, or theology. He thought he could show how to square the circle (to the derision of the geometers); he thought he could explain the truth of the doctrine of the Trinity, misunderstood for 1,500 years (to the derision of the theologians); he had, of course, reduced politics to a set of theorems where even Plato had failed. He could do everything. So, as well, he had to explain how his biblically soaked contemporaries had actually misunderstood their sacred text. But also, more seriously and importantly, there is nothing against the idea that God does not have a fundamental load-bearing role in the use of many methods, providing that these varying methods all produce the same answer. Hobbes, that is, can rely on a concilience of methods, just as we saw Hooker doing in the last chapter. I mentioned how both in the *Elements* [chap. 18] and also in *De Cive* [chap. 4], after establishing his new natural law, Hobbes inserts a chapter showing, as he calls it in the *Elements*, 'A confirmation of the same out of the Word of God'. God can confirm, but that does not mean that he bears the load (that the new natural law would disappear without him). If God is rational, what comes from reason is also what will come from God. We can establish things by experience, by the use of reason, by reading the word of God. We should, on perfectly traditional ideas about God, get the same answer. (If, instead, we have non-traditional ideas about God, then we have the answer anyway.)

Scientific Authority

Establishing Hobbes as a scientist, looking for natural knowledge, properly places God in his philosophy. However, it can lead to other misunderstandings. Thinking of laws of nature as we do now, as purely descriptive, may lead us to miss how Hobbes's natural study is still a normative (or prescriptive) study. The remark I quoted from *De Cive* about how philosophy studies morals does not mean that Hobbes is engaged in a merely descriptive study, of the kind we should now call the psychology or sociology of morals. Hobbes's account of natural law is still in this respect like Aristotle or Cicero, as described in the last chapter; it is natural but it is also law. There is, in addition, a related but more specific misunderstanding (or what I claim is a misunderstanding) that we have to be careful to avoid. With the presence of what anyone would call descriptive, scientific, material, and with both the *Elements* and *Leviathan* starting with sense perception, it is tempting to think that the foundations of Hobbes's political philosophy must lie in the area that we nowadays call natural science. It is tempting, that is, to think that we must first sort out Hobbes on body (on matter and motion) in order to understand Hobbes on the citizen (more matter and more motion). Some of what Hobbes himself says does indeed imply this. However, in the Preface to *De Cive* where Hobbes describes his overall scientific project, he also claims that this part can stand alone 'since it rests on its own principles known by reason' [19]. In Chapter 2 of *De Corpore*, Hobbes similarly claims that experience enables us to consider some of the later parts of the system (such as human emotions or political conflict) without deducing them from the earlier parts. I shall follow here Hobbes's claim of such independence between the parts of his overall project. The political thought can be considered a science; its conclusions can be deduced from generalisations justified by experience. However, it can also be thought of as a relatively free-standing science. The experience with which it starts is general experience of people and society rather than the movements of inanimate bodies or the mechanics of perception.

Of course, as I said, both the *Elements* and *Leviathan* start before this, but this produces a slow lead in to the proper political philosophy, particularly in *Leviathan*. Reading *Leviathan* for the first time (the greatest work of the greatest political philosopher), it is natural to start at the beginning. However, students who do this are liable to feel dragged through a series of definitions about language and the emotions without apparent point. They may well wonder what all the fuss is about. If instead they had read *De Cive*, they would have moved much more crisply into the political philosophy. Or if they start with *Leviathan*, they would be better advised to start at the equivalent point to the start of *De Cive* and fill in the earlier bits later. This is to start with Chapter 13 on the 'natural condition of mankind'. This way, they would rapidly run into the most famous phrase in the book, about life being 'solitary, poor, nasty, brutish, and short'. They would rapidly hit formidable problems and an urgent need for solutions. Then, with the next chapter (corresponding to *De Cive* chapter two), they would start on the construction of the 'natural laws' that were going to make it all work – the 'civil science', the 'theorems' of moral philosophy.

If something useful is to be taken from the parts before this, it is not so much specific material that can be built on but, rather, some general ideas and analogies. Among the general ideas is that of science itself, and Chapter 5 of *Leviathan* is called 'Of reason, and science'. Here we get Hobbes's idea that reason is a calculating (or 'reckoning') faculty, that it derives consequences, and that these consequences can be reduced 'to general rules, called theorems' [5.6, p. 20]. The account of perception may also work not so much as a foundation but rather as an analogy for the problems to be solved in morals. Hobbes is a proponent of the primary/secondary quality distinction. This is the latest science; it was in the air. Galileo before Hobbes, Descartes about the same time, Boyle and Locke after; they all espoused it. As Hobbes puts it in the *Elements*, 'there is nothing without us really which we call an image or colour' [2.4]. Moving on to sound, he explains that the clapper of a bell 'hath not sound in it but motion' [2.9]. In other words, what we think we see or hear can be analysed as really being motions of air or light. So science shows us that how it is really is different from how it seems. The bell itself is merely in motion; sound is the effect of such motion on us. Hence the naturalness of a move to scepticism, to the thought that nothing is really as it seems. It is the same for Hobbes with values. He again thinks that we are merely talking about the effects of things on us. Things are not really good in themselves but simply seem good to us. Hobbes says that 'whatsoever is the object of any man's appetite or desire, that is it which he for his part calleth *good*' [*Lev* 6.7, p. 24]. Goodness, like colour and sound, is the effect of things on people, and different effects on different people lead to different opinions about what is good. Hence conflict. Hence all the difficulty of constructing a proper science of morals.

However, even if we play down such considerations of body, optics, and perception, and even if we start with Chapter 13 of *Leviathan* rather than Chapter 1, we still start with a world prior to politics. We still start with social nature before moving on to an account of political nature. If we start *Leviathan* where I suggested, we start with a chapter describing the 'natural condition of mankind'. This chapter is still in the part of the work called 'Of Man' rather than the part called 'Of Commonwealth'. Similarly in the *Elements*, the corresponding chapter is in the part of the work called 'Human Nature'. As we saw, the first of the three parts of *De Cive* is about man, before Hobbes moves on to the citizen. So in all these cases, prior to the politics, we need an account of human, pre-political, nature. As part of our account of such human nature, we need an account of natural law. Then, given this, we can go on to construct civil (or political) society.

Self Preservation

First, therefore, the natural law. This, the rational foundation of Hobbes's thought, does not differ significantly in his three central works. His problem in all of them is how in a sceptical age to make statements of human reason that can depend upon something fixed, or generally agreed. In referring to Hobbes's analysis of the frightening sea monster, I started this chapter by suggesting that the agreed use of reason on which Hobbes relied was brute head-in-the-bed prudential self-concern. The problem I mentioned a bit later was how any such merely prudential basis could form the foundation for a body of material playing the role of traditional natural law. This must now be considered and resolved, both as to what actually is the basis of Hobbes's natural law, and also as to how much he wishes to recover the content of the traditional law. I shall start this consideration in the remains of this chapter, before, in the next, bringing the new Hobbesian natural law to its full problematic flowering, ready for the support of the new Hobbesian state.

Where Hobbes actually starts – the fundamental axiom of his new science – is that it is rational to seek one's own preservation. Or at least, to put it more cautiously, that it is 'not against reason'. In the *Elements*, he says 'it is not against reason that a man doth all he can to preserve body and limbs, both from death and pain' [14.6]. He notes that what 'is not against reason, men call RIGHT, or *jus*'. So from the fact that people seek to preserve themselves, that they do not find it unreasonable, we are into rights, into justice, into natural law. Our conclusions are the conclusions of 'right reason'. In his next work, *De Cive*, he says (here translated from the Latin), 'It is not there-fore . . . contrary to right reason if one makes every attempt to defend his body and limbs from death and to preserve them' [1.7]. 'Contrary to right reason (*contra rectam rationem*)'; it could be Cicero or Aquinas, as described in the last chapter. However, unlike them, Hobbes's con-tent is more obviously prudential than moral; it is preservation of the self rather than respect for others.

This is not just a blatant substitution of content. It is more craftily composed than this. To begin with, it is not just the general assertion of self interest, the claim that it is rational to pursue one's own interest. Hobbes has quite specific interests in mind, the avoidance of death and physical pain. It is not just an assertion of egoism. Even if we think in moral rather than prudential terms, it will usually be agreed that people are permitted to protect themselves. For example, it is usually thought immoral to attack or kill people, yet this normally immoral activity is permitted in cases of self-defence. Here, defending oneself against death or pain gives a (moral) reason for action. More contested is the case of whether a starving man in a remote forest is allowed to break into a cabin in a clearing to get the food inside; however, this is also usually thought to be excusable, permitted. So, at least in some cases, that something is conducive to survival is taken to be an allowable good reason for action. It is right reason – moral, natural law. So by examining some allowable excuses for action, we can see that Hobbes's promotion of the rationality of survival has backing from accepted moral principles.

On the other hand, working for oneself and one's own survival clearly is (or is also) a self-interested activity. Yet, even as such, it is now generally regarded as rational. Indeed, there is an understand-ing of rationality (so-called economic rationality) in which rational-ity consists precisely of maximising one's own interest. So to say that something is in one's interest gives one a recognisable good reason for action. This is not to say that it is necessarily the best or strongest, let alone the only, reason for action. It is just to say that it is univer-sally recognised as a good reason. Hence it is something that can be appealed to in justification and explanation of action. Furthermore, as was noted, Hobbes does not here have interest-maximisation as a reason but merely its necessary condition, self-preservation. So however variable or contested other elements of people's interests may be, they all have a clear interest in survival, since without survival they would not have any of these other interests.

Hobbes is attempting to construct a universally agreed and experimentally based natural law. So far, he has the rationality of self-preservation. We have seen that this is generally agreed to be a moral excuse and that it also fits neatly with so-called economic rationality – two natural uses of reason. However, self-preservation is also natural in another sense. It is how people actually, naturally, behave. It is what can be seen to happen if we observe the nature of the human species. For humans, as organisms, their function is survival. This is a description of actual, biological, activity. Now, just because people actually do something does not by itself show that they have a reason to do it; how things are does not necessarily tell us how things ought to be. However, one way the transition can be made in the present case is considering whether they could have done otherwise. Let us return to acceptable excuses (as an index of acceptable moral reasons). It is normally thought that if someone cannot help doing something, this provides an excuse for the action. Yet Hobbes thinks that we cannot help attempting to survive; it is our nature. Even with the advent of the state, he thinks that the prisoner condemned to execution will still struggle on the scaffold. The desire to hold on to life is so strong that he cannot help it; and, if he cannot help it, then he cannot be blamed for doing it. So we might say that if the struggle to survive is inevitable, then anything conducive to survival automatically gives a reason for action.

However, this kind of point has to be made with caution. Hobbes was a deterministic thinker. All our actions are conditioned, and hence can be explained; the will for Hobbes is merely the last cause preceding the action. Yet if everything is determined, we are in danger of not being able to distinguish those things that people cannot help doing (and are therefore perfectly excusable) and those things that they can help, and so have no excuse. If excuses are going to work, we cannot make everything that is actual thereby excusable, merely by applying determinism (complete scientific, naturalistic, explanation). This means that we have to be careful. Even so, the desire to survive can be held to be (observably) much more central to our nature than nearly any other activity. It is, as was seen above, a desire that is presupposed by nearly all other desires. It is practically unavoidable. Hence, following this desire is both more natural and also more excusable than following nearly any other desire. The centre of our observable nature gives us central reasons for action. Therefore the struggle for survival is natural for Hobbes in a double manner. First, as rational animals, we naturally think it to be rational, both in a prudential and also in a moral sense. Second, it is natural in that it is what we most basically strive to do. It is the way in which the species naturally, instinctively, behaves.

Given this rationality of self-preservation, we can continue. If we have reason to preserve ourselves, we have reason to avoid situations in which our life or limbs are under threat. War is such a situation. Hence we have a natural reason to seek peace. As Hobbes puts it in the *Elements*, 'reason therefore dictateth to every man for his own good, to seek after peace' [14.14]. This is at the end of the chapter on 'the estate and right of nature' and he follows it immediately in the first paragraph of the next chapter by talking of 'the law of nature'. For Hobbes, as he says here, 'there can therefore be no other law of nature than reason, nor no other precepts of NATURAL LAW, than those which declare unto us the ways of peace' [15.1]. So, at least for Hobbes, to find the dictates (or precepts) of natural law is to find the dictates of reason, and this is to find out which kinds of actions promote peace. The structure he lays down here in his first work on the topic is essentially followed in the later, more famous, works. In *De Cive*, he defines a natural law as a 'dictate of right reason (*dictamen rectae rationis*) about what should be done or not done for the longest possible preservation of life or limb' [2.1]. In *Leviathan*, he says that a 'law of nature' is 'a precept or general rule found out by reason by which a man is forbidden to do that which is destructive of his life or taketh away the means of preserving the same' [14.3, p. 64].

This all gives us, as he puts it in *Leviathan*, 'the first and fundamental law of nature, which is *to seek peace and follow it*' [14.4, p. 64]. Actually this follows from a more complex formulation (which again appears in much the same form in the earlier works), which is that 'every man ought to endeavour peace, as far as he has hope of obtaining it; and when he cannot obtain it, that he may seek and use all helps and advantages of war' [14.4, p. 64]. If you have to fight, then survival dictates that you fight as well as you can (not, that is, fairly, but, rather, successfully). However, it is much better (much more rational, much more conducive to survival) not to have to fight at all. So the law of nature dictates the search for peace, and it is in pursuit of such search, as we shall see, that Hobbes mounts his argument that it is rational for people without government to acquire one. This is the topic of the next chapters, and a central premise is that without government, people are in a condition of war; hence, from what we have already seen, they have, as seekers after peace, a reason to remove themselves from this condition and get government. Justification of government (and not just of government but of complete subservience to absolute authority) is the aim; the law of nature (or the rules of reasonableness) is the means of the deduction; and the starting point is a purportedly empirical understanding of the condition of people without government (that is, of people's human, as opposed to civil, nature).

War is what is to be avoided. Perhaps it is unsurprising that Hobbes's description of the condition of people without government is a description of a condition of war, of the war of all against all. It is a fearful state; it is a condition in which, infamously, life is nasty, brutish, and short. It is (in the main) a hypothetical condition, introduced for the purposes of argument. However, as we have seen, Hobbes, the fearful student of fear, was himself no stranger to war. He lived in turbulent times. There was nothing hypothetical about the wars, the civil wars, that form the background of his writing. There was nothing hypothetical about the clash or religions and biblical texts that brought them about. In the midst of this biblically inspired strife is the great beast Hobbes, the baited bear, the would-be calm producer of scientific theorems. Nature has describable laws, laws that (since they govern rational, human, nature) are the laws of reason. These are the resources that Hobbes wants and needs to deploy in the construction of his new philosophy without appeal to any kind of written authority, whether it be the word of God or whether it be the word of Aristotle. The term 'natural law', which Hobbes uses, is traditional. However, with Hobbes, the content is newly constructed from first principles, and is not dependent on any authority. This is why Hobbes's work still remains a foundation text in political philosophy and why it travels relatively easily from the classically trained and biblically imbued seventeenth century to our own period, in which neither of these kinds of books is widely known. That is, it travels if he can indeed produce such a rational foundation and construction. We have a little of the foundation already in place. In the next chapters, we shall see how the great beast of the state might emerge from it.

3

The State of Hobbes's Nature

We saw in the last chapter how Hobbes starts on his own construction of what he calls, using traditional terms, the 'laws of nature'. As well as the laws of nature, Hobbes also describes what he calls 'the state of nature'. For example, the place where he first proposes the foundational assumption of his law of nature – that 'reason' dictates 'to every man for his own good to seek after peace' – is in a chapter he calls 'Of the estate and right of nature' [*Elements*, chap. 14]. Before the laws of nature come the rights of nature, and these rights are exercised in the estate, or state, of nature. This supposed natural state, or, more precisely, this condition of people without government, is called in Hobbes's next work, *De Cive*, the 'state of nature' (*statum naturae*) [Pref. 11]. Hobbes seems to have invented this useful term. He thinks that the state of nature is a state of war; as he puts it in the *Elements*, 'the estate of men in this natural liberty is the estate of war' [14.11]. That is, he thinks that the condition of people without government is one of active or potential conflict (for Hobbes includes under 'war' not only actual fighting but any 'time wherein the will to contend by battle is sufficiently known' [*Lev* 13.8, p. 62]). So in Hobbes's state of nature, everyone is actually fighting or is threatened by fighting. It is the war of all against all (*bellum omnium in omnes* [*De Cive* 1.12]). It is an unpleasant condition. In the *Leviathan* chapter on 'the natural condition of mankind', he says that it is 'a time of war, where every man is enemy to every man', and, as such, it is infamously described as a condition in which life is 'solitary, poor, nasty, brutish, and short' [*Lev* 13.9, p.62]).

The unpleasantness of the state of nature is an important part of Hobbes's argument for the reasonableness of the state. Yet these principles of reasonableness – Hobbes's laws of nature – are meant to apply even before we have the state. So the state of nature is the background, not just to his construction of the state, but also to his construction of the natural law in terms of which the state is justified. The law of nature is meant to apply in the state of nature; that is why they are both called 'natural' (that is, not civil, artificial). The law of nature applies to people as such, to people whether or not they have government, and so also in the state of nature. However, in the state of nature, everyone is independent, and there is by definition no government or other human authority. So the problem is how, lacking any human authority, we can discover the principles of right reason that lay down what these independent people ought to do. Yet this is what Hobbes has to provide: he has to show what holds for these people without government in order to discover the constraints that apply as they attempt to leave the state of nature and gain government. Government gives authority, but we need a natural authority, a natural law, in order to give authority to government. The problems this presents form the substance of this chapter. We have the problem of the justificatory power, or otherwise, of Hobbes's so-called law of nature. We have the problem of whether his so-called state of nature is as unpleasant as he says. We have the problem of how we may use this law of nature to get out of the unpleasant state of nature to the supposedly better state of government.

In all three of Hobbes's main political works, he gives a full exposition of the 'laws of nature'. In the *Elements*, they are described and defended in Chapters 16 and 17. Towards the end of the latter chapter he reaches the conclusion that 'reason, therefore, and the law of nature over and above all these particular laws, doth dictate this law in general, *That those particular laws be so far observed, as they subject us not to any incommodity, that in our judgements may arise, by the neglect thereof in those towards whom we observe them*' [17.10]. In other words, if others 'neglect' to observe them, then I do not have to either, at least if observance would cause me any inconvenience ('incommodity'). That is, Hobbes's laws seem to have a hypothetical form. They are what people should do if, and only if, they can be sure that others will do it as well. Yet the problem is, or so at least Hobbes thinks, that we cannot be sure that others will perform unless they are forced to by a sovereign in a state. Hence it would seem that the law of nature should not bind in the state of nature. Yet we have just seen that the whole point of the law of nature is that it is something that does bind in the state of nature. This sharpens further the questions about the status of Hobbes's so-called 'law of nature' and about the relation between it and the state. Is the law of nature really a law in itself, or does it only become a law when there is a state to enforce it? And if the latter, how can Hobbes hope to use it as part of an argument that is meant to start without the state – that is, in his 'state of nature'?

Traditionally, as we have seen, God is the answer to the questions of the applicability and bindingness of the law of nature outside the state. God makes the law of nature and threatens punishment at the last judgement for non-performance. Hence God makes it binding on everyone whether they are in the state of government or in the state of nature. However, or so at least it was argued in the last chapter, this is not an answer that Hobbes himself can use (however much his language may echo the traditional language about the law of nature and God). For Hobbes does not allow that we can have natural knowledge of the intentions of God at the last judgement. Therefore, lacking this answer, Hobbes has a real problem of whether or how the laws of nature can bind without a state. Perhaps this is where their supposed hypothetical character comes in. Lacking the power of God's punishments, the laws bind each person in the state of nature, but only if every other person does what the laws require. However, since in the state of nature we cannot guarantee that they will, if we retreat to this hypothetical, we do not seem to be bound at all.

A more particular form of these questions is with respect to the bindingness of contracts, or agreements, and the importance of this is that Hobbes's central method of moving from the state of nature to the state is by means of a contract. So the more specific question is whether Hobbes thinks that we are really bound to keep our agreements on the basis of the law of nature alone and prior to existence of the state. If we are, then is this again merely a hypothetical binding, such as we are bound to keep our agreements only if the people with whom we have agreed perform as they have promised? And, if so, what, before the state, is to guarantee that others will perform? And if this is not guaranteed, how are we to use agreement (or contract) to get from the condition without a state to the condition with one?

One distinction that Hobbes uses in this context is the one between what he calls being bound *in foro interno* and being bound *in foro externo* – that is, between being bound before the internal tribunal and before the external tribunal. Thus, just after the remark quoted earlier from the *Elements* about not suffering 'incommodity' in the state of nature from others' non-performance, Hobbes says 'the force therefore of the law of nature is not *in foro externo*, till there be security for men to obey it; but is always in *foro interno*' [17.10]. So he puts together here the hypothetical character and the merely *in foro interno* force of the law of nature in the state of nature (where we lack 'security for men to obey'). By contrast, once we have the powers of the state, and so also have this security, we are then bound as well in the external forum and also bound categorically as opposed to merely hypothetically. So the question is again whether this merely hypothetical and *foro interno* force is going to be sufficient for Hobbes's construction of the state out of the state of nature.

Before trying to answer these questions about force and adequacy, let us first see some more of Hobbes's development of his law of nature. It will be remembered, as was stated at the end of the last chapter, that Hobbes's fundamental law is that 'every man ought to endeavour peace, as far as he has hope of obtaining it; and when he cannot obtain it, that he may seek and use all helps and advantages of war' [*Lev* 14.4, p. 64]. If you have to fight, you seek what help you can, but it is much better not to have to fight at all. Hence the shorter form of the law is to seek peace. The development of the rules that should be followed by rational people seeking peace constitutes Hobbes's law of nature. After deciding that they should seek peace, Hobbes continues that people may achieve it by giving up some of their natural liberty (or the right they have in the state of nature to do what they want). Hence he frames his second law in *Leviathan* as that 'a man be willing, when others are so too', as far 'as for peace and defence of himself he shall think it necessary, to lay down this right to all things, and be contented with so much liberty against other men, as he would allow other men against himself' [14.5, p. 65]. All are to retain the same restricted liberty; fair enough. We should relinquish some of the rights we have in the state of nature on condition that others do the same; fair enough. However, it is important to notice that this second law also has the hypothetical aspect commented on before. It is only if others do the same that we should give up some of our natural rights.

At the very least this creates coordination problems. There are two different places people may be in while still keeping the rules. They may go for efficient war and holding on to all of their liberties, or they may go for peace and relinquishing some liberty. Each person is only successful providing the others are doing the same. The overall rationality of seeking peace dictates that it is preferable for everyone to go for peace, but it is only preferable for any one person to seek peace if everyone else is doing so as well. If, instead, other people are not seeking peace, then (by the second part of his first law), you should not be seeking it either. 'The sum of virtue', as Hobbes puts it in the *Elements*, 'is to be sociable with them that will be sociable, and formidable to them that will not', adding that 'the same is the sum of the law of nature' [17.15]. The law of nature is to play peace to the pacific, but with the bellicose to fight to win.

At this point in his development of the law of nature, Hobbes turns in all three of his accounts to discussion of kinds of agreement (pacts, covenants, contracts). The third law of nature in *Leviathan* is 'that men perform their covenants' [15.1, p. 71], and such is the corresponding law in *De Cive* where it reads 'stand by your agreements (*pactis standum esse*)' [3.1]. It is also in the *Elements*, where it is 'every man is obliged to stand to, and perform, those covenants he maketh' [16.1]. If Hobbes is going to use agreement between the individual warring parties to get them out of the state of nature, then he will clearly want it as part of natural law that people stand to their agreements. It is clearly important for him, but it is also important to see whether he is correct. And even if he is correct, it is also important to see how much force the keeping of agreements has in a Hobbesian state of nature.

If Hobbes can derive the obligation to keep agreements from his fundamental requirements of self-preservation and seeking peace, then he has to show that we will not succeed in getting peace unless people stand by their agreements. The best attempt at this is in *De Cive*. He here says that 'since standing by agreements is necessary for securing peace . . . it will take its place . . . as a precept (*praeceptum*) of natural law' [3.1]. The problem is how this fits with the choice of going for war or for peace, the question why should I keep my agreements if

I think that others won't. Hobbes's answer to this here, for contracts of pure expectation in which the one party has to trust the other to perform (which is what he calls 'covenants'), is in fact that I am not obliged. That is, I am only obliged to keep my part if I am reasonably secure that the other party will perform. Again we get a hypothetical treatment, and again this puts into sharp perspective the problem as to how we can get out of the state of nature (where I do not seem to have security about anything) to the state (which would provide such security, enforcing contracts by law, if only I could reach it). It seems that we would only have real, enforceable, contracts with the state. This gives an incentive for reaching the state, but it means that we can't use contracts in the process. So there is the problem of why I should keep my word if I know that others will not. However, there is also the converse problem. If everyone else is keeping their word, and hence providing peace, why should I also keep my word, particularly if I would do better breaking it? This free rider question is the famous question posed by the character Hobbes called the 'fool' in *Leviathan* (or 'foole'; although I modernise the spelling in quotations, the 'foole' has become an icon of modern commentary in his primitive spelling).

This is to list, rather than to solve, problems, although solutions will be attempted. However, it already illustrates how Hobbes thinks that he can produce a law of nature from an absolutely fundamental base. In all his chief works, he adds several more laws at this point. The surprising thing about them is that they are very similar in content to traditionally conceived natural law. That is, although Hobbes seems to have a fundamentally different base (the self-interested rationality of survival), what he derives from this base would be recognisable in content to someone who thought instead that natural law is the moral truth imprinted on our consciences by God. This applies to the law just discussed, that people should keep their agreements. Many would think that this was simply morally right, rather than a rationally required means of achieving peace. Similarly with the precept that people should not to be judges in their own cause (Number 17 in *Leviathan*). This is precisely what people both then and now would think of as 'natural justice' (and is so treated by the civil courts) – that is, again it is fairly universally agreed to be morally right, rather than a prudential requirement for survival in a hostile world. Other laws cited by Hobbes reach even nearer the small change of traditional natural law, such as that envoys should be given safe conduct, or with respect to the rights of primogeniture.

More importantly, Hobbes sums up all his specific laws with the rule, 'do not that to another, which thou wouldst not have done to thyself' [*Lev* 15.35, p. 79]. This is our old friend, the golden rule, which we saw in the first chapter is a pre-eminent example of a natural law, as traditionally conceived. It will be remembered that there was a problem (considered, for example, by Aquinas) about the promulgation of natural law. This problem is how we may be bound by a law that we do not seem to have made or to have been given. It is the problem of our knowledge of the natural law. Hobbes considers it in all three works. In his first, he says that there is an 'easy rule to know upon a sudden, whether the action I be to do, be against the law of nature or not' [*Elements* 17.9]. He then gives a version of the golden rule: by imagining myself in the other person's place, I can test whether something is the natural law. Similarly in *De Cive*, the 'only rule he needs' is to 'think himself into the other person's place' [3.26]. In *Leviathan*, he again talks of people putting themselves into others' places, and says that the rule he quotes reduces all the laws of nature 'into one easy sum, intelligible even to the meanest capacity'. That is, the golden rule solves the problem of knowledge of the laws of nature; however mean someone's capacity, they may use it to know what is the law. Even if, as Hobbes puts it here, 'the most part are too busy in getting food and the rest too negligent to understand', they can still all acquire knowledge of the laws of nature by means of this simple test.

In the much later chapter in *Leviathan* on 'the kingdom of God by nature', Hobbes says that 'God declareth his laws three ways; by the dictates of natural reason, by revelation, and by the voice of some man, to whom by the operation of miracles, he procureth credit with the rest' [31.3, p. 187]. He calls this a 'triple word of God'. However, he says that universal laws are not given by the second means (revelation). The third depends upon 'faith', the first on 'right reason'. Nothing could be more traditional than this. God, promulgation, the word, right reason – all lined up in proper fashion and all issuing in the law of nature. It all sounds completely traditional, even if God has an uncertain role. However, if God does have an uncertain role, then we can forget revelation and faith. We are restricted to the first element of the 'triple word', right reason. Yet if we are restricted to right reason, it is important whether Hobbes is right that we can use the traditional golden rule as an answer to the problem of promulgation.

Hobbes's exposition of the laws of nature is traditional not only in its content but also in its form. It is connected in the same way with the law of God and with civil laws as in more orthodox accounts. In addition to the connections just mentioned, Hobbes says that the civil law must not conflict with natural law. He says that the sovereign is bound by the natural law. He says that as God's laws, the laws of nature are therefore immutable and eternal. In all these cases, Hobbes's new so-called natural law fits exactly into the place occupied by traditional natural law. Now such coincidence might merely be a helpful accident. Hobbes has a radical basis. If he nevertheless happens to achieve the same conclusions as in more traditional treatments, this can only help their acceptance. Radicals will follow him on his new ways; traditionalists need not dispute his conclusions. As noted in the last chapter, after his exposition of the law in both the *Elements* and *De Cive*, Hobbes adds a chapter showing that his natural laws are not in conflict with biblical revelation (we can now see that this is helped by their traditional content). It may help agreement, and it may help to camouflage his real intentions. However, if Hobbes lacks the traditional resources, the coincidence may make us wonder how he has managed to get such a traditional content from pure prudential practical reason. Also, if Hobbes lacks the resources of God, the question remains whether his law of nature is really a binding law at all, or, more generally, what reasons for action Hobbes's law of nature gives someone in the state of nature. There is a problem of knowledge, which might (perhaps) be solved by the golden rule. However, there is also a problem of motivation. Even if people in the state of nature can discover the law, there remains the question (at least for Hobbes) why they should bother to put this knowledge into effect.

Binding Force

To work, the law of nature must bind. As we saw, Hobbes says that the natural law does bind in the state of nature in that it binds *in foro interno*. However, he also seems to give it here a merely hypothetical force. When there is not a civil sovereign threatening punishment,

Hobbes thinks that I am not bound to keep contracts, or at least those of mutual trust. 'Such covenants are of none effect', he says [*Elements* 15.10]), or, as he puts it in *Leviathan*, 'covenants without the sword are but words and of no strength to secure a man at all' [17.2, p. 85]. The 'sword' here is the sword of state justice, such as the one the statue of justice carries over the Central Criminal Courts in London. Without security, mere words, no effect, no deal. The reason for this is that without the sword of state, I have no guarantee that other people will keep their agreements with me – that is, if I perform, the other party will as well. So the argument here seems to depend upon the assumption that people act self-interestedly, and this is an assumption that Hobbes certainly makes. 'By necessity of nature', he says in the *Elements*, 'every man doth in all his voluntary actions intend some good unto himself' [16.6], or, in *Leviathan*, 'of the voluntary acts of every man the object is *some good to himself*' [14.8, p. 66]. This, of course, is questionable, but it is not the only questionable assumption involved in the argument. As well as assuming that people's acts are self-interested, Hobbes needs also to assume that it is not in our interests to hold to agreements unless we know that we will be punished if we do not. For there could be self-interested reasons for keeping faith that do not involve avoiding punishment. Someone might, for example, wish to invest in their own good faith, building up a reputation which can later be cashed. Even if punishment (or something like it) is required, it does not follow (as Hobbes seems to think) that this requires the state (or God). Incentives similar to punishment might exist in the state of nature. There are many arguments against lynch mobs, but there is no problem about the power of the punishmentlike incentive they can provide (as opposed to their tendency to apply it in the wrong places).

So Hobbes may be wrong that (apart from God) only a civil sovereign can provide certainty of punishment and incentives to per-form. However, even if he is right, he still has the problem of how the law of nature binds before we have the state, the problem of what it means for me to be bound *in foro interno* even if I know that others will not perform. Perhaps it means that I am bound in con-science (the inner voice), bound before God even if not before the world. But if binding goes with a law-maker (someone to bind), and law-making goes with punishment (binding is by threats), then we get the conclusion that it is God's threatened punishment that binds us *in foro interno* in the state of nature, while the state's threatened punishments give us an additional *in foro externo* binding. In other words, we would get again the traditional account of God upholding the law of nature. However, at least as an account of Hobbes, this cannot be quite right. God's binding does indeed traditionally go with the individual conscience and the sovereign's binding with common, public authority. However, on this traditional account, God's binding is a full, objective, categorical binding. We are, that is, subject by God to a fully objective law of nature that applies to us whatever others do, and for which failure of compliance will be punished, whatever others do. So if this is what our conscience says, we should do it whatever others do. However, Hobbes says that if others don't do it, then neither should we. Therefore a different account is needed if we are to capture Hobbes's sense that we are not really bound when others do not perform.

As we saw in the last chapter, one way of producing this might be in terms of knowledge. We have insufficient knowledge to know whether or not we are bound by a sacred book or by the will of God. Of course, if I believe in God and the Bible, and believe that the Bible tells me to keep contracts, then I believe that I am bound in my individual conscience before God. I can criticise myself for failure since I believe that God will criticise me. However no one else may criticise me unless we happen to share this belief, and if I do not believe in God, then there is nothing to criticise. This interpretation would be possible for anyone favouring an atheistic account of Hobbes: we are not bound by God, because there is no God (although those who think there is a God will think themselves bound). However, it also works perfectly well as an interpretation even if Hobbes is an orthodox believer, following his account of our knowledge of God, as laid out in the last chapter. All that is needed is that we cannot be confident about the objective religious truth of the matter, whatever our own private beliefs might be.

God promises to bind, but (at least on the argument of the last chapter) cannot deliver. So let us try an account of binding that links it more closely with the hypothetical option. Let us try the notion that to be bound *in foro interno* merely means that we are bound if everyone else also performs. That is, I should keep my agreement if I can assume that the other party will, that I should pay my train fare if I can assume that others will, that I should speak the truth if I can assume that this is what generally happens in my society, and so on. Understood like this, I get the benefits that derive from a generally observed performance of these rules, but am not taken advantage of by people trying to free ride on my performance. We play the game as long as everyone else is playing it; as soon as someone tries to exploit us, we stop. Tit for tat, peace with those who show peace, otherwise war. Then Hobbes's point would be that it is not safe in the state of nature (which is a state of war) to start with the assumption that there is such peace and cooperation. We do not have sufficient assurance that others will be playing the following the rules game unless they know that they are liable to be penalised for non-performance. Yet this is just what we do not know in the state of nature. Once, by contrast, we have the state and sovereign, we do know that penalties operate, and so can be sufficiently secure. Therefore we should play the following-the-rules game in a state (even though, of course, we also know that there will be a small amount of divergence), because there we are bound in public, bound in *foro externo*. However, in the state of nature there is insufficient security, and we are therefore not bound *in foro externo*. Then the external forum can not criticise us for not keeping to our agreements, telling lies, and so on.

Again, however, this hypothetical account would not seem to capture the full force of being bound *in foro interno*. It is not just (as earlier) that we may also feel bound before God. It is also that quite independently of God, keeping agreements would seem to be a gesture in the right spirit, a gesture to the rule that we think everyone should follow. Hobbes in fact goes even further than this. He says that without security, the law of nature 'is always *in foro interno*, wherein the action of obedience being unsafe, the will and readiness to perform is taken for the performance' [*Elements* 17.10]. So I don't have to act, but I do have to have 'will and readiness'. Similarly in *Leviathan*, he says that 'the laws of nature oblige *in foro interno*, that is to say, they bind to a desire they should take place' [15.36, p. 79]. Here again, I have to have the will, the desire. It is not just that I should recognise that I am bound to something if others also do it. It is like a philanthropist who says that she will subscribe a hundred thousand to a good cause if a matching sum can be found elsewhere. She is not just binding herself hypothetically to pay if others do so as well. She is also expressing a desire that this should happen; she has the will and readiness to perform.

So where have we reached? We have it that there are reasons to seek peace, and this for Hobbes involves reasons to get ourselves out of the state of nature and into a position where these laws are enforceable by the power of the state. We know that it is in our interest (gets peace) if people keep their agreements. We know also that it will not be rational for people to keep their agreement unless they can be reasonably confident that the others will as well. So these rational considerations of peace tell us that we should keep our agreement only if the others will, but also that we are all better off if we are all in a situation where we can depend upon others' doing so. Hence we all have an interest in producing a state (the terrifying beast, the Leviathan) that punishes us for non-performance, so that we can all confidently rely on the mutually advantageous performance. In the state of nature, we have the *in foro interno* will and desire, but this is a will and a desire for things that require a state. It is a will and desire to give ourselves, in addition, an *in foro externo* reason. We desire the construction of a power that forces the external binding by terrifying us all into the security of performance. Uncertain of the application of the terrifying God for this role, Hobbes turns instead to the more certain terror of the state.

Counsel and Command

These are reasons for having a state, at least for Hobbes. They are the dictates of right reason, practical rationality. Hobbes calls such reasons laws, the laws of nature. However, we still have questions. We still have the question of whether these so-called laws are really laws in the state of nature. We still have the question of whether they really give us as much reason to leave the state of nature as Hobbes thinks that they do. We still have the question of the real nature of states and governments, of Hobbes's preferred solution to the problems of the state of nature. To answer these I shall now open up a discussion of the distinction between what Hobbes calls counsel and what he calls command. In Chapter 25 of *Leviathan* (entitled 'Of counsel'), Hobbes defines 'command' as when someone says '*Do this* or *Do not this* without expecting other reason than the will of him that says it'. In 'counsel', by contrast, the person may similarly say *Do this* or *Do not this*, but the anticipated reason for action is instead 'the benefit that arriveth by it to him to whom he saith it' [p. 176]. In both cases, one person says something, and because of this another person acts. In both cases, as Hobbes notes, the speech itself may be in the imperative mood. However the important difference is the reason why the person acts. In the command case, the reason for action is the will of the speaker, whereas in the counsel case it is the content of what is said. With command, we need only know that a superior wills something to have an adequate reason for action; knowledge of the source of the speech is sufficient. With counsel, by contrast, the speaker merely gives advice that the person may or may not choose to follow. When it is followed, this is because of what it is rather than because of the will of the person who gives it, because of its content rather than its source.

As Hobbes puts it at the start of the next chapter ('Of Civil Laws'), 'it is manifest that law in general is not counsel but command' [26.2, p. 137]. For Hobbes, command is the essence of law. Laws are obeyed because of the will of their maker rather than because of the goodness of their content. This is what happens (at least for Hobbes) with normal, positive law (the law of states). It is obeyed just on the basis of being the will of the sovereign. For Hobbes, when we have the commonwealth we have what he calls 'simple obedience'. We have, that is, obedience simply to the giver of the commands (the sovereign) completely independently of their content. With such simple obedience, we have what Hobbes in the *Elements* says 'may seem a paradox'. This is that the command of someone 'whose command is a law in one thing, is a law in every thing' [29.3]. Get the sovereign anywhere, and you get the sovereign everywhere. It is easy to see how this seems to follow from the idea of simple obedience. For if we have to obey what someone says, this shows that we have command rather than counsel. Hence we are obeying because of who says it rather than what is said. But if we obey simply because of the source of the saying, then we should obey anything else that emanates from the same source. Hence, if obedience in anything, then obedience in everything. Either we do not have obedience at all or we have simple obedience.

This sounds neat, and it is certainly what Hobbes wants from his sovereign Leviathan, but it is surely too fast. We might have a reason for obeying instructions based upon the source, but which only applied to a particular area of activity. For example, we might take as a reason for not driving more than thirty miles an hour that this is the speed commanded by the Highway Authority. That is, it is not because it seems to be a good thing to drive at this speed that we do it, but simply because that is the speed the authority commands. If instead of commanding thirty, it had commanded forty, this would have given us an equally good reason for going at forty. Source alone is sufficient, so this is command rather than counsel. However, obeying this particular command does not mean that we are thereby obliged to obey any other command the Highway Authority might give, quite irrespective of its content. If it commands us to slow down not only on the road but also in our sexual behaviour, we might say that this was none of its business (unless it was talking about sex while driving). So we have here command rather than counsel, and yet do not have simple obedience. We obey in some things without thereby being committed to obeying in everything; Hobbes's paradox does not apply.

Hobbes, no doubt, could dispose of this particular counterexample by deploying additional assumptions. For example, he assumes that there can only be one final authority in any one state. So he might say that the Highway Authority is only acting on behalf of the sovereign, and if the sovereign says to slow up sexually, we surely should. However, the putative counterexample suffices to show that simple obedience does not simply follow from the perfectly acceptable and recognisable distinction between counsel and command. In some cases, our reasons for action may be based on a combination of source and content; we obey because of the source provided the content meets certain conditions (we obey what the Highway Authority says provided it is about the highways). Even Hobbes himself says that 'subjects owe to sovereigns simple obedience in all things wherein their obedience is not repugnant to the word of God' [*Lev* 31.1, p. 186]. As might be expected (and as he wants to show after making the remark), this is much less of a limitation for Hobbes than it initially seems. However, we again seem to have a situation in which instructions should be checked for both content and source. It is not sufficient just to know that the sovereign has commanded something; we need also to know that it meets certain conditions of legitimacy (we obey just because the sovereign says it, provided that it is not contrary to the law of God).

In spite of these differences in consequences, the basic distinction between counsel (advice) and command (law) is one that we can recognise and accept. As Hobbes says, 'there are but few that see not that these are very different things' [*Lev* 25.1, p. 131]. In its terms, the problem of political obligation is why (or whether) there should be command as well as counsel. That is, the problem is whether we ever have a reason for following an instruction that is based upon its source (the will of the instructor) rather than upon its content. Hobbes says that 'the authority of writers, without the authority of the commonwealth, maketh not their opinions law, be they never so true' [*Lev* 26.22, p. 143]. What the writers say might not be bettered in terms of its content; it is 'never so true'. The writers have 'authority'. Yet this 'authority' does not make their opinions law. Their 'authority', it seems, differs from the 'authority of the commonwealth'. The writers advise, the commonwealth commands, and law is command. So we can distinguish between two senses, or uses, of 'authority'. Sometimes (as with scientific authority), people are authorities because they have good knowledge of an area and can give good advice and instruction. It is worth following what they say because what they say has a good chance of being right. The doctor advises me, and I do what she says; she knows better than me, and I stand a better chance of getting what I want if I follow her ideas rather than my own, unauthoritative, opinions. This is relatively straightforward, assuming that I can identify the experts. When I am told by the expert to do something ('take the tablets every morning'), this gives me a reason for action. It is also what Hobbes himself, the moral scientist, is doing. His words as a writer are 'never so true'. He is a scientist, an expert. However, what he is giving is not law but advice (take the medicine; do not question the sovereign).

The problem of political obligation is therefore to understand what other kind of authority there can be than the authority of experts; it is the problem of how the Highway Authority can be an authority. If it is, then, in Hobbes's language, it gives me reasons based on command rather than counsel. I do hope that the Highway Authority knows more than I do about the roads. It should have its hands on highway science, so it should be authoritative in the first sense. However, when it tells me to stop at a junction, I do not stop because I respect this greater knowledge. I stop because I respect its will. So it is also an authority in the second sense. It is not merely a writer of signs; in writing signs, it makes law. By contrast, Hobbes is merely a writer of books, and in writing his books he makes no law.

However, the fact that we hope that the Highway Authority is also an authority in the first sense (or the fact that we might be less inclined to obey it if we think that it is not) shows the complexity of making this distinction. It gives commands, but I take these commands to be based on knowledge. Conversely, the fact that the doctor has more knowledge than I do means that I may treat what she says as commands. I may do what I am told simply because she tells me. So now the distance between the Highway Authority and the doctor is starting to diminish. In both cases, my ultimate reason for following instructions might be that it is good for me to do what people say when they know more than I do. However, there still remains the important difference that in the cases of counsel, the final decision is made by me. I might be stupid not to follow the doctor's instruction about taking the tablets, but I am perfectly entitled to do so. Whereas if the Highway Authority is a legitimate political authority, then the final decision does not rest with me. I am not stupid but wrong if I refuse to stop when it says.

Now suppose that I discover that I do myself damage when I reserve to myself the final decision about whether or not to follow advice. Since the doctor knows more than I, it is silly for me to try and work out whether it is good advice before I follow it. However, if I reserve the final decision to myself, I might get tempted to try. In such circumstances, it would be sensible for me to bind myself to do whatever the doctor says without any further consideration of the content. So I could, for example, promise her that I will follow all her instructions. For Hobbes, this marks the shift from counsel to command. He explicitly says of someone that 'if he should covenant to follow it, then is the counsel turned into the nature of a command' [*Lev* 25.4; p.132]. Once I have promised (covenanted), the doctor ceases to be the first kind of authority and becomes the second. She now gives me commands.

The way that command can grow from covenant is important in Hobbes's general political philosophy, whereby people contract with each other in a state of nature to set up a state that commands. This will be looked at fully in the next chapter. However, before then, we still need to examine the possible bases of justification. We can see that superior knowledge gives a reason to follow advice, but (neither for Hobbes nor for us) can this by itself justify political authority. We can see that Hobbes thinks that promises change the situation. But

we have not, as yet, seen any reason why we should keep our promises
(that is, why the fact that we have promised in the past gives us, now, a
reason to do what we said). More generally, we have not as yet seen why
command gives a reason. Distinguishing command from counsel explains what needs to be justified. However, it does not by itself provide
any justification. Perhaps contract provides the reasons. Or perhaps
we can get the reasons more simply from the ways in which command
seems to merge with counsel. Let us look at this first. Consider another
case, in which we do not agree to obey the expert doctor, but the state
commissions an expert and gives him discretionary control over a particular area. For example, during an outbreak of animal disease, the
state gives a veterinary expert the power to control the movements
of animals. Here again, there is command rather than counsel. Only
this time it is not a command created by contract (for the expert's
power is created by the state). Nevertheless it may seem that, as with
the doctor, the ultimate reason for obedience is that the person is an
expert. We obey because of the probable goodness of what he says.
So it might seem that all justification of authority ultimately came
down to content. That is, when we obey just because it is someone's
will, this is only because it is an indirect way of reaching the right
content.

However, whatever justification may be made for political authority
in this way, it is not one that Hobbes can use. Hobbes, that is, could
not hold that political authorities are merely substitutes for scientific
authority, so that all law is ultimately advice. For Hobbes does not think
that political authorities necessarily know better than anyone else. For
him, the Highway Authority would still be an authority even if it were
quite ignorant of highway science. So any reason he gives for following
commands cannot be that they are concealed advice, or indirect ways
of acquiring advice. The examples presented show that we can have
different mixes of reasons for action partially based on the content
of the reasons and partially based on their source. Sometimes we may
follow source as an indirect way of achieving content. However, with
Hobbes, by contrast, it is source all the way down. His reasons for
having political authority at no stage depend on the superior wisdom
of such authority. The sovereign is supposed by Hobbes to enforce the
law of nature; indeed, Hobbes wishes to argue that from a practical
point of view, everyone else should regard what the sovereign says as

declaring what is the law of nature. However, this is not because the sovereign has superior understanding. It is not because the sovereign is more likely to get the law of nature right. On the contrary. Hobbes's sovereign does not need any special expertise.

The reason for having the sovereign (and political authority) is to have single judgement. Yet all that is needed for this (or so at least Hobbes thinks) is that we have some mechanism producing the singleness of judgement, and such a mechanism may be quite independent of any consideration of its correctness. We can see this in an old Greek metaphor (or tale) that Hobbes uses in this context, the story of the Gordian knot that Alexander cut with his sword. The separate judgements of separate people can be thought of like the separate threads. Left to ourselves, we all go off in different directions, having differing and disagreeing judgements, and the result is a tangle. This knot is sorted out for Hobbes by the sovereign. However, the sovereign does not (or, at least, may not) do this by having a special, stronger thread that is more securely fastened to the truth and that can therefore be used to sort out the others. Instead, the sovereign may solve the whole business with the sword. Hobbes uses the story in his discussion of interpretation of the civil laws. He says that for the sovereign, 'there can not be any knot in the law' since he can either find the ends 'to undo it by, or else by making what ends he will (as Alexander did with his sword in the Gordian knot), by the legislative power' [*Lev* 26.21, p. 143]. He does allow here that the sovereign could find the natural ends and untie the knot. However, his main point is that the sovereign does not need to do this. For if he does not find the natural ends, he can simply produce them. Rather than being better, the sovereign is simply stronger. The knot is not untied by superior wisdom but is instead cut by superior power. So power is what the sovereign provides, and the reason we obey the sovereign is given not by superior wisdom but by superior power. As was seen at the start of the last chapter, the point of Leviathan is that there is no power like it on earth. The same holds, it would seem, for God himself. We do not obey because of God's superior wisdom but because of his formidable power. Being master even of Leviathan is enough (and such, as was seen, is God's answer to Job). Hobbes says that 'the right of nature, whereby God reigneth over men . . . is to be derived . . . from his *irresistible power*' (*Lev* 31.5, p. 187]. Or, as he puts it in *De Cive*: 'sure and irresistible power gives the right of ruling' [1.14]; or, in the *Elements*, 'irresistible might in the state of nature is right' [14.13].

Natural Reasons

Let us go back to counsel and command. Following this distinction, the answer to whether the law of nature is really law would seem to be 'no'. These so-called laws of nature are really truths of practical reason, truths that some (scientific) expert in the field such as Hobbes can lay out, and that sovereigns and others may then apply. And this is indeed what Hobbes himself says. Without modesty (here as elsewhere) he says that what he had written is 'evident truth', but that 'though it be evident truth is not therefore presently law . . . for though it be naturally reasonable; yet it is by the sovereign power that it is law' [26.22, p.143]. In other words, it is advice, needing someone with the power of command to make it law. This fits in with the 'theorems' that Hobbes says he is deducing, both in his chapters setting up natural law and also when he later looks back at what he has done. Here (again without undue modesty) he claims that 'neither Plato nor any other philosopher hitherto have put into order and sufficiently or probably proved all the theorems of moral doctrine'. Hobbes has now done it. But having done it, what he hopes is that his writing will 'fall into the hands of a sovereign' [31.41, p. 193]. Only the sovereign can make it law.

This is an inference as to what Hobbes could be expected to say. However, he also says it directly. In *Leviathan*, he specifically says of the laws of nature that 'these dictates of reason, men use to call by the name of laws, but improperly: for they are but conclusions, or theorems concerning what conduceth to the conservation and defence of themselves; whereas law properly is the word of him that by right has command over others' [*Lev* 15.41, p. 80]. In other words, everything seems to line up: counsel not command, theorems not laws, part of the moral science produced by scientist Hobbes, rather than a code enacted by a legislator. Indeed, if we take Hobbes's firm statement that law is command, and if we see the so-called laws of nature as deduced truths of practical reason, then there is no other way to understand it. As Hobbes puts it later, 'the laws of nature . . . in the condition of mere nature (as I have said before in the end of Chapter 15) are not properly laws, but qualities that dispose men to peace and to obedience' [*Lev* 26.8, p. 138].

This is what Hobbes says he said before. However, even this can be disputed. For after the remark first quoted (and to which he refers back), he adds, 'but yet if we consider the same theorems, as delivered in the word of God, that by right commandeth all things; then are they properly called laws'. If we bring God back in, then we have a commanding power, and so as well as the reason coming from content we have the reason coming from imperative will, a will with a frightening power to enforce. Then, if we properly have God, we properly have law; we have command, not counsel. Similarly, in *De Cive*, he says that 'properly speaking, the natural laws are not laws, in so far as they proceed from nature', but then, again, adds 'in so far as the same laws have been legislated by God in the holy scriptures . . . they are very properly called by the name of laws' [3.33]. I do not need to repeat the arguments of the last chapter about how far God can properly enter as an independent element in Hobbes's philosophy. Given certain religious beliefs, it is easy to see how the law of nature becomes law. It is the divine law, or the law that is laid down positively in the Bible. However, lacking this supernatural belief, we are left with the so-called law of nature as not being really a law 'from nature'. We are left with good reasons that, however, do not have the force of law. And when Hobbes came to rewrite *Leviathan* in the Latin version, he dropped the reference to God here, and left it as the bald statement that they were not properly (*proprie*) laws, exactly what he later describes himself to have said in both English and Latin versions.

So, in the most coherent reconstruction of his thought (as well as what, most of the time Hobbes actually says), these so-called laws of nature are not really laws. However, this does not mean that they are therefore of no use, or that his attempt to reconstruct natural law is doomed to failure, or that we cannot have any reasons in the state of nature to guide our exit from it. For, although not laws, they are still good reasons. As Hobbes puts it in *De Cive*, 'natural laws' can be taught 'in two forms' – either 'through natural reason, deducing natural right and natural laws from human principles and human contracts' or else 'in the form of laws, by divine authority' [17.13]. Even if we dispense with the latter, we still have the arguments, the 'theorems', the new civil science that Hobbes has constructed, and these are still (for Hobbes) conclusive reasons about how to act. Several other distinctions that Hobbes makes are also relevant here. He distinguishes between 'equity' and 'justice' and between 'sin' and 'law'. What is against natural law is wrong, even in the state of nature (and even without God's positive commands), It is not equitable, not fair. It also (particularly if we reintroduce God) may be designated a sin. As Hobbes puts it in his late *Dialogue Between a Philosopher and a Student of the Common Law*, 'injustice is the transgression of a statute law, and iniquity the transgression of the law of reason' [70]. This is a technical, limited, distinction, but it is applied in a similar way in the more major works. In *Leviathan*, for example, he says that although nothing a sovereign can do to a subject 'can properly be called injustice', nevertheless his action (such as, for example, putting a known innocent subject to death) could 'be against the law of nature, as contrary to equity' [21.7, p. 109]. It is not unjust, but it is wrong. There is not a (real) law against it, but there are still good reasons not to do it.

So Hobbes's 'laws of nature' provide good reasons in the state of nature even if they are not really laws. These reasons are reasons for having, or creating, a superior power, and once we have (with the state) such real power, we will then also have real laws. With the state and these real laws, we then have additional good reasons for action. We have, that is, reasons for having such additional reasons – that is, reasons for having the state. Since no one has sufficient power to protect him or herself in the state of nature, and since God is a hidden or absent God not to be relied on for protection, we need for safety to be able to create a new power that will protect us. This, for Hobbes, is the state. We have reasons to do this, reasons we can use. They are the ones with which Hobbes starts his new law of nature and which were laid out at the end of the last chapter. We have, that is, an overwhelming reason to seek peace as a means to seeking our preservation. Indeed, as described, for Hobbes our nature is such that we cannot help doing such a thing. In the *Elements*, he says that anyone wanting to live in the state of nature 'contradicteth himself. For every man by natural necessity desireth his own good' [14.12]. In other words, since we naturally, necessarily, seek our own good, we would be contradicting this most central part of our nature if we did not seek peace or attempt to escape the state of nature. So we have natural necessity and reason enough to attempt to get out, to attempt to construct for ourselves that mighty Leviathan or mortal god who by his supreme power offers us the security our most central nature necessarily craves.

So we have reasons in the state of nature, even though these reasons are reasons for getting out. They are reasons for having the state, and once we have the state, our need to preserve ourselves gives us additional reasons. For the mighty Leviathan we construct has formidable power, power of life and death over us. Hence our fear of Leviathan gives us reason to obey Leviathan's law. This reason, which is a reason for everyone, secures the law (or so-called law) in a way that cannot be accomplished in the state of nature. Hence we can each more securely rely on the behaviour of others, and hence our observance need no longer be merely hypothetical or *in foro interno*. The reasons for having the state are not just the greater power that the state provides, although this is important. In Chapter 26 of *Leviathan*, Hobbes says that the laws of nature become proper laws in a 'commonwealth', and describes what is added 'when a commonwealth is once settled'. For then these laws of nature are now also 'commands of the commonwealth'; so we now have command, real law. We now have 'the sovereign power that obliges men to obey them' – that is, we have the right kind of power, a power that imposes obligations on people. As Hobbes puts it, 'there is need of the ordinances of the sovereign power, and punishments to be ordained for such as shall break them' [26.8]. So an important part of the point is that we have real power, a power that uses punishment to enforce its will. However, this is not the whole point. For without such a single sovereign, people will disagree about what is the right course of action, about what is the law of nature. The state gives determination and certainty as well as the power of enforcement. As Hobbes puts it in *De Cive*, 'thus one learns what *theft* is, what *murder* is and *adultery*, and generally what a *wrong* is, from the civil law' [6.16]. When we have the civil law, we have an increase of knowledge as well as an increase in power.

These are all reasons for having the state or commonwealth. Increase in power of enforcement and increase of knowledge about what to enforce can only be good things. Earlier it was discussed whether we are naturally obliged to keep our agreements. However, whether we are or not is of little practical consequence, for these agreements cannot be relied on. Mere knowledge of what we should do is not enough. As Hobbes puts it in *De Cive*, 'the natural laws do not guarantee their own observance as soon as they are known' [5.1]. With the state, it all becomes clearer. What is inequitable now becomes unjust, since there is a sovereign to declare the law. We now have the power of punishment, forcing us to keep our agreements. So the state adds security of performance. However, it also adds another kind of determinacy. It tells us what a contract is – that is, which agreements should be kept. So it gives us double determinacy, double security, double certainty. With the state, we get good reasons for action. Hence, wanting good reasons for action, we have good reasons to have the state.

Naturally Nasty

The state is a good, but, even so, Hobbes' argument will only work if the commonwealth is better than the state of nature. And it will only be better if the state of nature is as bad as Hobbes thinks that it is. So Hobbes's argument only works if he is right that the state of nature is a state of war, a war of all against all. For it is only if the state of nature is a thoroughly bad and dangerous place that we have (self-preserving) reasons to hand ourselves over to the uncontrollable power of the mighty Leviathan. Therefore we must now examine this crucial piece of the argument, the argument that things are inevitably 'nasty' if people are left in their 'natural condition', the argument of Chapter 13 of *Leviathan*. In this famous chapter (on 'the natural condition of mankind'), Hobbes says that there are three reasons why people fight – 'competition', 'diffidence' and 'glory' [6]. These, he says, make people invade, respectively, for 'gain', for 'safety', and for 'reputation' [7]. Of these, 'diffidence' (fear) is to some extent secondary. If conflict is caused by other reasons, then 'diffidence' will give an additional reason. In the *Elements*, Hobbes talks of 'a general diffidence in mankind, and mutual fear one of another' [14.3]. So if there is mutual fear, then there are additional reasons for everyone to secure themselves. But why should there be fear? Here, the first and third reasons are sufficient. People sometimes want the same things ('wives, children, and cattle', as it is listed at this point in *Leviathan*), and fight for them. Or they want glory; they want to be best. This is an essentially competitive, positional, good. Not everyone can have it. ('Glorying, like honour, is nothing if everyone has it' is how he puts it in *De Cive* [1.2].) So if some want it, there will be competition, and therefore, at least for Hobbes, there will be fights over 'trifles, as a word, a smile, a different opinion' [*Lev* 13.7, p. 62].

The exact account of people's 'natural condition' (and whether it even makes sense to describe an a-contextual, pre-political, 'human nature') does not matter so much here. All that is needed is that there be some disposition to conflict. So we could dispense with 'glory' as merely part of the swagger of Hobbes's world. In the *Elements*, (written in the middle of a frightful struggle in England that led to the civil war) Hobbes thinks that it is sufficient to observe that 'since men by natural passion are diverse ways offensive one to another, every man thinking well of himself, and hating to see the same in others, they must needs provoke one another by words, and other signs of contempt and hatred' [14.4]; or, put several people together into a room, and conflict is inevitable. In the previous section, he similarly describes 'how some are vainly glorious, and hope for precedency and superiority above their fellows'. However, we might think that this was not as inevitable as Hobbes makes out, that people might not always be necessarily striving for glory or precedence, or that their very diversity necessarily made them hate each other. So perhaps we might drop 'glory' as an essential aspect of human nature. However, we still have what Hobbes calls 'competition', and there would seem to be potential for this as long as there are conflicts of individual interest. (In *De Cive*, he says that 'the most frequent cause why men want to hurt each other arises when many want the same thing at the same time' [1.6].) Given this, 'diffidence' (or the additional things that our mutual fear leads us to do) takes over. If I have a well-based fear that you might take something, then I have an additional reason to get it first. If I think that you are going to attack me, then I have an additional reason to devote energy and care to defence. Wherever the conflict might start ('glory' or 'competition'), once there is potential for it, fear of it ('diffidence') will lead everyone to attempt to secure themselves; and these attempts may in turn provoke additional fear. When trouble threatens, it pays to be pre-emptive, and when Hobbes first mentions 'diffidence' in his *Leviathan* 'natural condition of mankind' chapter, he says 'there is no way for any man to secure himself so reasonable as anticipation' [4].

Hobbes, as part of his empirical claim that the state of nature was a state of potential war, points out in this chapter how different sovereign countries (which, lacking a political superior, may be said to be in a state of nature with respect to each other) 'are in continual jealousies and the posture of gladiators, having their weapons pointing and their eyes fixed on one another, that is, their forts, garrisons, and guns upon the frontiers of their kingdoms' [12]. All this is expensive and, it might seem, pointless. Surely two adjacent countries fixed into this gladiatorial posture would mutually do better by dropping all these guns and garrisons and putting the money to better use? It is not, as it stands, there for 'competition' (as a means to getting another bit of land), for it is purely defensive. It is not, as it stands, there for 'glory' ('my guns are bigger than your guns'). The reason is what Hobbes calls 'diffidence' – that is, mutual fear. As long as each thinks the other might invade, they have reason to defend. So, in 'anticipation' of an invasion that might never come, they expend money and effort on defence. Even if neither wishes to invade, they still get locked into a mutually expensive posture of defence.

These are the parts of the account that lend themselves to modelling in modern games theory, such as the so-called prisoners' dilemma. In this modern games theory, each player is taken to think in a purely self-interested way, and a matrix is constructed of the order in which outcomes would be ranked in terms of this interest. The possible application of this to Hobbes is that Hobbes also seems to have everyone acting self interestedly, indeed, holds that it is inevitable. Now Hobbes claims that in a state of nature, this self-interested action leads everyone into war. He claims that he has empirical support for this in the guns and garrisons that sovereign states have on their borders. This is the claim that, it seems, can be translated into games theory. Given that guns and garrisons are expensive and that each state would (self-interestedly) prefer not to have them, how do they get into this position? Let us rank some other possible outcomes. The worst position for a state to be in is if it drops its own guns and the other state then invades; the best position to be in is if the other one drops its guns so that it can itself invade. Hence we can argue as follows (which is the structure of the classic prisoners' dilemma). There are two ways the other side can play: either it drops its guns or it does not. If it drops its guns, you are better keeping yours (your first choice against your second). If it does not, you are again better off keeping yours (your third choice against your fourth). Hence, whatever the other side does, you should keep your guns. But the argument is exactly the same for the other side. Hence they should both keep their guns. Hence we end up with the expensive guns and garrisons on the frontiers, just as Hobbes described. This is so even though it is for each of them their third best choice rather than what is for each of them their second best choice. That is, both sides go for the worse option even though a situation is available (mutual disarmament) in which they each would do better. Why? Diffidence, as Hobbes calls it – mutual fear. Fear of the worse leads them to secure themselves against what might happen, and hence, in avoiding the worse, they also miss the better.

This provides some of these reasons for having a common external power in order to avoid such mutually destructive (or at least sub-optimal) fear. However, we already have a puzzle. For the example of the military defences of sovereign countries was an example that Hobbes cites as a real-life example from his own world, and is indeed one that is still with us today, several centuries on. Yet, if rational self-interest is really as Hobbes describes, whereby people placed in a state of nature have reason to escape to the greater security of the state, then it might seem that the separate sovereign states should also have escaped by now into the greater security of a single sovereign world government. Individuals have done it (according to Hobbes), but states have not. So if his account is to work, something has to be different at the state level. In fact, it may not be the rationality of escape that is different but rather its possibility. For just because it is better to be out of the situation does not mean that this is what will inevitably happen, as the crude modelling of the prisoners' dilemma illustrates, where we do not end up in the better situation.

It might be thought that the whole problem here (both of the state of nature and also of the prisoners' dilemma) arises because the individual parties think and act separately. It might be thought that if they could only communicate and agree, things would be improved. Thus, in the example given, seeing that they would mutually benefit from disarmament, it might seem that they could agree not to invade each other and so reach a better position (cheap non-invasion rather than expensive non-invasion). However, the same game works in exactly the same way once again if we now ask whether each party should honour such an agreement (that is, if we now look at the payoffs for keeping the agreement if the other one does, and so on). Again we see that each would do better if it breaks the agreement. Hence, each would break the agreement, and so we are back again with the guns, with the state of nature as a state of war. Here we only have mutual trust to enforce the agreement, and yet, as we saw Hobbes observing, covenants without a sword are mere breath.

States therefore cannot escape the dilemma by mere agreement, but nor, it seems, can individuals. For both, there is the question of whether, if the state of nature is as bad as Hobbes says, it is possible to exit it. Certainly Hobbes's own favourite strategy of doing so by mutual agreement looks problematic, given that agreements in such a condition are 'but words'. However, as well as analogies there are also dis-analogies between states and individuals. It is important for Hobbes that in the state of nature everyone be effectively equal in strength (as he stresses in all three of his treatments) and that they are all equally weak. As he puts it in *Leviathan*, 'the weakest has strength enough to kill the strongest' [13.1, p. 60]. Even the strongest sleep. So no one (at least for Hobbes) has sufficient strength for security. They need a greater strength; hence they need the artificially constructed strength of the great Leviathan. This, however, does not apply to states, at least not obviously so. The weakest here cannot topple the strongest. States do not go to sleep. Hence, at least for some of them, there is both the possibility and the desirability of going it alone (that is, defending themselves by their own exertions) in a way that has no analogue with respect to individual people. (Hobbes himself also mentions how the defences of states help the industry of their subjects, again something without an analogue for individuals.)

The mutual relations of sovereign states were introduced because of the difficulties of providing empirical description of individuals without government. Hobbes also tries anthropology, taking, as was said, the state of nature as being the condition of the indigenous American peoples, whom he believed to be in a continual state of war. But lacking much empirical evidence, we would seem to be pushed back into a priori models of human nature, which are even harder to control. Finding it hard to observe empirically whether people are always actually competing for advantage, we instead model it in games in which we assume a priori that each party is trying to advance its interest as much as possible. Then, or so it seems, we can prove deductively how Hobbes's 'diffidence' leads to continual conflict, exactly his conclusion. However, one problem about this route to his conclusion is that although Hobbes does think that people act self-interestedly, he has one specific interest that drives the arguments of his political philosophy, the interest of survival. This is an unusual and special interest, which, as we saw in the last chapter, has a much more secure base than the mere advancement of interest. Once our survival is secure, we do not necessarily have a good reason to exploit others merely for our own further gain; certainly it would not be a reason of the same kind So it is not obvious that Hobbes's reasons (as given in his laws of nature) will translate into the kind of situations modelled by the prisoners' dilemma. For that depends on the assumption that we are always trying to advance our interests, however secure we are. For example, once the other side disarms, which would be enough to give us security, we are nevertheless assumed to prefer seizing things from it rather than leaving it alone (hence we are taken to prefer keeping our arms; and so reach the situation in which neither side disarms). A model in which only security was the goal might more readily result in stable situations without either prisoners' dilemma sub-optimality or a strong government forcing universal conformity.

Alternatively, we may cast our naturalistic descriptions more widely in our attempt to capture human essence. Taking natural history seriously, we could try situating people among the animals. Hobbes is aware of the threats that this might pose to his position, being eager in both the *Elements* and *Leviathan* to distinguish between people and such social insects as ants and bees (which, as he observes, Aristotle called political creatures). The question is, as he puts it in the *Elements*, why 'may not men, that foresee the benefit of concord, continually maintain the same without compulsion, as well as they?' [19.5] With the social insects, we see individuals naturally living together in harmony without government, and if that is the state of nature for ants and bees, the question properly arises why people in the state of nature should be any different. Competition is not inevitable, any more than the conflicts or glory; diffidence can be overcome. 'That little creature, the bee' shows that we can have complex, mutually beneficial, and coordinated activity without any government, any superior power, or any great Leviathan.

Hobbes has therefore to distinguish between us and the ants and bees, which he does in Chapter 17 of *Leviathan*. The first difference he notes is glory – that is, the human 'competition for honour and dignity' [7]. However, as we have seen, this is possibly dispensable in the human case (even though Hobbes thinks, as he puts it here, that 'man, whose joy consisteth in comparing himself with other men, can relish nothing but what is eminent'). Perhaps we could rub along with each other as the ants do, and without bothering about who is eminent. Another of Hobbes's points is that the agreement of these 'creatures is natural; that of men is by covenant only, which is artificial' [12]. However, this is just what Hobbes has to demonstrate, and so cannot properly be assumed as part of the argument. He has to show that there cannot be natural agreement and harmony between people; hence that we cannot have peace in the state of nature; hence that we have by covenant to construct the artificial creature, the great Leviathan to give us agreement and peace. However, before this last effort comes a string of points that are significant. These develop the obvious difference between people and insects, sophisticated linguistic ability. Language means, thinks Hobbes, that people are able criticise governments, but this striving 'to reform and innovate' leads to 'distraction and civil war' [9]. (By trying to fix it we break it; this is all written after the English civil wars and the destruction of the king and his state.) The use of language means that people, unlike ants, represent 'good in the likeness of evil' [10], and furthermore that 'irrational creatures cannot distinguish between *injury* and *damage*' [11]. This all arises not just from the use of language but, more specifically, from the use of language to make moral evaluations. With people, we get language, and with language, we get criticism. The government is criticised, and so upset. Other people are criticised, and so upset. There is dispute over the good; hence argument, conflict. When I am affected and hurt, I sometimes feel moral resentment; I judge that it is wrong, and this motivates me in a special way to do something about it, leading again to conflict. That is, in Hobbes's terms, I distinguish between injury (that which is not *jus*, is unjust, morally wrong) and damage (that which is mere hurt). The latter happens if I am hit by the branch of a tree blown by the wind; the former happens if someone improperly hits me. And if I think that someone has improperly hit me, I hit back, and we are into war. The ants merely bump into each other, and bumping into each other, they bump along. Bumping into another ant is no different from bumping into a twig. However, if people bump into each other, we are into conflict, war. For they have language, and so get morally aggrieved by the bumping; they feel resentment and so fight back. Or so at least thinks Hobbes.

So the primrose path to the hell of civil conflict is paved with good intentions – that is, intentions about the good – moral evaluations. The plurality of these moral evaluations produces the intellectual disagreements that Hobbes identifies as the most insidious causes of civil war. 'Intellectual dissension too is extremely serious, that kind of strife inevitably causes the worst conflicts', he says, noting that 'the bitterest wars are those between different sects of the same religion and different factions in the same country' [*De Cive* 1.5]. This is where we came in: the conflict of the books, the contested interpretations of the Bible, rational scepticism, disputes about authority, civil war. What Hobbes wants to end is such a plurality of voices, and yet plurality is all that the state of nature can provide. So here is another reason to exit the necessarily conflicting and contested state of nature into a condition in which this plurality of voices can be reduced to unity. For Hobbes, this comes with the state, because, for him, in the state we achieve monopoly of judgement. Hobbes's sovereign has authority over the interpretation of scripture, reducing the biblical babble to a single voice. He has authority over the content of natural law, so avoiding intellectual dissension about what is right or the destructive scepticism of not knowing how to act. With the state, all this is perfectly clear: you do what you are told, and the great power of the Leviathan provides everyone with fully comprehensible reasons (just like God's original answer to Job).

This sovereign (as we have seen) gives command rather than advice, making something a reason just because of his will, and once we have command we can stop wondering about what is right. This is the Hobbesian conclusion, and yet it contains an obvious paradox. Once we have the state, we no longer need nor may properly use private judgement; once we have command, we no longer need advice (counsel). However, Hobbes, who is writing in the state, is himself giving advice. He is just a particular, private, voice, expressing his own individual view about what is right. On his own account, even if what he says is true, this does not make it the law. So how can Hobbes do this? That is, either he is right about leaving it all to the sovereign, in which case he shouldn't be giving his own views about natural law, or else he, like others, may give such an account, in which case the sovereign should not, after all, be granted a monopoly of judgement. More particularly, if we get out of the horrors of civil war and save our skins by ceasing to think for ourselves, then Hobbes should not be continuing to think for himself (even if the content of his thought is that we should not think for ourselves). There are similar strains in Hobbes's attitude to the universities: sometimes he thinks that they should be closed down as sources of sedition; sometimes he thinks that it would be all right if only they would teach Hobbes. He couldn't really allow them to encourage people to think for themselves; yet it would only be if people thought for themselves in the contemporary universities that they would discover Hobbes (writing from outside the academy) rather than the Aristotle pushed into them by their teachers.

In these circumstances, what Hobbes needs above all is a doctrine that can universally be recognised to be correct. He needs reasons that can be recognised as such despite peoples' other positions in the discordant babble of different ideas. This is what Hobbes hopes to provide by his new natural law; reasons that will apply in all contexts (in the state of nature and in the state, whether you believe in Rome or Geneva, whether you follow Aristotle or Galileo). Hence it is founded on prudence, on the rationality of self-preservation. This is something that everyone can see to be right. Even if we have language, so that our thought is essentially moralised, we can see that this provides justification. Life, survival, is our deepest need. This is the state of nature's law. Our rational response to our deepest need is to move from the state of nature to the state of law. We do this by artificially constructing the state. Or so at least Hobbes holds. In the next chapter, we shall have our last encounter with the great Leviathan by examining and criticising Hobbes' construction.

4

Hobbes: The Birth of Justice

Whether our thought is based on the word of God or on natural reason, Hobbes wants to show that we have nothing to do but obey, no other place to go than to submit ourselves to the authorities. Respect, but do not criticise, Leviathan. The greatest threat, in Hobbes's age, to such uncritical respect was religion; hence Hobbes wants to show that there is no religious way round this truth. However, it is exactly the same for him with more secular bases of thought. Here also there is for Hobbes no alternative to political authority. We might try to appeal to the Bible, to the precept that we should obey God rather than man. Or, alternatively, we might try to appeal to our natural reason with its understanding of the objective truths of justice, supposed to be accessible to everyone's individual conscience. Either way, we might think that in so doing we could reach to something beyond the present local authority, something that would justify resistance or rebellion if that authority is found to be wicked, irreligious, or unjust as measured by these independent standards. However, what Hobbes wants to show is that this is not so. There are no such independently accessible standards. Of course there is natural law. Of course there are the truths of justice. Of course there is God commanding right action. (We have seen that whether Hobbes himself really thought that this last was an 'of course' is a matter of debate, but this does not affect the fact that all he needs to do is to suppose it to be common ground for the purposes of his argument.) Of course there are such things. However, what Hobbes wishes to show is that there is no way of reaching any of them independently of the local political superior, and so show that none of them can be used against this superior. There are, of course, truths of justice, but the truths of justice are what the sovereign says they are.

Where Hobbes starts is with disagreement. Disagreement makes justification difficult, by making it hard to see what is objectively right. However, the fact of disagreement also provides the problem that any such justification has to solve. It is precisely the plurality of voices that poses Hobbes's most pressing problem, and it is the reduction of this plurality to the single, authoritative, voice of the state that is Hobbes's central solution. The Hobbesian state of nature is a place of profound and continuous disagreement, and disagreement leads to war. His solution is the artificially constructed commonwealth, or state. With the state, we have a way of blending wills so that we may achieve a single will. With the state, we have a way of consolidating judgements so that we may achieve a single judgement. With such a single judgement, we no longer have conflict. So with the state, the problems of conflict are avoided; we have a political solution to an intellectual and a moral problem.

It is definitional of Hobbes's state of nature that in it there is only private judgement. In this condition, says Hobbes, 'everyone is governed by his own reason' [*Lev* 14.4, p. 64]. We start, as was seen, with a right to preserve ourselves, hence with a right to anything needed for such preservation. But who, in the state of nature, is to be the judge of such necessities? Since everyone is equal and there is no authoritative superior, there is no alternative to everyone judging these necessities for themselves. Hence, as Hobbes puts it in the *Elements*, 'every man by right of nature is judge himself of the necessity of the means, and the greatness of the danger' [14.8]. Our natural right (or liberty) when we lack a political superior is a right of judgement. As he puts it in *De Cive*, 'by natural law *one is oneself the judge* [*ipse* iure naturale *iudex est*]' [1.9]. However, if each person judges for him or herself, then we have a plurality of views about the right answer. Hence conflict arises from disagreements about what is right.

Hobbes makes it 'a precept of the law of nature' that 'every man divest himself of the right he hath to all things by nature' [*Elements* 15.2]. To get the single public will, we each give up some private rights. But which ones? Hobbes says that it is the right to all things, but what, more specifically, should I give up to get the state? One possibility might be the right to private enforcement of my other rights. So, rather than each of us doing by ourselves what it takes to give us security, we each instead divest ourselves of this right and permit it to be done instead by the sovereign (the state). We transfer to the state an initial private right to punish. Put in this way, it sounds more like Locke than Hobbes, and, as such, will be looked at later. In Hobbes's terms, it would be better to say that we each give up our right to self-protection, but better still to say that we each give up our right to judge the best way to ensure our safety. Then, instead of the plurality of private judgements, we have the single public judgement of the sovereign. As Hobbes puts it in the last chapter of the *Elements*, 'in the state of nature, where every man is his own judge' we get differences and 'breach of peace'; hence 'it was necessary there should be a common measure of all things that might fall in controversy'. Hobbes then notes that 'some say' that the common measure is 'right reason'. In other words, we might think that we could reach for our reason as this 'common measure'. However, Hobbes immediately adds that 'seeing right reason is not existent, the reason of some man, or men, must supply the place thereof; and that man, or men, is they, that have the sovereign power' [29.8]. For Hobbes, our own reason is not 'right reason' and cannot provide a 'common measure'. Only a political sovereign can provide right reason, common measure. Rather than reason being sovereign, the sovereign is reason.

We can take Hobbes's claim here that 'right reason is not existent' in two different ways, which are however equivalent in their practical effect. We could understand it ontologically, as making the claim that there is no 'right reason' – that is, no natural law. Hence, lacking natural law, we have instead to make do with the only law we can get, the law provided by the sovereign's will. Or, alternatively, we could understand Hobbes's claim epistemologically, as making the claim that although there is 'right reason' (natural law), our only means of identifying it is by the actual reasoning processes of actual people. Then the question becomes whose reasoning processes we should use for this purpose. Since different people's processes disagree, if we regard everyone's process as equal, we will reach no answer ('where every man is his own judge, there properly is no judge at all' [*Elements* 17.6]). The alternative is to take just some or just one of these people as judge, and this is what Hobbes does with the sovereign. So, again, we

reach the sovereign. Therefore, whether on ontological or epistemological grounds, we need the state (sovereign) to gain applicable right
reason – that is, justice. Hence for Hobbes, the birth of the state is also
the birth of justice. Justice demands a 'common measure', and states
provide common measure. As he puts it in the *Elements*, 'it belongeth
also to the judgement of the same sovereign power to set forth and
make known the common measure by which every man is to know
what is his and what another's, what is good and what is bad, and what
he ought to do and what not' [20.10].

So, for this and other reasons already discussed, Hobbes thinks that
we should escape the state of nature and construct the state (or, if we
are already in a state, we should be glad that we are). But how is the
construction to proceed? However rational the will to make it, how in
fact can this will be constructively applied? This is the point at which the
original contract is meant to work. We are meant to will the state into
existence by agreement with each other ('a creation out of nothing by
human wit' [*Elements* 20.1]). We each exercise our independent will
and make an agreement that constructs the mighty Leviathan. Thereby
we create both the desired single will, or common measure of justice,
and also the almighty punishing power that gives it its effect. It is to be
created by contract. Yet, as we have seen, the problem for Hobbes is
that contracts seem to lack any effect before we have the state. We need
a binding contract in order to construct the state, but we also seem to
need the state in order to construct a binding contract. Without state
power, we have no security of enforcement, and without such security,
contracts do not seem to bind. This was the problem described in the
last chapter, but the point can also be put in terms of the considerations
about common judgement just discussed. Only with the state is there
a common measure as to whether we have a contract – that is, an
authoritative voice as to whether a contract has been made, its exact
terms, and how it should be enforced. As Hobbes puts it in the *Elements*,
'when there shall be such a power coercive over both the parties, as
shall derive them of their private judgements in this point; then may
such covenants be effectual' [15.10]. So we have a seeming circle: for
contracts we need the state, and for the state we need contracts.

At the start of the Introduction to the *Leviathan*, Hobbes describes the creation of the 'artificial man', his Leviathan (commonwealth,
state). He whimsically traces several parallels between this 'artificial

man' and natural men. Thus 'equity and laws' are taken to be 'an artificial reason and will' (it will be remembered that 'equity' is for Hobbes the law of nature that can hold before the state, giving good reason, whereas law is created by will, command). Then he gets to the birth of the artificial man – that is to the birth of his Leviathan. Here we need a divine creative act, something corresponding to 'that *fiat*, or the *Let us make man*, pronounced by God in the creation' of natural man. For this crucial creative act, he proposes 'the *pacts* and *covenants* by which the parts of this Body Politique were first made, set together, and united'. In other words, the artificial political body (that is, the state) is created by pact and covenant. (Both 'pact' and 'covenant' are terms specifically used by Hobbes to indicate those contracts in which there is not immediate mutual performance and in which there is therefore an element of trust; there are, that is, contracts of expectation.)

So the great beast, the almighty state, is to start with contract, and before looking further at the particular details of how Hobbes does it, we should note some of the more general attractions, as well as the possibly alarming consequences, of starting with contract. The attractions are particularly apparent in the sort of sceptical age that Hobbes inhabited and in which the content of all duties is doubted. For, with contract, rather than trying to discover the content of pre-existing rights and duties (given by God, objectively there, engraved on everyone's hearts), we instead create our own obligations. Yet, if the normative world we inhabit is not merely externally given but is instead something we ourselves create, then it is much easier to see how it applies to us. The two standard problems of duty are content and force – that is, what our duties are and how they move us into action. However, if instead of our obligations just being there, we construct our own, then both these problems become much more tractable. We know the content of our duties because it is a content we choose for ourselves. This content also naturally connects with our will and action because our will is involved in its construction; in willing its content, we also will its application. Hence the attractiveness of the idea that there is, as Hobbes puts it, 'no obligation on any man which ariseth not from some act of his own' [*Lev* 21.10, p. 111]. We are bound because we bind ourselves.

To see how this might work in a particular example, let us consider Hobbes's views of the rights of conquerors. Hobbes thinks that when a conquered people is bound to obey its conquerors, 'it is not therefore the victory that giveth the right of dominion over the vanquished but his own covenant. Nor is he obliged because he is conquered, that is to say beaten, taken, or put to flight, but because he cometh in and submitteth to the victor' [*Lev* 20.11, p. 104]. This is, I think, an implausible account of obligation to obey conquerors. However, the point to notice for our purposes is how Hobbes, wanting the conquered person bound, does not depend for this upon the conqueror's power, but instead upon a supposed covenant by the conquered. He wants the person to be bound, and so he thinks that the person must therefore have bound himself. Hobbes thinks that the person is obliged, and so supposes that the obligation must arise from some act of his own. So Hobbes assumes it is because the person covenants or submits that he is under obligation.

We are bound only because we have bound ourselves. This, at least at times, is true for Hobbes even with the kingdom of God. It might be thought that God, the greatest conqueror of the lot, has sufficient power to make all people his subjects. But, again, Hobbes distinguishes between those who are subjects of this kingdom and those who are mere enemies or aliens. Hence, for Hobbes, atheists are not subjects. In *De Cive* [15.2], he notes that inanimate things are not subjects because they cannot understand, and then immediately goes on to say that atheists are not subjects either, claiming that 'the only persons to be numbered in the kingdom of God are those who accept that he is ruler of all things'. Neither trees nor atheists accept or agree; neither is a subject. This does not in fact, for Hobbes, stop action against atheists. However, any action of God (or his lieutenants on earth) against them is not action against disobedient subjects, but rather action against an alien enemy. Therefore God is sovereign of all in two different ways: 'he is king of all the earth by his power, but of his chosen people he is king by covenant' [*Lev* 12.22, p. 58]. This duality of power and covenant will be more closely scrutinised later, but the point to notice here is how, even with something as powerful as God, Hobbes is looking for covenants, for how people are bound because they have bound themselves.

So Hobbes is constantly looking for agreements when we would not expect them and where we cannot obviously observe them. Another example is Hobbes's claim that a child's obligation to obey its parents arises from its own consent. This constant discovery (or implication) of agreements where we might not expect them has important consequences. For, because Hobbes thinks that people have created their obligations for themselves, he also thinks that they can therefore be held to them. Hence, for Hobbes, because we ourselves constructed the state, we are therefore bound to it. For Hobbes, whatever awful things the state does to us, no injustice, no wrong, can be involved. We chose it; it is our state, our action; we willed it and hence cannot complain. Hence subjects of a sovereign are not allowed 'to make war upon, or so much as to accuse of injustice, or in any way speak evil of their sovereign, because they have authorised all his actions, and in bestowing the sovereign power, made them their own' [*Lev* 24.7, p. 128]. Everything follows from our 'authorisation'. We chose it, and hence cannot (properly) object. We may be criticised for stupidity if we choose something harmful, but we cannot complain that the harms are unjust. In this way, the absolute state (or sovereign) gains purchase in Hobbes; we may start with complete liberty, but we soon find that we have willed ourselves into a condition of complete subjection, with no room left to complain. We can notice how here in Hobbes (as before, in fact, in Grotius), an apparent initial position of freedom in which we can will and construct what we like leads to an absolute government in which all possibility of willing is removed. We are only bound by what we choose, but once we have chosen the state, there is no subsequent scope for further choice.

The legal and moral maxim on which Hobbes can and does rely here is that people cannot wrong themselves in their own freely chosen actions. The standard Latin legal tag that expresses this is *volenti not fit injuria* – that is, what someone does voluntarily is not an injustice to him. (Hobbes quotes this tag in Latin not only in his Latin work *De Cive* [3.7], but also in his English work, the *Elements* [21.3].) Hence, as he puts it in *Leviathan*, 'whatsoever is done to a man, conformable to his own will signified to the doer, is no injury to him' [15.13, p. 75], or, even more strikingly and strongly, 'to do injury to oneself is impossible' [18.6, p. 90]. Here, as always, we have to remember the special legal sense of 'injury' that Hobbes is using; how the Latin tag about *injuria* is standing behind the English, so that the English 'injury' here means something more like 'injustice' – the claim is not that you can't hurt yourself, but rather that you can't be unjust to yourself in your own actions. So for Hobbes, as also in a legal commonplace (albeit not one fully recognised in modern English law), if we create our own obligations, then we cannot properly object to any of the consequences. We chose it, and hence cannot complain. For Hobbes, the absolute power of the Leviathan is something that we created. Hence we cannot object to the consequences; hence we have no ground to object to any use of its absolute power. Leviathan may, for example, tax us, tax us without representation (which is just what the king Hobbes defended did in the contentious run up to the English civil war). However, the king is our own constructed sovereign. Hence we have no proper ground for complaint.

If we instead had made a bilateral agreement with this sovereign, then perhaps we might have a proper ground for complaint. In agreeing, we would still have been acting voluntarily in a way that subsequently bound us. But so also would the sovereign, and if the sovereign broke the agreement (for example, not to tax us without representation), then we too might be released from our obligation (for example, to pay taxes). However, this is not the way the agreement works in Hobbes. The contract is not with the sovereign but with each other. It is we alone who do all the making, and because we alone make, it is we alone who are subsequently bound. As Hobbes puts it in the chapter on 'the rights of sovereigns' in *Leviathan*, the process by which the sovereign arises is 'by covenant only of one to another and not of him to any one of them', and hence, according to Hobbes, 'there can happen no breach of covenant on the part of the sovereign and consequently none of his subjects . . . can be freed from his subjection' [18.4, p. 89]. Therefore, once we have the state, we are, as he puts it in the preceding paragraph, 'bound, every man to every man, to own and be reputed author of all that he that is already their sovereign shall do and judge fit to be done'. All Hobbes's terms of art need careful watching. Here it is 'author'. For Hobbes, each of us is the 'author' of what the 'sovereign' does. We need authority, we get it by authorisation, and authorisation requires an author. In Hobbes, we are the authors of our political fate. We are the 'author'. Hence the sovereign is authorised; hence we cannot complain.

Constructing the State

So there are both natural attractions in the idea that we are only bound because we bind ourselves and also disconcerting absolutist consequences. With this in mind, we will now move to a closer examination of how the idea is actually put into effect by Hobbes in his state construction. As we do, it will be helpful to remember the problems that have been exposed even by this rapid survey of the attractions and dangers of the idea. It is central for Hobbes, as he has just been quoted as saying, that we do not covenant with the sovereign but only with each other. However, if so, there is a problem of how the account of obedience to conquerors is supposed to work. Hobbes wants us bound by our own agreement. However, if there is any agreement after conquest at all, it would seem to be an agreement with the conqueror rather than, as Hobbes wants, with each other. Also, it is all very well to have fantasies of state construction from nothing, but the problem is how this is meant to fit with actual obligation in actual states. Perhaps, that is, in some fanciful hypothetical scenario, I might 'authorise' the sovereign, but the problem is what has that to do with obedience to the actual historical King Charles who is now taxing me in an outrageous manner. Bad King Charles is clearly my present political fate, but it is difficult to see how I could have been the 'author' of him, or it. For, whatever the origin of Charles's kingship, it certainly did not emerge from everyone's getting together in some primeval English wood and contracting with each other to have a king called Charles.

These problems need to be solved in Hobbes's account of how the state construction is actually to proceed. Also, even if we bind ourselves by making contracts, we still have the problem of why contracts bind. It is all very well to say that we bind ourselves by making contracts, but this only works if (valid) contracts bind, and that (valid) contracts bind cannot itself be the result of a contract (an agreement to keep our agreements), otherwise we are into a vicious regress. This shows, incidentally (at least if we are thinking, like Hobbes, of contracts), that not all our obligations are created by us, for the obligation to keep contracts is not. More pertinently, the claim that we choose our own obligations is no help with the perennial problem of why contracts bind in the state of nature. For we cannot just choose to make them bind by means of an agreement that contracts should bind, since the same problem recurs as to whether this second-order agreement itself should bind. (In a games theory reconstruction, everyone might agree to keep their agreements, and then not do so.) So we still have the problem of the seeming circle between binding contracts and a binding state.

In meeting these problems and discussing Hobbes's actual state construction, let us start with the problem of who the parties to the assumed contract are supposed to be. In fact, Hobbes has not one but two stories of state construction (or political obligation), and the remarks about conquerors come from the second story. His first story is what he calls a commonwealth by institution, but he also has a second story, which he calls a commonwealth by acquisition. The first story is the familiar fantastical one by which the commonwealth emerges from everyone's contracting with everyone else in the state of nature. The second story is the much more usual occurrence of state creation by conquest. However, Hobbes thinks that both are normatively in the same position. In each, there are the same obligations of subjects and same freedom of sovereigns. For in both cases, he thinks there is an agreement that authorises the sovereign, and the political obligations that the people have to this sovereign are taken to follow from this agreement.

Before turning to the first story – the classic original contract one – let us look further at the second story, Hobbes's account of the commonwealth by acquisition. His crucial and primary distinction here is between a slave who has to be forced to do what he does and a subject who agrees to it voluntarily (and who is therefore subjected by his own act). If I am chained and pulled into action, for Hobbes I am under no obligation. If I can, I may escape my conqueror, I may disobey, I may even kill. My relation to the conqueror is merely one of war, and it is up to the conqueror to watch me as he might a dangerous dog. Everything changes, however, if instead of being bound by the conqueror's chains, I have bound myself by my own agreement. Then (as the price of life) I have agreed to obey; hence for Hobbes I am obliged not to escape or kill. With my agreement, I have authorised the actions of this sovereign, and, as such, cannot complain.

Yet if all that is needed to put myself under obligation is acquiescence, not killing when I can, then it would seem rather easy to get most sovereigns authorised. Bad King Charles has not chained me up, and even so I have not killed him when I could. So perhaps I have shown myself to be a subject rather than a slave. But it is a further step to suppose that by not killing King Charles when I could, I thereby make myself obliged to follow his will, authorise his taxation policy, and so on. If this is all it takes to acquire obligation to current kings like Charles, then obligation comes rather easy, although, to be fair, I am here reading this account *into* Hobbes rather than *out* from his actual text. Hobbes's conqueror spares the life of his captives, and it might be argued that King Charles does not spare my life (nor me his) in this way. The conqueror had them at the end of his sword; he had a particular occasion to kill, but then decided not to. However, if this is all the extra that is needed to produce the obligation, then before bad Charles taxes me, he first has to terrify me. Anything sufficiently terrifying becomes sovereign, and we are back to the formidable biblical beast, the great leviathan who is 'king over all the proud' chiefly because he is so frightening.

Hobbes's second story shows that we need no original forest in which people agree with each other in order to get an authorised sovereign. For we get it in the case of conquest (of commonwealth by acquisition) when an individual or group by sheer power subjugates the people in an area and so constructs there a state, a state in which, as we have seen, Hobbes still thinks that these people are subjected by their own agreement. However, such an agreement, if it exists at all, seems to be an agreement with the sovereign rather than of everyone with everyone. The sovereign agrees to give me liberty and I agree to give the sovereign obedience. However, here Hobbes brings another device into play. When he discusses whether the sovereign is bound, he says that even if the sovereign had made an agreement with the subjects, this would not bind him at all since 'the opinion that any monarch receiveth his power by covenant, that is to say on condition, proceedeth from want of understanding this easy truth, that covenants being but words and breath have no force to oblige, contain, constrain, or protect any man, but what it has from the public sword' [18.4, p. 89]. Another way of putting this point is that the relationship between sovereign and subject is for Hobbes a state of nature relation, and that in the state of nature, promises are but 'words and breath' (as we saw in the last chapter, he says that they are 'but words and of no strength to secure a man at all'). So whether or not we think that there was an agreement between sovereign and subject in the conquest case, the sovereign for Hobbes is not bound. Yet, either way, we have agreed, and so we are bound. In one of these readings, the sovereign might also have agreed, but this does not matter since, being a mere state of nature, it does not bind.

However, if so, this returns us to the problem of the seeming circle between binding contracts and the state. This problem is even more obvious with the first story Hobbes tells in which we all, in the state of nature, agree with one another to have a sovereign and a state. This classic account is at the end of chapter 17 of *Leviathan*, the chapter on 'the causes, generation, and definition of a commonwealth'. This is the chapter in which Hobbes describes how we can have 'the multitude so united in one person' that it 'is called a commonwealth, in Latin, civitas'. In showing how individual people (a multitude) can construct a commonwealth, he wants to show how this initially disorganised crowd can nevertheless 'erect...a common power, as may be able to defend them from the invasion of foreigners and the injuries of one another and thereby to secure themselves in some sort'. (In other words, the desired exit from the miserable state of nature.) They do it by conferring 'all their power and strength upon one man, or one assembly of men, that they may reduce all wills...unto one will'. So we reach the single, artificial, will, giving the desired monopoly of judgement and reduction of the lethal discordant babble of competing wills that exist in Hobbes's state of nature. With the single will we get the single, artificial man. We get the sovereign, who could, as he has here just said, be either a single person (a king) or else an assembly of persons (a governing parliament).

Hobbes says that the multitude achieve this single will because they 'appoint one man, or assembly of men, to bear their person' and everyone has to 'own and acknowledge himself to be author of what so beareth their person...and therein to submit their wills, every one to his will, and their judgements to his judgement' [17.13, p. 87]. So we have submission to the sovereign. But, again, this submission flows from the acts of the people themselves. They submit because they have to acknowledge that they are the 'author' (the authorising source) of the sovereign. This, as Hobbes puts it, 'is more than consent or concord; it is a real unity of them all in one and the same person, made by covenant of every man with every man, in such manner as if every man should say to every man, *I authorise and give up my right of governing my self to this man, or this assembly of men, on this condition that thou give up thy right to him and authorise all his actions in like manner.*' Here, close together, is every element of the Hobbesian story: the contract of each with each, the pacts and covenants that Hobbes said in the Introduction unite the body politic, and the explicit act of authorisation by which each separate individual becomes the author of what the single king or assembly does.

Keeping the Contract

In Hobbes's earlier exposition of his new natural law, after he reaches his first conclusion that all rationally ought to seek peace, he lays it down as a law that everyone should give up a right that was causing war, on condition that everyone else should do so as well. We have seen how the right of separate, independent judgement was (for Hobbes) such a cause of war. So, by this law of nature, everyone should be prepared to give up this right (providing that everyone else does so as well). They should give them up and instead achieve the single will and judgement provided by a state monopoly. Here we see Hobbes's first account in *Leviathan* of how this is supposed to work. We do it by contract, by a contract we make each with each that we will give up our right providing that the other does so as well. Yet, because we do it by contract, we have the problem of how it is supposed to work, since the contract happens in what is still the state of nature. Being in the horrible Hobbesian natural state, it may be desirable to get out; however, just because it is so horrible, we are not able to depend upon contracts. As we saw, if we model Hobbes's account of international relations as a game in which separate nations are locked into state of nature type of conflict, they won't get out of it merely by each contracting with each that they will stop the warfare (for the same, mutually destructive, game merely replays itself if they do).

Hobbes continually says that we are bound by our own acts, by our agreements, by what we have 'authorised'. But given that on Hobbes's own account, such binding seems extremely fragile ('of no strength to secure a man at all'), we need a better explanation of how such binding is supposed to work. As we saw in the last chapter, there are in fact reasons that Hobbes can provide to show why we should keep our covenants in the state of nature. First, Hobbes can use the traditional, God-backed, natural law that holds that people should stand by their agreements. Here the reason for observance is God's insight into its rightness, or, alternatively, his will that we should do it, or, alternatively, that he will punish us if we don't. Then there is, second, Hobbes's new natural law in which those things that promote peace give us reasons for action. Here, keeping to our agreements promotes peace, and is accordingly number three of the new natural laws expounded in *Leviathan*. Keeping agreements promotes peace because it stops the aggravation and resentment of people who are abused by the breach of their protected expectations. However, it also, more specifically, promotes peace by being the means for the construction of the state that enforces the peace. Here the reason for keeping agreements is prudential, self-interested; the justification is that it leads to our self preservation. We need the peace that is given by the state. We need to respect contracts to reach the state. Hence we should respect contracts as part of our natural search for peace.

In addition to these two different kinds of Hobbesian reasons for keeping our agreements, Hobbes provides a third, quite different, ground. This, so far undiscussed, account he gives in almost exactly the same way in all three of his political philosophy books, and in each case it occurs when Hobbes first introduces the idea of laying down some rights on condition that others do the same. The central idea of this account is 'absurdity', a term (as he explicitly says in all three places) he borrows from the traditional processes of formal argument in the contemporary universities ('the schools'). Breaking an agreement is for Hobbes a prime example of injustice (or 'injury'); indeed, at times, he says it is definitional of injustice. He now wishes to show that such injustice – that is, such breaking of contracts – is wrong. He does this by comparing it to what is called 'absurdity' in the contemporary university disputations. As he puts it in *Leviathan* (the shortest account), he says that as it is in the 'disputations of scholars . . . called an absurdity to contradict what one maintained in the beginning, so in the world it is called injustice and injury voluntary to undo that which from the beginning he had voluntary done' [14.7, p. 65]. In the earlier *Elements*, he is somewhat fuller. Here, after mentioning the 'great similitude' with 'that which is called *absurd* in the arguments and disputations of the schools', he declares that 'there is in every breach of covenant a contradiction properly so called' because 'he that violateth a covenant, willeth the doing and the not doing of the same thing at the same time; which is a plain contradiction' [16.2].

This, if it worked, would be a knockdown argument showing that we have to keep our agreements. However, it is highly questionable as to whether it does work. The language of 'absurdity' is something we can still understand, even without memory of Medieval disputation, for we still talk of *reductio ad absurdum* arguments. We still, that is, use the Latin 'absurdum' to describe an argument in which a set of premises is shown to be inconsistent by deriving from them a contradiction (an absurdity). In Hobbes's *De Cive* (written in Latin), 'absurdum' is the word he uses at the corresponding point. He talks of 'someone in the schools who is reduced to absurdity (*reducitur ad absurdum*)' [3.3]. Anything that results in contradiction is thereby shown to be questionable (or reduced to absurdity). With Hobbes (and the Medieval scholastics), we may accept this. The problem, however, is why breaking an agreement should be of this kind. Hobbes says that it is because it is a contradiction in the will, such that someone breaking an agreement both wills A and also wills not-A. But someone who has both these wills only provides a problem if he has them simultaneously. Take the analogous case of belief. There is no corresponding problem about belief if I believe something on Monday (for example, that Hobbes is a consistent thinker) and something incompatible with it on Friday (for example, that Hobbes is not a consistent thinker). This is not an absurdity, a defeat for the rational intellect. All it means is that I have changed my mind. Since such a change may well be on the basis of additional evidence or additional thought, there is nothing absurd about it. So we only get into absurdity (or significant contradiction) when both of the opposing elements are held at the same time. Perhaps it does not make sense to say that I believe at the same time both that Hobbes is consistent and also that he is not consistent; at least such a description makes it difficult to tell what I really believe. Yet the normal examples of making and then breaking agreements seem much more like believing something on Monday and believing something else on Friday. For, standardly, I agree on Monday (that, for example, I will lecture on Hobbes on Friday) and then on Friday I decide not to deliver. Again, it would seem, I have changed my mind. As before, I have said or done something that contradicts (or, at least, goes against) what I said or did before, but in both cases this may be for good and comprehensible reasons.

However, presumably to meet this problem, Hobbes in his *Elements* account says that the two competing wills happen at the same time. For (in the quotation I gave earlier), he says that someone breaking a covenant 'willeth the doing and the not doing of the same thing at the same time'. Hence for Hobbes we do not have the will on Monday to do something on Friday, but rather some kind of statement on Monday that there will be will on Friday. What Hobbes actually says is that 'he that covenenteth willeth to do, or omit, in the time to come'. This ambiguous sentence is neutral between the two competing readings. 'He wills in the time to come' could mean 'he now wills A in the time to come', or it could mean 'he now agrees to will A in the time to come'. However, if we give Hobbes the credit of the latter reading, then we find him having both of the wills on Friday (the agreement has him willing A on Friday; breaking it has him willing not-A on Friday). However, we then run into another obvious problem. The agreement can only be construed as an agreement that results in a future will if it is also presumed that agreements should be kept (that if I agree now, the will to keep it will be there in the future). It presumes that agreements are efficacious in connecting the present with the future. Yet whether agreements do this is precisely the point that is under discussion, which is whether making an agreement today commits us to the corresponding will tomorrow.

If, because of its question-begging nature, we reject this reading, then we are back in the temporal hole. I show willing in the present, but the putative performance is in the future, and Hobbes has to explain why I am not allowed to change my mind in the interim. Even if this temporal hole can be filled, an additional problem arises in that a contradiction (or 'absurdity') in wills does not seem to be quite the same thing as a contradiction in beliefs. For it seems much easier to make sense of someone's having two incompatible desires (or wills) than someone's having two incompatible beliefs. This follows from the standard metaphor used here of direction of fit, whereby beliefs should fit the world, whereas the world should fit our will. Hence if I have incompatible beliefs, I know that at least one of them must be wrong. It is hard to say what I am believing if I seem to hold on to both, knowing that they are inconsistent, for it seems hard to say of both that they are sincerely aimed at the truth. By contrast, I can easily want two things even though I know that I cannot have both. I may want Hobbes to be simple enough to understand and also complicated enough to be interesting, even though, as it happens, I cannot have both, so that any account I give of Hobbes is in fact going to be either oversimple or else oversubtle.

Nevertheless, we can at least say that there is a pragmatic problem in breaking agreements. The point of making an agreement is undercut if I do not do what I say, in a loosely similar way to that in which the point of making a statement is undercut if I do not say what I believe. In the one case, I am using an authoritative means to fix my will; in the other, I am, on my authority, declaring how I see the world. Too much insincerity in either case destroys the authority and thereby the instrument that I am using for my insincere purposes; too much change of mind means that these implements will no longer be there for the mind to use. As Hobbes puts it in *De Cive* (as translated), 'in making an agreement one denies by the very act of agreeing that the act is meaningless. And it is against reason knowingly to take away the meaning of anything'. [3.2].

I should not knowingly take away its meaning. But, as we saw in the last chapter, the best Hobbes can do for state-of-nature agreements is an *in foro interno* reading, which means that we all wish to keep them (providing that, which we wish as well, that everyone else does). More than that, they do not bind. Indeed, in the very same paragraph of *Leviathan* in which Hobbes introduces the idea of 'absurdity', he says that agreements have no strength in the state of nature. As we have seen, binding for Hobbes requires reliable sanctions, and these only come with the state. It seems therefore that however elegant an account we may give of 'absurdity', we still have the brute and brutal problem of how Hobbes can reach the state by use of binding agreements.

Only power matters. Only with the sword do we have proper contracts. So does this not destroy the whole original contract program, the idea that the normative content of the state proceeds from our own wills, so that we are bound by the state because we have bound ourselves? Not immediately; for even if we think that in the end, only power binds (and that only overwhelming power binds absolutely), we nevertheless have to see where this power comes from. The state, for Hobbes, is an artificial construction. The great Leviathan is an artificial man. It is constructed by us. Lacking power in the state of nature, we make for ourselves a greater power. So Leviathan comes from us, and having power, Leviathan binds us. Hence we are, after all, bound by our actions, or rather we are bound by our actions if we can by these actions reach the great Leviathan. However, the pieces of Leviathan are only to be put together by agreement. So surely we have to have the binding that puts Leviathan together before we have the power that Leviathan brings? Well, it all depends; it all depends on how exactly the construction is supposed to proceed. Let us follow Hobbes in thinking of two different versions of state construction: construction from nothing and construction by conquest (the invasion of a superior power). In the latter case, we already have power, the power sufficient to enforce agreements. So if we make agreements with the conqueror (or anyone else), the sword is there and we are bound. The agreements can be enforced by the conqueror and so we can be relied on to keep them. By contrast, the conqueror is not bound because there is no power that can force the conqueror; hence we would just be foolish to rely on the conqueror's word; this, therefore, is not a normal, bilateral, agreement.

So much for creation by conquest, the easier case. This leaves the harder one, the creation of a state from nothing. However, is not clear even here how much we in fact have to depend upon mere mutual trust, and hence on the things that, for Hobbes, need the power of the sword. For what is to happen here is that all except one simultaneously lay down their weapons, leaving that one with the power of the sword. This could perhaps be programmed as a present act: a circle of people round the potential sovereign, each with spears, agreeing to throw them into the centre at the feet of the potential sovereign, not only at the same time as the others, but as they see the others doing it. Of course, we still have the possibility of a dummy, whereby at the very last moment a spear fails to leave someone's hand, and, modelled by the sort of games theory discussed briefly in the last chapter (which depends upon people not just saving their skins but getting maximum advantage), each person would do better playing dummy. Hence we might have everyone making the dummy and then holding on, an entertaining example of choreography, but not a means of escaping the state of nature.

We think of consent, as in the particular cases of contract and covenant, as some kind of legal agreement, and wonder how it can bind (before we have a proper, enforceable, law). But all we need here to get the spears into the centre of the circle is not 'consent' in the sense of a quasi-legal engagement, whereby someone explicitly binds him or herself, but rather 'consent' in the sense of when people merely happen to agree. In its older sense, still used sometimes by Hobbes, 'consent' means such mere coincidence of judgement or will. (This follows the etymology of the word, coming from the Latin *con* and *sentire*, thinking or feeling together, having the same sentiment.) For example, Hobbes defines the term in the *Elements* as 'this concourse of their wills is called CONSENT' [12.7]. Later he explains that 'it is not the consent of passion, or consent in some error gotten by custom, that makes the law of nature' [15.1]; here he merely means having the same passion, or the same custom-based error. 'Agree' in modern English has the same duplicity: it can mean something that merely happens to be similar ('we agree that the wine is better than the food'), or it can mean an intentionally constructed and obligation creating meeting of minds ('I agree to bring the food if you will bring the wine').

To get the actual power of the sovereign, all we need is the former sense; all we need is that most of the people happen to have the same idea. For if they happen to transfer making judgements to one person (or group), then this person (or group) has power, and with power we have binding force and so have solved the problem. So all that would be needed to escape the horrible state of nature is that the obvious rationality of so doing makes most people renounce their original right of judgement. Then we have a consent of wills, which thereby produces the power to enforce explicit agreements. Here, there is no problematic circle. Nor is it necessary that everyone agrees; the consent does not have to be universal. For the problem here is not a moral problem of the entitlement of the state to bind people without their consent, but rather the practical possibility of getting enough power to make agreements stick also *in foro externo*; and for this we merely need that most of the spears happen to leave the hands.

The Foole

Yet if I know that this might happen, it may well then not be rational for me to end up in the reneging minority – that is, to acquire the reputation of being someone who will only keep his agreements if forced to do so. This is one way to approach the notoriously controversial passage in *Leviathan* in which Hobbes answers the 'foole' (as I shall spell him here in order to identify this particular argument). The problem is put by Hobbes as that 'the foole has said in his heart, there is no such thing as justice; and sometimes also with his tongue' [15.4, p. 72]; the foole thinks that 'breach' of covenants, which he allows 'may be called injustice', 'may not sometimes stand with that reason which dictateth

to every man his own good', Since Hobbes takes himself to reply con-
clusively to this foole (that is, to show that he is indeed a fool), we
now seem to have exactly what we have been seeking – namely, an
argument in which Hobbes shows how it is irrational to be unjust and,
more specifically, to breach covenants. Furthermore, since the foole
only accepts self-interested rationality, this seems to be exactly the self-
interested defence of keeping covenants that we needed. At last we
would seem to have the argument why, after all, thinking of nothing
but our own good, we should nevertheless keep faith with others.

The passage is, as I say, highly controversial, so no one interpretation is going to be conclusive; indeed, it is probably a property of such
much argued over passages that they fail to tell a stable single story
(and so allow different, incompatible, emphases). However, a few possible ways of being misled can fairly confidently be headed off. We
might be misled by the implied, but altered, biblical reference of its
start. Psalm 14 (in the standard fifteenth-century English Coverdale
translation) starts, 'The fool hath said in his heart: there is no God'.
Hobbes clearly knows this, and indeed later in this passage itself he
remarks that 'the same fool says that there is no God'. So the question
is whether it matters that 'God' has been replaced by 'justice'. I do not
think that it does. The psalm (as also the highly similar Psalm 53) goes
on that 'there is none that doeth good, no not one'. God looks down
from heaven and finds that everyone is 'altogether abominable'. So
the consequence of these fools thinking that there is no God is that
everyone acts wrongly. The negation of God leads to the negation
of justice, and the question (in either case) is whether this is indeed
foolish.

The next thing that may mislead is that after his opening biblical
remark about the foole, Hobbes then spends a page-long paragraph
laying out his case. Since the opinions described sound much like
what Hobbes says elsewhere, it is easy to assume that this is just another
statement of his own views. However, we are not entitled just to assume
that here Hobbes is speaking in his own voice, for at the end of the
long paragraph he says 'this specious reasoning is nevertheless false'.
That is, Hobbes himself declares that what he has just said is false.
Therefore, it cannot simply be taken at face value. Somehow, it has to
be interpreted. We have to find something wrong with it, either the
opinions or their application.

Now, it might be the opinions. The foole here argues that 'every man's conservation . . . being committed to his own care, there could be no reason why every man might not do what he thought conduced thereunto; and therefore also to make or not make, keep or not keep, covenants was not against reason when it conduced to one's benefit'. Yet, even though placed in the mouth of the foole, this sounds exactly like Hobbes himself, at least with respect to the state of nature: how we have to reason for ourselves as to what provides our safety ('conservation'); that reason tells us to pursue our own good; that, as the foole puts it here, 'the voluntary acts of men tend to the benefit of themselves'; and so on. Since this is so like Hobbes himself (that is, so much in tune with what he says elsewhere), I do not think that it is plausible to claim that Hobbes thinks these opinions of the foole are wrong.

However, if this is so, then what Hobbes finds specious in the foole's argument must not be these ideas themselves but rather their application. The next paragraph, which starts the demonstration of why the 'reasoning is nevertheless false', is:

For the question is not of promises mutual where there is no security of performance on either side, as when there is no civil power erected over the parties promising, for such promises are no covenants. But either where one of the parties has performed already, or where there is a power to make him perform, there is a question whether it be against reason, that is against the benefit of the other, to perform or not.

I have quoted at length in case it is thought that I am hiding something; and, at this length, it all now seems simple the other way. Of course, there is a problem about keeping agreements made in the state of nature, but Hobbes here seems to be saying that this is not the situation he is discussing. Instead, he is considering the situation where there is 'a civil power', 'a power to make him perform'. It would seem therefore that in answer to the foole, Hobbes takes the case where there already is a commonwealth. Yet if we already have the commonwealth, then we have the sword and, even on Hobbes's only-for-your-own-good account, someone breaching covenants would indeed be a fool. So, at least at first sight, the foole's mistake is quite simply in thinking that state-of-nature applications of rationality still apply when we have the powerful punishing state in place. So, or so it seems, we have a resolution of this notoriously controversial passage.

However, as the reply proceeds, it ceases in fact to be this simple (which is why we get controversy, as different bits go different ways). For, in showing that 'it is not against reason' to keep agreements, Hobbes ceases to rely on such state punishing power. He first makes an intermediate point, which we can accept, that what counts as a (self-interestedly) rational action depends upon how it may be assessed before it happens. The rationality of action depends upon the consequences we are entitled antecedently to predict rather than what, by mere fluke, may actually happen. Of course, people breaching contracts might actually get away with it, but the question is whether it is antecedently predictable that they would, and hence whether it was rational for them to attempt it.

So now the question becomes whether we can show that people getting away with breaking their word are merely lucky, and have no right to expect that injustice would in fact pay. Hobbes says not, for he 'that breaketh his covenant, and consequently declareth that he thinks that he may with reason do so, cannot be received into any society that unite themselves for peace and defence but by the error of them that receive him'. According to Hobbes, the contract breaker has no right to assume that society will make such an 'error'. So the reply to the foole seems now to be that people may invest in their reputations, and it is foolish for someone to do something that is liable to damage his reputation. He might of course be lucky and get away with it, but he has no antecedent right to expect this. However, the answer to this is not to be found out, to have a policy of only breaching secretly, and so on. That is, the foole may agree that he has an interest in not being thought to be the kind of person who breaks promises, but hold that he needn't be such a fool as explicitly to declare that this is what he does; he just happens to break promises quietly, and this only 'declares' his views to others if they notice. To which Hobbes's reply would seem to be that the foole has no right to assume antecedently that they won't.

This is familiar argument and counterargument about investment in reputation. However, I think that Hobbes's reply here may be more directly related to the context of commonwealth than this. Hobbes talks of being 'received into society', which sounds today like having the right birth or manners to make one socially accepted in a particular circle. For Hobbes, however, peoples are purely groups of individual persons, disorganised multitudes, unless and until they have a sovereign, and are therefore, because of the single will of this sovereign, formed into a commonwealth. If 'society' is a group of individual people, then 'being received by society' means being received by every individual person. It could mean this, and here the arguments about investment in reputation apply. However, in the present context, it sounds much more like being received by people organised into a state. For this passage is about 'security'. It is about people who 'unite themselves for peace and defence', and in Hobbes, such uniting can only be by the state (otherwise there is a mere multitude, and neither peace nor defence). His standard term for the opposite to 'the state of nature' is 'civil society'. So the question again is whether people may reasonably expect to get the necessary co-operation with others in civil society if they declare themselves to live by another law. The answer is, again, clearly that it is not reasonable, so the foole is a fool.

With the state, it is too hot for the foole: he has to succumb to its sheer power. Without the state, it is too cold to move him: he may well feel he can get away with dissembling amidst its anarchic jumble of conflicts. However, there is also a Goldilocks answer to the foole: something that is neither too hot nor too cold; something that is between mere state of nature and an already formed state. This is where people are engaged in the process of state formation, such as is described in the original contract argument. In this case, we have an additional reason for people's being prepared to co-operate in that they have an interest in not being the one who didn't co-operate if the state happened to succeed. If for any reason (accident, trust), a sufficient number combine to produce effective state power, the others will find themselves in an unpleasant position, having declared themselves to live by another law. Of course, they may not be found out or remembered, but in such a case, if someone lives 'in society, it is by the errors of other men which he could not foresee, nor reckon upon'. Antecedently, this could not be reasonably anticipated. It is more likely that having shown themselves untrustworthy, they 'cannot be received' in the new society, and hence be in what is for Hobbes the (nasty, brutish) most miserable of conditions. Therefore prudence counsels co-operation.

So much for the foole, and whether or not some of the answer to the foole can be deployed in this way to answer questions about state formation, it is clear that the standard modern ways of modelling the choice as some sort of prisoner's dilemma are misleading. The idea of rationality deployed in both the foole's argument and also more generally in Hobbes is certainly a self-interested one, in which it is taken to be rational for people to pursue their own good, and it is also assumed that this is what, as a matter of fact, people will do when left free to act. However, as I showed in the last chapter, it does not follow from this that they are therefore always assumed by Hobbes to be maximising their interest or pursuing any advantage. For Hobbes's argument is driven by fear, and so some goods are taken to be much more important than others. What Hobbes's agents want is life, not optimisation; they are aiming to preserve themselves. This is what it is rational for them to attempt to achieve; hence (in Hobbes's terms), it is rational for them to do whatever it takes to get a commonwealth as the only means of doing it. The important thing for them is that others disarm, and it is not important for them whether, if they do, they can still keep their own arms. It is much more important for them to pursue any chance of getting the most important thing (general disarmament) than to bother about the slight hope of getting something that might arguably be better than this (everyone but themselves disarming). This means that they need not have any particular preference for staying armed if the others disarm. But if this is so, the preference for staying armed no longer dominates the preference for disarmament (that is, it is no longer the better option, whatever anyone else does), so we lose the prisoner's dilemma situation. (Since it is no longer better for each to hold arms, whatever anyone else does, they no longer have an incentive to stay in the armed situation, which is worse for them all.)

Will and Power

The arguments just given put together questions of justification and questions of possibility. We justify the state by showing that it emerges as a result of people's will, then worry over the possibility of their will's being efficacious. Some answers to this worry have just been given. However, we can also get answers by separating the questions of desirability and possibility. Possibility was merely a means to an end – what we basically want to know is whether the state is desirable. If we can show that the state is something that we would choose to enter if we were not in it, then this gives grounds for thinking it to be desirable. The principle here is the same as in the *volenti* maxim quoted by Hobbes – that whatever we ourselves wish, cannot be deemed an injustice to us. What we would choose is what we have reason to support and approve. Yet this retrospective, hypothetical question – whether we would choose the state if we were not in it – can be distinguished from the practical problems of moving from the one condition to the other. The practical problems depend in part on the power to enforce contracts. However, we are already normally already in states when we ask questions about justification. So we already have the power to enforce contracts. We are not asking about the practical possibility of getting out of the state of nature, for that is not our problem. Instead, we are asking about its desirability, and hence about the desirability of the condition we are already in.

This hypothetical way of taking the contract shows that Hobbes's argument, which embraces a fairly fantastic story, need not come apart on mere practicalities. However, even if we restrict ourselves to justification, we still have the question of how important a justifying device Hobbes thinks the original contract to be. Clearly he thinks that there is a difference between everyone's agreeing explicitly to set up a state and a mere harmony of wills, which just happens by chance to produce it. Even if, accidentally or otherwise, we achieve state power, we still, for Hobbes, seem to need the appropriate will. We still have the question of authorisation, the idea that my state is only legitimate if it acts by my authority. So there are still questions of the relations of power and will to be disentangled. Where we left this problem was that we found that Hobbes took will further than we might expect by reading it into situations like that of the conqueror, which seem at first sight to be ones of conspicuously unequal power. If we obey the state because of its power, this is deemed to be because we have willed it. We solve the problem of apparent lack of will by taking it to be implied in situations of unequal power. However, we now run into the converse problem. For if we can assume will this easily, what now remains of the claim that we are only bound by our own acts? What is left of the distinction that Hobbes wants to make between being overwhelmed by a superior force (like a chained slave) and agreeing to be subjugated (like the unchained servant)? For Hobbes thinks that these are very different. Yet both are produced by power.

Will and power are meant to be very different, yet when we look further into the relationship in Hobbes between will and power, we notice two features that tend to reduce the distinction between them. First, as we have seen, we find Hobbes introducing will where at first sight we have nothing but power. However, second, we also find him giving power a role where, at first sight, we have nothing but will. Although, at least at first sight, these seem to be moving in different directions, they combine to reduce the contrast between will and power. The first feature is present in Hobbes's account of why children are obligated to obey their parents. We might think that this was founded on generation: the parents made the child, hence the child is obliged to the parents. However, this, as Hobbes says, would not make the child obligated to the father more than to the mother. It would not, that is, explain contemporary assumptions. Indeed, as Hobbes also points out, if we allow knowledge to play a role in establishing the obligation, then the obligation would be to the mother, since she is the more certain parent. More promising, at least from a Hobbesian point of view, would be to try sheer power: the child has to obey its terrifying, enormous parent, just as we have to obey any other enormous monster we are placed close to by fate (this only contingently happens to be a parent). This is what we might expect from Hobbes, and indeed this does play a part. However, as we saw earlier, even here Hobbes seems to feel that he has also to introduce the will of the obliged in order to explain the obligation. Paternal dominion, he says in his chapter on the subject in *Leviathan*, is 'from the child's consent, either express, or by other sufficient arguments declared' [20.4, p. 102]. It is in the same chapter that Hobbes explains obligation to conquerors who acquire the sovereign power by force, and the explanation in each case is much the same: the dominated submits himself to the superior force.

The thing to notice is that superior force is still here doing work. Hobbes says here, of a child, that 'it oweth its life to the mother, and is therefore obliged to obey her', noting that 'every man is supposed to promise obedience to him in whose power it is to save or destroy him' [20.5, p. 103]. That is, what at first looked like pure choice is in fact explained by superior power. We start with an implausible claim that children explicitly choose to submit themselves to their parents and would not be obliged to obey them unless they happened to have gone through this particular, historical, act. Then it is allowed that consent need not be 'express' (that is, overt, explicit), but can instead be by 'other sufficient arguments declared'. So we now need to find the acts by which the child otherwise indicates consent. In fact, it is not found in any specific act of the child but in the mere situation of being in the power of life or death of someone else. If that person deigns to spare the child (as the powerful mother normally does), then, says Hobbes, the child is supposed to have promised obedience. So an argument that looks as if it is all about will or consent ends up in fact as an argument that is all about power. Once there is sufficient disparity of power, the promising is merely presumed. Indeed, in the *Elements* (in the corresponding chapter on 'the power of fathers'), Hobbes weakens the ground for the presumed promise from the receipt of life to the receipt of food. He says that 'it is to be presumed, that he which giveth sustenance to another, whereby to strengthen him, hath received a promise of obedience in consideration thereof' [23.3]. This is not quite receipt of benefits putting someone under an obligation (although this, in effect, is also one of the laws of nature that Hobbes described earlier), for here we do not have any old benefit but only the particular benefits (food) that are needed for life. However, it shows that an obligation that seems to be based on will and promise is in fact based upon something else.

In *De Cive*, Hobbes says that 'without his personal consent and agreement, either explicit (*expresso*) or implied (*subaudito*), the right of legislation could not have been conferred on anyone' [14.12]. Here we have another declaration that all rightful legislation over us follows from our will. But again we have to tease out the exact details of how it is put, as again it turns out that the agreement may only be implied. Hobbes here explains what he means by 'implied' (*subaudito*) by giving an example. This is 'when they accept the benefit (*beneficio*) of a person's power (*imperii*) and laws for protection and preservation (*conservationem*)'. So again we get benefits, more particularly benefits of preservation. And again the mere receipt of such benefits means that we are taken to have implicitly given consent. So, again, but this time in the case of the state, it is the receipt of benefit from superior power that is doing the work, rather than our consent to this power. An argument that looks as if it is about will is in fact founded upon unequal power.

This reading in of consent works with the tentative hypothetical account suggested earlier. For if we, looking back, say that we would have agreed to submit ourselves to the superior power, then it is both the fact of superior power that founds the obligation and also the fact that we would have agreed that makes this obligation palatable. With superior power, we have an argument that we cannot refuse. We cannot refuse to do what the superior power says, and we cannot refuse to agree that it is better for us to do what that power says than to be demolished and disposed of. However, just as with later arguments based on supposed hypothetical consent, it may be difficult to keep the two parts together. Sometimes power alone does the work, so that we are bound by the inequality of power even if it is false that we would have agreed.

On the other hand, there are cases of apparent explicit consent to something in Hobbes that are not deemed by Hobbes to be really cases of consent after all. That is, we can think that we are consenting (explicitly and not implicitly; categorically and not hypothetically), and yet Hobbes says that this is not what is really happening. So again the real work is not being done by apparent consent. One example is Hobbes's claim in *Leviathan* that 'a covenant not to defend myself from force, by force, is always void' [14.29 p. 69]. Given the number of unpleasant things that Hobbes allows us to agree to, starting with the mighty Leviathan, this sounds strange. Of course it might be stupid to covenant not to defend myself, but what is to stop me here from being stupid, creating my own obligatory situation by use of my own will and covenant? (I might – perhaps equally stupidly – covenant to obey the conqueror.) Why, that is, may I not give people permission to attack me, when, as we have seen, Hobbes holds that I cannot object to any injustice in the prince, however nasty he proves to be to me, since I constructed him by my will and hence 'authorised' his actions? In fact, the explanation comes with a slightly earlier claim by Hobbes where he says that 'a man cannot lay down the right of resisting them that assault him by force to take away his life, because he cannot be understood to aim thereby at any good to himself' [14.8, p. 66]. This presumably distinguishes (for Hobbes) these cases from the cases of the construction of the sovereign by will, since the motive of that construction is the good of the constructors (escaping the terrible state of nature), whereas here it has no good consequences. However, what is pertinent here is that Hobbes is not allowing someone to construct by contract what he thinks he is constructing. I can say that I agree not to resist; I can think that this is an agreement or contract. But for Hobbes, this is not a contract. It is not a contract because it is not a real expression of will. It is not a real expression of will because in making it, I am not aiming at my own good. In other words, it is taken as definitional of (real, intended) human action that it is aimed at the agent's good, hence anything else is not really intended.

However, in this example we would seem to have as clear and explicit a statement of will, or of the desire to contract, as can be gotten. It does not depend upon any tacit consent, or upon any reading of agreement into the implicit facts of the situation. We have an attempt, in explicit and understood words, by someone of full age and understanding, to reach an agreement: 'I, John Doe, hereby contract not to resist your attacks'. Of course such a contract (or apparent contract) may have been extracted through fear, and, as such, might be held to be invalid. However, this can not be Hobbes's objection. He thinks that 'covenants entered into by fear, in the condition of mere nature, are obligatory' [*Lev* 14.27, p. 69]. This has to be so for him, otherwise he would lose the whole original contract construction of the state, for these original contracts arise from fear in the state of nature. So also do the covenants to obey a conqueror. As Hobbes puts it, 'in both cases they do it for fear' [*Lev* 20.2, p. 102]. So Hobbes has to have another reason for holding the contract invalid than that it is extracted by fear. His reason is that it is not really a contract at all because it does not express the person's real will. As he puts it just after the remark about not being able to lay down the right of resisting assault quoted earlier, 'If a man by words or other signs seem to dispoil himself of the end for which these signs were intended, he is not to be understood as if he meant it, or that it was his will' [*Lev* 14.8, p. 66]. So you can try and be as explicit as you like in expressing your desire to agree; Hobbes will not allow you to know what it is that you are saying.

This shows, I think, that something other than agreement is here doing the real work. It is, as Hobbes says, the person's own good. Someone's own good will give that person a reason for action, and something being a good for someone will justify it. This gives the real reasons, the real obligations, the real facts that explain and bind. Against this, what someone seems to wish, or try to will, is irrelevant.

Hence, again, will and power, seemingly so different, start to merge, yet here it is from the other end. In the earlier story, what seemed to be arguments based merely on respect for power, were construed by Hobbes as implicit signs of will. In this later story, arguments that seem to be about explicit will are in fact reconstructed so that it is power that does the work. For if I cannot be deemed to will something that is not my own good, then I cannot be deemed to will anything other than respect for power, since respect for power is for my own good. We have a mighty sovereign and a terrified subject. We ask why the subject should obey. The official answer is because of will: the subject has willed the sovereign, authorised its actions. However, we then find that anyone subject to sufficient power is automatically deemed by Hobbes to will obedience. On the other hand, if people attempt to will something that is not in their own good, then they are deemed not really to have willed. So, either way, what we are taken to have willed is whatever is good for us. Therefore, what really does the work in these arguments is what is, or is not, good for someone. Once this base is in place, then a superstructural description in terms of will can be erected. The mighty Leviathan may seem to be morally tamed and all its terrifying actions properly authorised. But we only need to lift the mask to see sheer power still doing all the work. It is only authorised because it is so powerful (just like the conqueror or parent with the power of life and death); any attempt to will that is not aimed at the person's good are disregarded and dismissed. Since it would be stupid to want to resist Leviathan, I am deemed not to have attempted to do so.

So now we can see how great nature changes its course. We start with a 'state of nature', which is explicitly, and by definition, not the political state. In it there is a 'natural law', a law that we can construct with our 'natural' reason, the reason we have as human and not merely political animals. The natural reason counsels us to seek peace, and the rational laws are laws about how to achieve this supreme piece of prudence, the laws about how to achieve peace. They do not arise from experience; they are part of science, which, like arithmetic or geometry can be proved a priori (*Lev* 20.19, p. 107). They tell us to seek peace, and, rationally, we want therefore the single will and judgement that provides it. Hence we (rationally) want the state; we want to escape the state of nature and enter the political state in which we can therefore have justice (and property and all other good things). We also want the power that enforces it and makes it real (which makes contracts that bind *in foro externo*). Both ways, we rationally (that is, naturally) want the state.

We naturally want the state. Hence, starting with the state of nature, we naturally wish to exit from it. The state of nature is a natural condition, which, equally naturally, turns into something else. It is like the uranium isotope, which, natural as it is, naturally turns into something different. It is like the natural caterpillar, which naturally becomes a butterfly. So also the state naturally arises. As Hobbes puts it in the *Elements*, someone desiring to live in the state of nature, 'the estate of liberty and right of all to all, contradicteth himself. For everyone by natural necessity desireth his own good, to which this estate is contrary' [14.12]. So wanting to be in the state is a 'natural necessity'; it is something our nature naturally reaches. Otherwise put, it is something that is rational for us, and it is rational because it is for our own good.

So the state naturally arises because it is naturally good for us. The state has utility. With the single judgement and power it gives we get justice. With justice we get many other good things. A prominent example of this for Hobbes is property (which he calls 'propriety'). So, for example, he says at the end of his chapter on the 'natural condition of mankind' (that is, on the state of nature), there is in it 'no propriety, no dominion, no *mine* and *thine* distinct [13.13, p. 63]; or, in the *Elements*, 'before the institution of sovereign power, *meum* and *tuum* implied no propriety' [27.8]. By contrast, once we have the state, we not only have keeping of contracts, or justice, we also have property. So the state is good for us and, being rational, it is therefore something that we, rationally, will into existence. The birth of justice lies in the rational construction of politics, and the point of rationality is that it is good for us. This justification of things (the state, property) because they are good for us is a theme to which we will return.

5

War and Peace: Grotius and Pufendorf

In our discussion of Hobbes, we have seen the problems posed by moral and political scepticism and the radical nature of his response. In the first chapter, it was noted that Hobbes first became aware of the force of this problem, and started formulating his answers while in Paris in the 1630s in the circle around Marin Mersenne, whose best known member is Descartes. As we saw, the Mersenne circle was reacting to the French sceptics of the previous generation such as Montaigne and Charron, who held that we should live by the appearances, follow the customs. The problem was that this seemed to abolish the objectivity of justice. As Charron put it (and was quoted in the first chapter), 'laws and customs are maintained in credit, not because they are just and good, but because they are laws and customs: this is the mystical foundation of their authority, they have no other'. With Hobbes, we have seen one response, first formulated in Paris, to get beyond such mere customs and to refound a universal natural law. In this chapter, we shall look at two other responses, those of Grotius and Pufendorf. Since the problems and the time are the same, there are similarities as well as important differences between these treatments and Hobbes; however, I shall not in general make comparisons. This is a new shot at the problem, to be treated on its own terms.

The first main work considered in this chapter is another intellectual production from Paris, after the time of Montaigne and Charron, but in the decade before Hobbes's meetings with the Mersenne circle. Written in Latin and dedicated to the King of France, it is called

On the Laws of War and Peace (*De Jure Belli ac Pacis*). Its author, a Dutchman recently escaped from prison and in exile, is Hugo Grotius. It starts with the question of scepticism, which sets the problem: People think that there is no such thing as justice; they think that everyone only acts in his own interest; what is called justice is merely the interests of the stronger; and so on. Grotius then takes the problem on. He will show that there is justice, both in peace and in war. In particular, he will show that there are obligations with respect to how war should be started and how it should be conducted. He is writing in the middle of ferocious wars, conflict. As with Hobbes, the question is again deeply practical, and the problem is again to find a standpoint, a truth, that can be applied to all of the competing parties.

The importance of the law that Grotius wishes to discover is not only to find something as supposedly immune to moral scepticism as Descartes' later answers were supposed to be to metaphysical scepticism. This would be prize enough. However, it is also important that the law is one that applies between different states, that applies to all states, indeed that applies to all conflict, both internal and external. It is universal and international. Its conclusions cannot therefore be derived from the laws or customs of different states. They are not propounded by any human legislator, for there is no person or people in control of the whole world. If there is a true law of the whole world, it does not derive from the will of a legislator but must instead be based on independent moral truth.

Of course, as well as the customs of particular peoples, there are also international, perhaps universal, customs. There are agreed, conventional, practices of warfare, at least in Christian Europe. The players in Grotius's day had played the game with each other so often that they had evolved implicit rules of play. Grotius recognises this, but also distinguishes it. This he calls the law of nations, the *Jus Gentium*. It indeed follows from the common (explicit or tacit) will of peoples. However, as well as this he asserts that there are principles of justice not dependent on anyone's will but that are true merely by the nature of things (or the nature of humanity). This is the law of nature, the natural law (the *Jus Naturae*; *Jus naturale*).

Montaigne says that 'the laws of conscience, which we say are born of Nature, are born of custom' (*Of Custom*). Grotius's challenge is to show instead that nature does not reduce to custom. It is to show that there is a law independent of custom. It is to show, as against Charron's claim about the law's depending upon custom, that its authority depends upon custom-independent moral truth. If this can be done, scepticism is answered, and reason and justification for political action provided. As we saw, this was done by Hobbes in a prudential manner. However, if Grotius succeeds, he promises the possibility of a fuller, more moralised, answer. Universal justificatory rules do not need to be reduced to mere prudence. Some laws are wrong, and some things done in a war are wrong, not just because they are imprudent (silly), creating more harm for their perpetrators than their enemies. They are wrong because they are not just. Whether this can be done, and its implications for political philosophy, is the central topic of this chapter.

Hugo Grotius was born in 1583, making him five years older than Hobbes. Through the first part of his life, the Dutch were fighting for their independence from Spain. They were also involved in confrontation with the Spanish with respect to trade to the East Indies, and Grotius's first main work, the *Mare Liberum*, is a defence of the freedom of the seas. It argues against the Spanish attempt to close the Indies to outsiders (it was in fact the Portuguese who had had the original claim, but Spain succeeded to it when it took over Portugal). Grotius's *Mare Liberum* (which in fact is extracted from a much larger work only published centuries after his death) is an initial attempt to appeal both to his enemies and also to neutral states. For this, Grotius has to find and use argumentative resources that do not depend upon a single country, or set of customs, or religion. Instead, as a citizen of a Protestant country fighting for independence from its Catholic masters, he has to find something common to both. Hence his frequent citation of the opinions of Spanish writers.

After the end of the war with Spain, Grotius was actively engaged in Dutch politics. However, his side lost, his leader was executed, and Grotius himself was imprisoned and in danger of his life. It was during the forced leisure imposed by imprisonment that he composed the *De Jure Belli ac Pacis* (DJBP). Among other things, it is a wide-ranging survey of the literature of the subject, classical and modern. Literature was useful to Grotius in another way in that he escaped from prison in a hamper purporting to be his supply of books, and so went into exile in Paris. Thirty-five years later, another work written in prison was published. This is the *Elements of Universal Jurisprudence* (EJU), published in 1660 and written by the second main philosopher considered in this chapter, Samuel Pufendorf. He also had gotten into temporary political trouble, this time for being an ambassador on the wrong side.

In EJU, his first work, Pufendorf lays out the first principles of natural law. Then, in 1672, he wrote his major work (another massive compilation), *De jure naturae et gentium* (DJN – *Of the Law of Nature and Nations*). The next year, he published an epitome of this, the *De officio hominis et civis juxta legem naturalem* (DOH – *On the duty of man and citizen according to natural law*). This was extensively used as a university teaching text. Earlier, Pufendorf had been, in Heidelberg, the first person to hold a chair in natural and international law. So Pufendorf professed officially the subject that Grotius had in effect created. Born after Grotius's great work was published (in Saxony in 1632), Pufendorf comes from a later generation. Grotius lived through war; Pufendorf lived in relative peace. The Thirty Years War ended in 1648 with the Peace of Westphalia, which regularised the system of states (and their wars). The English civil war was over by 1660; the French had settled down; the Dutch had established their independence. Also, intellectually, we have consolidation and systematisation. The new natural law has come to stay.

Grotius is now taken to be the modern founder of natural law. This is a retrospective judgement. This is how it looks to Pufendorf, and particularly to Grotius and Pufendorf's great French editor and translator, Jean Barbeyrac. However, as we have seen, natural law existed in many ways and with many varieties before Grotius. Although his work was taken in retrospect to be a new theory of natural law, it still has much in common with classical and scholastic predecessors. Like them, natural law is understood to be a law that is true for all times, peoples and places, and whose truth follows from the nature of humanity (Christians would add, as created by God).

Grotius's *De Jure* is massive. It is much more a collection of quotations from all sorts of writers and authorities than it is any kind of new, let alone deductive, exposition of natural law. Indeed, it could well be used as a dictionary of quotations with respect to the topics it deals with. The first quotation (with thousands to follow) is from Cicero. Cicero's work is in fact a good example of some of the ideas on natural law that were around before Grotius, and on which he could draw while fermenting his rich brew of authorities. Cicero in his *De Legisbus* (On Laws) said that the nature of justice must be sought for in the nature of man. He said that it was right reason (*recta ratio*), reason being the first common possession of man and God. Cicero also says that the foundation of justice is our natural inclination to love our fellow men.

All of this is also claimed by Grotius and Pufendorf. They hold that there are truths about human beings as such. For them, all human beings of whatever race, religion, or people are equally human. People can recognise each other, can relate to each other socially, because of their mere common humanity and not because of some more specific communitarian tie. People are citizens of a single world. Grotius even occasionally talks of the single state (*civitas*) composed of all nations. Terence's remark about nothing human being alien is frequently pressed into service; Grotius remarks in *Mare Liberum* that if we only observed it 'we would surely live in a more peaceable world'. From all of this follows a basic, minimal, natural law.

The Basis of Natural Law

So far so good. But how is this natural law to be extracted from nature? One problem is getting any kind of evaluative truths from a naturalistic basis. We tend to think of this problem in terms of G. E. Moore's 'naturalistic fallacy', but as a criticism of Grotius, it is much older than that, featuring prominently near the start of Rousseau's *Social Contract* where Rousseau says that Grotius's 'usual method of reasoning is constantly to establish right by fact' [I,2]. Describing natural facts will not give us natural right. This is a natural criticism of naturalism, but I do not think that it should be seriously worrying for either Grotius or Pufendorf. For they do not assume that all natural instincts should be followed, or just endorse how things actually are. On the contrary, they have a more familiar view of morality whereby much of what people do, and are naturally inclined to do, is quite wrong (especially for Pufendorf, who is particularly resistant to the idea that people ought to give in to their sexual appetites or desires for luxury). The law that Grotius and Pufendorf delineate is critical rather than descriptive.

One example will bring this out. The section on natural law in the great compendium of Roman law, Justinian's *Institutes*, gets off on the wrong foot by referring to an opinion of Gaius's about the procreative instinct that men have in common with animals. This sort of comparison is one that both Grotius and Pufendorf specifically reject. It is not the nature and desires that people have in common with animals that counts with them. Rather it is what distinguishes them. It is (as with Cicero) reason. As Pufendorf puts it, 'there is a great difference between natural instinct and the dictates of reason' (DJN 6.1.3). So if natural law follows from the nature of humans, it follows from the nature of humans as reasoning creatures; it follows from the nature of reason. And if reason is in itself normative, this makes it much harder to convict it of the naturalistic fallacy. Reason is essentially justificatory and not merely descriptive.

So, if natural law is founded on nature, it is founded on what can naturally be used as a reason. It is founded on what is naturally justifying. But what is? In the Thirty Years War, when one of the marauding armies arrived at the gates of a town, it would send in a piece of paper with the words 'Fire. Fire. Blood. Blood.' on it. They burned the edges just to make sure the town got the point. Naturally (as we would say) the towns tended to see reason (as we would say). They opened up and supplied food to save themselves being put to fire, sack, and pillage. Similarly, the Mafia chief may talk of presenting someone with an argument which he cannot refuse, before putting a horse's head in his bed as a reminder about whose head might follow. Argument, reason, natural justification. This all works. But so far this is all Hobbes. Can we do better? Are there any other naturally justifying reasons than the ones that appeal to people's self-interest (their desire not to be burned by marauding soldiers or end up entombed by gangsters in the concrete foundations of a motorway overpass)?

If instead of threatening the persons themselves, we threaten their children or parents, they may again (as we say) see reason. Natural reason; it would be unnatural not to react. Parents are naturally concerned for their children. Siblings similarly have natural ties, naturally shared sentiment. So may people who grow up together in the same shared space. However, the whole point for Grotius is that we do not rely on special ties, special kinship, special position; rather we are meant to find nothing human alien (foreign). How do we get this indifferent concern for all human beings from nature? Is Shakespeare right when he says, 'one touch of nature makes the whole world kin' (*Troilus and Cressida*)? Also, even if he is right, how do we get this from the nature of reason rather than from natural sentiment (otherwise we would again be putting people back with the animals)? We still have a problem of what can be correctly be counted as right reason.

To resolve this, let us look at a particular example, that people should keep their contracts. Why, if it is, is it naturally reasonable to do so? Why is this not just a custom? The example is not taken by chance. We have already seen the importance of contract in Hobbes. So also in the theorists looked at in this chapter. Contract is an absolutely central concept for them, explaining our obligation to political superiors and to the laws of particular states. For these obligations are supposed by them to arise from contract (or agreement) and can be explained if contracts really oblige. But do they? Hobbes has an answer: once Leviathan's sword is in place, we shall suffer too much if we don't keep our agreements. However, here we are seeking an alternative, more moralised, answer. If we can find one, we shall have found a basis for natural law.

Not that these thinkers wanted natural law to do all the work. Indeed, the attraction of contract for them is that it enabled them to explain and justify most aspects of our political life without using natural law. It is easy to see the attractions of this in an uncertain age. For if we are uncertain about what is the objectively right thing to do, it is attractive to think that rightness flows from our own will. We have a minimalist natural law, a basic set of values that we hope can be generally accepted. This is only thin bread. Most of the work, the thick filling of our thin-bread sandwich, will be done by agreements, which create all the other politically and legally important values. We have seen how both Grotius and Pufendorf have a minimal natural law (the *Jus Naturae*). They both also have matters on which people have generally agreed, the law of peoples or nations (the *Jus Gentium*). Lastly, there is by far the largest part of the law. This is the civil law, sometimes called 'municipal law' (the *Jus Civile*). For Grotius and Pufendorf, this largest part of the law is created by agreements, either explicit or tacit.

However, for this to work, this super-structure of justified political society and civil law has to rest on the natural law. More specifically, it has to rest on its being true that people are obliged by the agreements they have made. Even in civil law, this is not straightforward. Agreement alone does not automatically make one obliged. Other things are normally thought to be necessary as well (and discussed by Grotius and

Pufendorf), such as that the agreement was not extracted by improper force or deception. However, and more problematically, agreements may also be held to be void on grounds of content. Agreements to do something illegal or immoral may be held not to oblige, on the grounds that they were agreements beyond our power to make. Therefore, even if we bracket out force and fraud so that we have a genuine agreement, this still may not be sufficient to produce obligation. I may agree to the state, but was it in my power to make such an agreement? This is one reason why agreement alone cannot do all the work. We need also an account of obligations and permissions that does not depend upon agreement.

In the last chapters, we wrestled, along with Hobbes, with the problem of why people are obliged to keep their agreements. If we say that it is because we (explicitly or tacitly) have agreed to keep agreements, we are in an infinite regress. So some other source of obligation is needed. We might try the notion that God has commanded that we keep faith. However, this raises a whole string of familiar difficulties, of the kind Grotius and Pufendorf wanted to avoid. To discover God's will, we have to interpret sacred text (or other revelation), and this is contentious. Also, as the text of a particular religion, the Bible lacks true universality. Even if we accept the Bible, the injunction to keep our pacts is not prominent (it is not in the Ten Commandments; it is not invoked by Christ in the way that loving our neighbour is). Indeed, God himself (as recorded) seems at times to be a less than perfect example of keeping agreements. So this route is best avoided.

In any case, Grotius and Pufendorf wanted a natural law that did not depend upon special revelation of God's will. The most notorious thing Grotius says in the *Prolegomena* to his great work is that some remarks he had just made 'would have a degree of validity even if we should concede that which cannot be conceded without the utmost wickedness, that there is no God, or that the affairs of men are of no concern to him' (Sec. 110). This so-called *etiamsi* ('even if') clause inevitably led to trouble in a riven and theologically driven age. It has also been taken (out of context) as marking the foundation of a new secular natural law, independent of God. Later, Pufendorf starts his epitome, the *De Officio*, by setting out in the Preface a 'careful delineation' of the 'boundaries' of natural law. Again the central idea is to separate natural law from theology and from the 'particular revelation of the Deity'. Their aim here is to describe a law that does not depend upon any particular understanding of the Bible or of the traditions of the church.

We shall return later to the position of God in the theory. However, at least for Grotius and Pufendorf, we must find a more secular foundation. We might try the idea that something is good for us, that it has utility (which also peeped through at the end of the last, Hobbes, chapter). Utility features largely in Grotius and Pufendorf's accounts of the civil law. They, like Hobbes, assume that people generally will what is in their interest. So they expect the civil law to serve utility. Utility can therefore be used by them in evaluation of the civil law. However, utility is not why the civil law obliges. Rather it obliges because it is constructed by the will of the people themselves. It therefore obliges if people are obliged by their express will, if they are obliged to keep to their agreements. So the question for utility is not the justification of particular civil arrangements but rather whether it can justify keeping agreements.

Keeping agreements does in general promote utility. If we have a rule (or general obligation) to keep our promises, and the rule is generally observed, we shall as a whole do better. This need not be a merely prudential argument. It is a utilitarian argument: any particular individual's interests may not be promoted, but we shall, as a whole, get more utility if everyone follows the rules. So this avoids free-rider problems, and might work, making the natural law a command to maximise utility. We will come back to this possibility in Chapter 9.

However, again, whatever the intrinsic merits of this, it is not Grotius and Pufendorf's way, at least not directly. Pufendorf points out that we will fail to get utility from promises unless we keep them, and they both agree that it is good for us to be able to have, make, and keep agreements. However, they both claim that although being just promotes utility, they are not to be identified. Grotius, for example, resists the idea that it is permissible to increase people's utility by force, against their will (DJBP 2.21.2). He says elsewhere that just because something is less useful does not make it unlawful (2.5.12). Indeed, his whole project of replying to scepticism about justice can be more narrowly described as resisting the identification of justice with utility. Right at the start of the *Prolegomena* to *De Jure Belli*, he says that the work is 'necessary because . . . on the lips of men quite generally is the saying . . . that . . . nothing is unjust which is expedient' (Sec. 3). He then takes a particular sceptic, Carneades, as his target. Carneades was notorious in the ancient world for having argued both in favour of and against justice, but what Grotius focuses on here is the claim he attributes to Carneades that laws arise from expediency (Sec. 5). Or, as he also puts it here, 'there is no law of nature, because all creatures . . . are impelled by nature towards ends advantageous to themselves'. The words translated here as 'expediency' or 'advantage' are all translations of the Latin *utilitas*, or its cognates, so the view contested here is the view that justice reduces to utility.

Utility cannot therefore be for Grotius the basis. We must try something else. For Grotius and Pufendorf, the basis of natural law is the nature of human beings as rational and social animals. Let us first try rationality. What we want here are pure a priori principles, derived from the nature of rationality alone, showing how rational creatures must reason (when they are reasoning correctly). Grotius himself talks of a priori methods. He says, for example, (DJBP 1.1.12) that there is a 'proof a priori' that demonstrates 'the necessary agreement or disagreement of anything with a rational and social nature'. But why is keeping faith something that 'agrees' with us as a rational creature? Perhaps the point is that we can just know, by direct intuition, that it is so. Grotius considers the question why we should keep faith in the very last chapter of *De Jure* (3.25.1). Here he says that 'the bond of good faith is manifest of itself' (*per se manifestum est*). In other words, it is intrinsically evident. Once we understand what a pact is, we understand that pacts should be observed. There are familiar arguments in this area, on each side. Let me just note here that it is one way we may derive the law of nature, by a priori intuition. Grotius talks in the *Prolegomena* (Sec. 39) of referring the 'proofs of things touching the law of nature to certain fundamental conceptions which are beyond question'. These fundamentals he holds to be 'manifest and clear'. In other words, we have a supposed basis in intuition and an implicit axiomatic method.

Grotius wants to use both a priori and a posteriori methods; both prove things directly and also cite masses of practice and authorities. A posteriori claims may help to persuade, and in argument it is useful to be able to cite things on which both parties agree (as we saw Grotius citing texts written by his enemies, the Spaniards). However,

general agreement on something is neither necessary and sufficient to
demonstrate that something is natural law. It is not necessary as people
may be mistaken, as both Grotius and Pufendorf were only too aware.
It is not sufficient since there are other explanations of agreement
than the objective truth of things. Both Grotius and Pufendorf clearly
distinguish between natural law and the *Jus Gentium*. Yet the principles of the *Jus Gentium* are agreed principles. Hence agreement is not
sufficient to prove that we have natural law. The relationship between
agreement and law can go in either direction. In the natural law case,
we can explain the agreement because of the law. In the *Jus Gentium*
case, we explain the law because of the agreement. Here, as Charron
says about all law, agreement is all there is to it.

Let us return to a priori methods. Can we do better than saying
that if you understand what a contract is, you thereby understand that
it should be kept? We should next try adding what is necessary if we
are to be able to live as social beings. Early in the *De Jure*, Grotius
has another, very short but intriguing, argument as to why we should
keep our agreements. In Section 15 of the *Prolegomena* to the work, he
notes that municipal law arises from pacts. He says that this is possible 'since it is a rule of the law of nature to abide by pacts'. He then
gives a quick remark in support, which, even though it is only a single
line in an enormous book, is still, I think, full of interest. 'For it was
necessary', says Grotius, 'that among men there be some method of
obligating themselves one to another, and no other natural method
can be imagined'. How I see this working is as follows. We have an idea
of obligation, and we also wish to use such things (this is part of the
original nature of what it is to be a rational being; if we don't understand this, we don't get started). Yet as well as standing obligations, it
is also very useful to create obligations (to bind ourselves and others).
So we need a method of creating obligations. Here Grotius says he
cannot imagine another method, which is always a dangerous type of
philosophical argument (just because we can't imagine alternatives
does not mean that there are not any, and if there are alternatives,
the argument that supports something as the necessary means toward
a desired or necessary goal fails). It would be better to reconstruct
this by saying that contracts (pacts, promises, agreements; the Latin
here is *pactum*) are whatever it is whereby people agree in obligating themselves to each other. Then we don't need imagination about

alternatives. We just need the simple fact that people wish to create mutual obligations.

The next question is why people wish to do this, and the answer, at least for Grotius, is because people are social. They are social and rational animals; they wish to maintain the social order (*societas*). From this, Grotius gives (in Section 8) a quick list of the basic elements of law: abstaining from that which is another's, making good of losses, keeping of promises, and inflicting penalties according to desert. So, as well as breaking agreements, it is also unjust is to harm people in certain basic, minimal, ways. Similarly, Pufendorf says that the 'first among the absolute duties is the duty not to harm others' (DO 1.6.2). Or, otherwise put, people have certain basic, natural, rights. If such harm or injustice has occurred (if these rights are interfered with), then restitution and penalty is in order. As Pufendorf puts it, 'harm inflicted by one man on another ... must be made good by the person who may rightly be held responsible' (DO 1.6.4). These basic natural rights are needed for a basic sociability, which, it will be remembered, applies to all people as such and does not depend upon their being members of the same more particular community. Such basic sociability is needed for being fully human, and these natural rights are the basic human rights (rights that all people have merely by virtue of being human).

The centre of this sounds like a tautology, or pun. Injustice (*injustitia*) is lack of respect for right (*jus*). Interfere with someone's right (their *jus*), and we then have no *jus*. We have *injustitia*. The two interdefine: if we can say what rights are, we discover what is injustice, and vice versa. This is the structure: the content is clearly a right not to be harmed in certain basic ways. It is also a right to hold on to 'my own'. This, however, demands a notion of property. Yet, since neither Grotius nor Pufendorf thinks that there is such a thing as a naturally acquired right to property, strictly speaking (as opposed to a natural right to the property I acquire conventionally, for example by agreement), this does not immediately produce as much as might be expected; we shall come back to property later.

This is the basic minimum core of natural law. We may disagree about details of the content, but the central idea is to specify the minimum necessary for people to live in peace with one another. Just after outlining the first duty, described earlier, not to harm others, Pufendorf comments, 'I can live in peace with a man who does me no positive service, and with a man who does not exchange even the commonest duties with me, provided he does me no harm'.

So the basic claim is not to harm, and the basic philosophical point about this is that this is a claim about an obligation. For it is being able to understand the idea of obligation that distinguishes people from animals, that gives expression to the point that these are laws of human rationality rather than natural animal instinct. As Pufendorf puts it, 'although many actions of men and beasts are very much alike . . . as a matter of fact there is a great difference between them, since among beasts they come from the simple inclination of their nature, while men perform them from a sense, as it were, of obligation, a sense which brutes do not have' (DJN 2.3.2). We have a quite independent moral understanding of a moral world. At least as Pufendorf sees it, the moral entities and qualities of this moral world are imputed. We can't understand an object as property by conducting a physical analysis, decomposing it into its chemical constituents. Rather, it depends upon understanding it in terms of these imputed moral properties. It involves understanding it in terms of obligations, in the case of property obligations created by ourselves.

We saw earlier that for Grotius and Pufendorf, obligations are chiefly created by contract (or agreement). In the account of contract there, we did not go into details (as both Grotius and Pufendorf do) as to what constitutes a valid contract. However, a fundamental aspect is the desire to create an obligation; it is an understanding of the idea of an obligation that makes the whole thing possible. We use this special, un-animal, humanly recognised thing, and bind ourselves with it.

Natural Rights

This central notion of obligation thus creates rights: the right not to be harmed, and the right to have agreements kept. Again, more important than the precise content is the logical shape into which this content fits. We have here a theory of natural rights, in a full evaluative sense. My rights are things I have, rather like possessions. Grotius talks of how 'a right becomes a moral quality of a person' (1.1.4) – that is, it is not just a moral sort of thing but is also something the person has. He says that a right is a 'power' (*potestas*) over others (1.1.5). So these rights have immediate implications about other people's actions. They should not interfere with my rights. If they do, then there is injustice. Certain such rights are supposed to be possessed by human beings as such. These are the natural, or human, rights. Any interference with them breaks the 'law of nature'. It justifies forcing the interferer to restore the situation, as well as meting out punishment.

In this way, Grotius can justify war, and also outline a law of war from first (natural) principles. Between states, there is no human superior, so we can't appeal to someone to decide conflicts or to lay down laws for states. All states are sovereign, supreme, law-makers. Hence, if there is a law that binds states, it has to be either natural law or else what Grotius called 'divine positive law' (that is, commandments from God, acting as legislator for all people and all states). If the natural law is as Grotius supposes, then people have a basic right not to be harmed in their lives, bodies, and possessions (even though who actually possesses what may have to be conventionally established). They have a right to have agreements kept.

When this does not happen, there is injustice, and where there is injustice, restitution and punishment are permitted by natural law. Hence states, lacking a superior (under God) and bound only by natural (and divine) law, may justly declare war and attack, destroy, and seize the people and property of other states when that state has acted unjustly. The central notion here is one of permission. Normally we would not be permitted to attack, destroy life, or seize property. This would be against the (natural) law. However, if the other has already offended, then I gain permission to do what would otherwise be forbidden. I can now legitimately defend myself, even if this involves killing people. I can also attack and destroy to get my property back, or to punish. As Grotius puts it, 'do not prohibit all use of force, but only that use of force which is in conflict with society, that is, which attempts to take away the rights of another' (DJBP 1.2.1).

Hence we can get a law of justified war (which gives both the legitimate grounds for starting war and also the legitimate ways in which it can be waged). The theory also applies to individual inter-personal relations so far as people are still in a relationship to each other, bounded by the law of nature. Among the rights possessed in this state of nature is the right to punish. This may be more familiar to people from Locke, who, although he upholds it, recognises that it is a 'strange Doctrine'

(*Second Treatise*, Sec. 13). However, strange or otherwise, the doctrine also exists quite clearly in both Grotius and Pufendorf (which is, of course, where Locke found it). It is this that particularly does the work in licensing warfare. Although Grotius's great work is often thought of as a piece of humanity, attempting to limit and control the prevalent warfare of a violent age, it still gives a lot of reasons and defence for warfare, and punishment is prominent among them. Pufendorf also has no squeamishness about a right to punish (or permission to do to people what would otherwise be forbidden). In a train of thought that may again be more familiar to people from Locke, he says of someone who attacks me that 'by his avowing himself that he is my enemy... he gives me, so far as he is able to, an unlimited freedom of action against him' (DJGN 2.5.3). (Compare Locke, who says that someone using 'unjust violence' has 'declared War against all Mankind, and therefore may be destroyed as a *Lyon* or a *Tyger*' [Sec. 11].)

Even though Pufendorf talks in terms of the person to be punished setting himself in war against me, the argument here is not just an argument for self-defence, nor does it depend upon the same grounds. I do have the right to defend myself. Grotius and Pufendorf set this out, both thinking that I have a right to kill someone attacking me or my property. However, they also both think that I have a right of self-defence against innocent attackers. If, for example, we are both drowning and there is a single plank that can support only one of us, for Pufendorf I have the right to push the other person off and cause their death (DO 1.5.21). Both agree, less controversially, that I have the right to knock over an innocent person in the way while fleeing for my life. In these cases of innocent threats, I am only allowed to act to save myself, and one's right to save oneself is the justification. It is different in the case of punishment. Here we have a guilty party. That is, we already have had an offence against natural law. Grotius and Pufendorf think that the law will not be effective unless offences are punished. The argument in Pufendorf is that in willing the law, God also wills the means to put the law into effect. (Locke also comments – section 7 – that the law of nature would 'be in vain' without a '*Power to Execute that law*'.)

So we have a natural right to punish. This applies well enough between full, sovereign, states, which are supposed to be still in a state of nature with respect to each other. However, what bearing does it have for individuals? The people with whom we live are no longer in a 'state of nature' with us, if indeed they ever were. In states, we are subject to different obligations. In a civil state, for example, I am not allowed to invade my neighbour's house, killing all in my path, to get back some object that is unjustly being withheld from me. This state, and the way in which it so restricts us, has to be explained. As in Hobbes, the explanation is in terms of a movement from state of nature to state, effected by agreement. However, things are different from Hobbes. This time, people start with full rights in the state of nature. Even so, by will they place themselves in subjection to the authority of a state. They have a reason. States are more efficient in the execution of the (natural) law, and we have seen that the law needs execution. So, by subjecting themselves, people get better protection. Conversely, whoever protects them (the sovereign) has a duty to enforce this law. In subjecting themselves, people specifically surrender their natural right to punish to the sovereign. The sovereign institutes punishments and so creates civil law. Whatever the basis of natural law, there is less mystery about the human law. It is instituted by human will, the will of the sovereign (which, of course, does not have to be a single, absolute, prince but might be a democratically representative council).

The next question, therefore, is how natural law and civil law fit together. Both Grotius and Pufendorf hold that the civil law can't validly work against natural law. Given their premises, one way this could be argued for is the following. They assume that civil society, and hence civil law, arises from agreements. Yet in civil law principles of contract, a contract to do something illegal does not oblige. 'Taking out a contract' (an agreement to kill someone for money) is not a contract enforceable at law. So it could be argued that no one could validly contract to do anything against natural law. Hence they cannot construct (by contract) a civil law that conflicts with natural law.

This is the way we would expect it to go. But on the other hand, Grotius has many examples where the natural law would suggest one conclusion and yet civil law says something else. Here are some examples. An agreement made during the life of a spouse to wed someone else after his or her death is, says Grotius, valid under natural law (which holds that agreements should be respected) but not under civil law, because, says Grotius, 'public utility' is against it (presumably because it might encourage the murder of spouses, or at least inhibit

attempts to preserve them). Another example is the rights of the un-
born (2.4.10). For Grotius, they have none by nature, yet civil law can
give them rights by what he calls a 'fiction'. A further example is the
rights of husbands over their wives' goods (2.5.8). This applied in many
jurisdictions both then and also long afterwards, but, says Grotius, it is
not a right derivable from natural law.

Now the problem is how these examples are legitimate, given that
civil law cannot validly propose something against natural law. The
last two are fairly straightforward. Here there are spaces in natural
law that civil law can fill in. A right does not exist by nature, but it is
not against natural law to have such a (civil) right. A husband has no
natural right over his wife's property, but then civil law gives him the
right. This example can be applied more widely. In neither Grotius
nor Pufendorf are there any natural property rights. Property derives
from human will or convention – that is, active or tacit agreement. We
can contract with each other to divide up the world, or we can contract
into government to do it for us, but no such arrangement is naturally
unjust. So, for example, a wife may give her husband rights to all her
property by her specific marriage agreement, or she may live in a civil
state that has decided this arrangement.

This leads to another answer. This is that rights may be changed by
human will. Having an initial set of rights, we may then by contract
and agreement dispose of them. Clearly there is nothing in itself problematic in contract creating rights or in rights being surrendered by
agreement. If, for example, I contract to sell a piece of land, I thereby
create the right to be paid by the other party and I also surrender
the bundle of property rights connected with the land. So there is no
intrinsic problem in alienating rights by agreement.

However, if I can surrender all my natural rights, it would seem
that there would be no scope left for saying that natural law trumps
civil law. On entering civil society, I voluntarily gave away the trumps.
On the other hand, if I can't surrender natural rights, then it seems
that the construction of states described in Grotius and Pufendorf
cannot work. It is because I suppose that I do better with states that
punish on my behalf, I agree (either explicitly or tacitly) to have
states do the punishing for me. Hence I give up one of my natural
rights in order to better secure the others. This no doubt seems like
a good bargain. It is a piece of prudence. So, if only prudence counts

(self-interest, utility), then we can provide a Hobbesian sort of justification. If, however, we think that as well as prudence, there is also natural law, matters are not so straightforward. For we now have a justice whose truths are independent of mere human decision and control. Hence our ability to maximise our interest is curtailed. We must not offend against natural law.

In our decisions, therefore, we must respect human rights, and the question is whether this prevents our alienating our rights at will. We must respect other's rights, but how far do we have to respect our own? If a right is something I can alienate at will, it is an area of sovereignty, or free control. By contrast, rights might be considered to be particularly important and specially protected goods, goods that I have to respect whether they are my own or someone else's. A good example to test which is the best account is voluntarily contracting oneself into slavery. Both Grotius and Pufendorf think that I may do this (DJBP 2.5.26; DJN 7.3.1). In fact, although they both think that slavery is legitimate (people may have property rights over other people), for them this is the only way in which it can occur. As against Aristotle, that is, they hold that no one is a slave by nature. Here again, although there is not a natural right to something, the right can be created by human agreement. The view of rights implied by this fits with their general analytical account. We saw earlier that Grotius considers my rights to be personal possessions that give me power over others. In the same place, he also says that they give me freedom. So the view of rights being implied is that of sovereignty: they mark areas of free choice by me, where I have, according to this choice, control over others. Only, of course, the way I may exercise this free choice is by relinquishing it: among my rights is the right to decide to make myself a slave.

There seems therefore to be no limits to our will. Whatever we are initially given, we may will it away. Will creates the moral universe. We still have natural law constraining civil law, but this now means that we cannot do things to people against their will. If they will, it is legitimate. Yet, for Grotius and Pufendorf, the state is created by such will. Hence, in creating the state, it seems that I can alienate any right I may possess in the state of nature. Hence I alienate my right to punish. Hence, perhaps, a wife may alienate her right to hold property. Hence, perhaps, I alienate my right during my spouse's lifetime to contract to marry someone else on his or her death. It all depends on what the particular state is whether these agreements are, or can be, made. However, nothing is beyond my will. So nothing is beyond the state's powers. That is, nothing is beyond my authorisation of these powers.

This applies also, particularly and importantly, to the power of the state and its officials over me. It applies to its powers of decision and to my right to exercise private judgement. That is, I may legitimately contract into a state in which everything is decided by an absolute prince. Here I have alienated any right of my own to decide and also, as in a slavery contract, any right to withdraw if I don't like what follows. Both Grotius and Pufendorf specifically allow such absolute states and specifically make the analogy with enslaving oneself. In other words, even though we start with much richer moral materials than Hobbes, we may nevertheless legitimately reach a Hobbesian Leviathan in which all scope for private judgement is surrendered.

But here we have moved too fast. Consider the following two claims by Pufendorf. First (from DO 2.10.1), 'consent of subjects is required to constitute any legitimate government'. That is just what we have been saying, and would expect. However, now try this from the longer work, of which we have just quoted the epitome (although it is not from the corresponding place): 'the statement that all government is based on the consent of those who are governed is utterly false' (DJN 3.4.4). This sounds like a flat contradiction (in works by the same author at the same time). Yet there is an answer. The answer is God. God governs us, without and independent of, our consent. (Indeed, for Pufendorf, God's authority is needed to create the fundamental obligations of natural law, which we do not create for ourselves.) And if it starts from God, we can suppose that God may have purposes for us, running beyond our will. We are God's creatures, and so it is not just up to us to decide whether we can let things go to waste or spoil. It seems that, after all, our will is limited, and we may not, after all, legitimately construct the whole of our moral world.

Let us take another example to test this, this time suicide. If rights are just areas of my own control, placing obligations on others but not on myself, then the legitimacy of suicide would be simple. I have a right to life, which means that others have an obligation not to harm me by killing me. However, this would not on such an account also apply to me. That no one else can kill me legitimately does not prevent my full, free, control over myself, including self-destruction. So that is how, in Grotius and Pufendorf, and analogous to their accounts of voluntary slavery, we might expect it to go. However, it does not. Here Pufendorf says that 'we deny the absolute power of a man over his own life' (DJN 2.4.19). At least some suicides are ruled out; people who kill themselves through mere weariness or fear of what is to come should be judged 'to have sinned against the law of nature'.

The idea that since we are creatures of God, God limits what we may legitimately do with ourselves is one thing that could have been used to limit the voluntary agreements into which people enter. God may not want his creatures to destroy or enslave themselves. However, as seen, this possible limitation does not work for Grotius or Pufendorf. Voluntary slavery is allowed, and once slavery is allowed, all kinds of political absolutism easily follow. There is, however, another way out. This is to query not which agreements are possible but, rather, which agreements have actually been made. The actual obligation comes from the actual agreement. Inevitably (just as with Hobbes himself) there is some lack of nerve with these two thinkers at the crucial point. Hobbes thought that I could struggle on the scaffold when the state decided to execute me (for it was my security that led me to set up this mortal god in the first place). When Grotius and Pufendorf find things working badly to my detriment, they can suggest that this cannot be supposed to have been part of my original agreement. I actually agreed otherwise. My agreement placed side constraints on the uncontrolled exercise of absolute power. They are, however, very cautious about this way out. One reason (as in Hobbes) is the thought that once private judgement starts, government rapidly becomes impossible. The unified state becomes a dissociated mass of individuals (*dissociata multitudo*, DJBP 1.4.2).

One use of these hypotheses about what people must be supposed to have agreed is Grotius's handling of the question as to whether people in extreme want can take what would normally be considered other people's property. His claim is that in such conditions, the property reverts to its original common status (in Grotius we start with common use of things and construct private property by agreement). His argument is that 'we must consider what was the intention of those who introduced private property, which we must suppose to have been to remove as little as possible from natural equity' (DJBP 2.2.6). The details do not matter as much as the form of the argument, whereby we suppose that people must have made a particular kind of agreement, otherwise they would have been irrational. (As regards the particular argument, Pufendorf refutes it by pointing out that since Grotius thinks that people who take things in such circumstances should still make compensation for what they take, he is acknowledging that the things taken are still private property and have not reverted to common use.)

Once we allow this kind of argument, the suppositions about rationality are, it would seem, doing more work than the hypotheses about agreement. Another example in Grotius is with respect to the right of the state to take the goods of its citizens. Here Grotius allows this because 'those who founded civil society must be supposed to have intended' that private ends give way to common utility (DJBP 3.20.8). This may be the rational thing to do; it may be the right account of the state. However, the justification does not really follow here from (hypothetical claims about) agreement: these hypotheses are merely devices to purchase the desired results. Just as with Hobbes, what looks as if it is founded entirely on will actually turns out to have another ground.

The Authority of Princes

The desired result is the power of the state and the power of the prince. This is also achieved by an important distinction for Grotius and Pufendorf between things being wrong and what I may legitimately do about it. The prince may be wrong, but this does not mean that I can refuse to obey, let alone punish. I have surrendered my right to punish. Even if an absolute prince is wrong, even if an absolute prince clearly does something against natural law, the judgement of this and any sanctions or punishment that arise from this has to be left to God. Grotius thinks that bad kings arise only infrequently, that when things happen infrequently, we should hold to the general rule, and so it is just bad luck. In any case, we ought to endure rather than resist. There is some doubt about extreme situations, and just as with someone starving, the material is available for him (and mentioned) whereby necessity can override normal law. However, he is reluctant to use it, even though it would provide him with another way of limiting obedience.

Here again the result is very similar to Hobbes, even though the premises and initial structure are different. In Hobbes, there are no agreements between prince and people. Leviathan, as we saw, cannot be bound down by contract (or indeed by anything else). It is different in Grotius and Pufendorf. In Pufendorf, there is an explicit double contract in his model story of the evolution from the state from the state of nature (EJU 1.12.27; DJN 7.2.7; DO 2.6.7). He has three stages. First (as in Hobbes), there is the contract of all with all to have a state. Then there is a decree, or agreed declaration, about the form of the proposed state. Finally there is a contract with whomever is sovereign according to this decree. For example, if the decree is to have an absolute prince, then there is an agreement between the people and this prince. In the first contract, people agree with each other. In the second contract, they agree with the sovereign. Since there is here an agreement between sovereign and people, this means that (unlike Hobbes) we can say that the sovereign has behaved unjustly. We can say that the sovereign has not kept to a contract to which he was a party. This position is very unlike Hobbes. Here the sovereign may be wrong, whereas in Hobbes such an idea makes no sense. Nevertheless, the consequences are the same. There is nothing (or, at least, practically nothing) we can legitimately do about the acts of the sovereign.

This is how it is in Grotius and Pufendorf. They do not think that absolute princes are the only legitimate form of government; whatever is agreed upon is legitimate (so it could, for example, be a democracy). However, they both think that it is the superior form – that is, it provides more utility. These absolute princes may be petitioned and may take advice. They may commission inferior magistrates. However, they are subject to no legal control in their own territories. The moral materials from which the argument is constructed differ from Hobbes, but the results are much the same. By divine right theory, God may install a monarchy that we, the people, are not permitted to question. Naturally, contemporary kings were fond of this doctrine. Hobbes did not have such a theory. His monarch arises from human, not divine, will. However, his monarch is still beyond question. Similarly, Grotius and Pufendorf did not support divine right theories. Again the political theory was working without the particular interventions of God (*etiamsi*). However, for them also we do not need a God to install monarchs with a divine right of judgement that we, the people, may not question. We don't need God because we, the people, can do it for ourselves.

That is, if we do it by agreement, and if such agreements are legitimate. But even if it is agreed that such agreement is legitimate, this type of justification still runs into the problem of whether it actually, as a matter of fact, applies. Only actual agreements obligate. We may hypothesise about what agreements might have been or should have been; it is something else to show they were actually made. It is one thing to show that this is a possible source of government; it is another to show that it actually applies in any particular case. If justification depends upon choice, then the choices have actually to have been made.

Agreement, as Grotius and Pufendorf handle it, is either explicit or tacit (*tacitum*). Since we have little explicit agreement, and since they themselves were prepared to handle the original contract in a purely hypothetical (or non-historical) way, the weight then falls on tacit consent. Here the scope they allow to it goes, I think, further than most of us would find plausible. It is one thing (Pufendorf's example) to hold that when a stranger enters a country 'in the guise of a friend', he is tacitly agreeing to abide by its laws (DJN 3.6.2). Someone who knows that these laws apply, who acts freely in choosing to live in the country, and who makes no sign to cancel this natural assumption may be deemed to have implicitly consented.

We may even (another Pufendorf example) in using language be deemed to have tacitly consented to have agreed to call things by their familiar names (that is, in speaking English with you, I am tacitly consenting to mean chair by 'chair', and so on). However, this is now becoming the claim that I have tacitly consented to any custom that is established and that I understand and to which I do not explicitly object. Here, my own will (and hence my own responsibility) is being attenuated, and more is made of what is customarily (or naturally) there. If this works, then any established government, customary and not criticised, is taken to have the tacit consent of its people, and hence they are taken to be bound to it by their own will. Many arguments can be given why such a government should be obeyed (the powers that be are ordained of God; de facto by default is de jure; it is customary and custom is all there is to justice; there would be disutility in trying to change it; it does the basic work of keeping the peace; it co-ordinates expectations; and so on). However, it is not clear that the right argument in such a case is that the government should be obeyed because we have agreed to it with our tacit consent.

A good test for this, I think, is the question of why children should obey their parents (which we discussed with Hobbes). The contemporary opponents of the idea that the just foundation of government is in the consent of the governed drew heavily on the obligation of created things to their creator. Political authority was modelled after parental authority; and in both cases we were supposed to be born into subjection, rather than willing ourselves into it. The commandment to 'honour thy father and mother' was widely glossed as commanding obedience to all secular authority. Hobbes, by contrast, makes children's obligation a matter of agreement. So does Pufendorf. Having said that 'paternal power' is 'the oldest as well as the most sacred form of authority' (DO 2.3.1), he then goes on to say that it has two bases, natural law and 'the tacit consent of the child'.

Here, Pufendorf's first basis, natural law, is enough for his conclusion. The argument is that a necessary condition for the reproduction of society (for people as social creatures) is that someone has care of children, that this naturally is the parents, and that such care requires a measure of authority or control. However, Pufendorf also wants to add a second basis, tacit consent. This shows how strong is the need of these thinkers to rest all subjection in the will of the subjected. However, here it seems to be implausible. We run into similar problems as we did with Hobbes's similar idea. Merely because a child has not run away from its parents, are we really to suppose that it has therefore 'tacitly' consented to their authority? As in the analogous case of obedience to established government, 'tacit' consent seems to be merely a loose wheel, idly turning. It is something added by someone in the grip of a theory about the necessity of consent when the real work of justification and explanation goes on elsewhere.

So other arguments seem to be at work here as well as the explicit contracting-into-government ones. And, as we saw earlier, even if similar conclusions to Hobbes seem to emerge, these same conclusions are reached by use of different moral materials. Since the materials are different, other conclusions may be possible. This will be seen in the next chapter. Pufendorf also makes another advance on Hobbes of future use. This is with respect to the understanding of 'society'.

As used at present, the term 'civil society' is unfortunately ambiguous, having almost reversed its meaning from the seventeenth century. At the time of Hobbes and Locke (and Grotius and Pufendorf), it stands for a society that is civic – that is, in a *civitas* or a state. It is political society. Nowadays it tends to stand for that nexus of social relationships (for example, economic ones) that stand over and against the political. The term is therefore tricky, but that there are two possibilities is important. For even if, as a hypothetical thought experiment, we start with a 'natural' state of isolated individuals and examine the construction of 'society', we have two options about where we have reached. We can imagine people forming relationships and coming together in a non-political way. Or we can imagine their starting without a political superior and then constructing one, thereby creating political society. Hobbes does it all in one jump. But we can imagine two stages, and this is what Pufendorf does. Put differently, we can have a use for the term 'people' to mean an identifiable group in social relationships with each other and inhabiting a piece of land, quite independently of the question whether this 'people' has any political organisation, or any sovereign.

This point about the meaning of 'people' is a useful analytical point and, as I said, the insights of these thinkers into analytical and structural points have a validity independent of the particular content they propose. This also applies to another distinction they make, which in Pufendorf's terms is that between perfect and imperfect obligations. He also talks about perfect and imperfect rights. Grotius's similar distinction is between what he calls a 'faculty' (*facultas*) 'when the moral quality is perfect' and an 'aptitude' (*aptitudo*) 'when it is not perfect' (DJBP 1.1.4). Perfect rights are what we normally think of as rights. They are the rights described in the previous account. When I have a right (a perfect right), this automatically places an obligation on others. If they do not keep it, then there has been injustice (I have been done an injustice). This is against the (natural) law, and is sufficient grounds for restitution and punishment. This is the story so far. However, both Grotius and Pufendorf add to this story things that we are expected to do, and that it is praiseworthy for us to do, but that do not bind us in the same way. These are the imperfect obligations, the requirements of what Pufendorf calls 'humanity', as opposed to the requirements of justice. For example, if someone very poor owes (rich) me something, justice says I should take it; humanity may say that I shouldn't. On the one hand, we have perfect obligations and rights, justifying interference by force when not met (restitution and punishment). On the other hand, we have imperfect obligations and rights, which merely justify censure if not met. If I take the beggar's bowl from him and he starves, this is injustice. I should be punished. If I fail to put something in the bowl, the worst that should apply to me is public lack of esteem (and perhaps also the dim view of the Almighty).

There are at least two reasons why Grotius or Pufendorf wants this distinction. The first is to try and keep the natural law as minimal as possible. To live in society, we need a basic set of minimal rights, which are mainly concerned with not harming each other for no good reason. On top of this can be placed other requirements, which vary with time and people. Groups may form, create states, and impose additional obligations on themselves. These obligations, however, only apply for these groups. Similarly God, as lawgiver, may impose obligations, either on everyone, or on a particular people. Thus, Grotius thought that the law laid down in the Old Testament (such as the Ten Commandments) was not, as others thought, God's statement of the natural law, but just a law that God gave to a particular people, the Jews. Hence it binds the Jews, but does not bind others (he notes how commandments in the Old Testament often start 'Hear, O Israel'; it is only Israel that is supposed to be listening). By contrast, the New Testament might be supposed to bind non-Jewish, Christian, Europe. However, Grotius thinks that Christ did not lay down a law but made recommendations (that is, in Pufendorf's language, imperfect obligations). As Christians, Europeans are supposed to do more. But this is not a law. It recommends generosity, humility, and such like. We can try and inculcate these traits. We can condemn their lack. However, we should not punish it. Ingratitude is a sin; it is not injustice.

This is the first reason for the distinction – namely, it helps to keep the natural law minimal and therefore true for all times and all peoples. The second reason, which Pufendorf urges, is quite different. It takes the form of trying to prevent a crowding out of goodness. If everything were required by law, thinks Pufendorf, then people would not have the opportunity to display their good qualities. They would not have the opportunity to display merit, and so to earn praise.

Here is another consequence of the minimalism. Perhaps surprisingly (but like other legal theorists), although he writes at length about law, Pufendorf nevertheless wishes to cut back on its normal scope. Keep law to the basics. Don't keep requiring things of people. Give them room to be good. If people do things just because they fear punishment, they may be doing the right things, but they are doing them for the wrong reasons, and this is wrong. (The next step in this argument, only taken later, would be that the identity of an act depends on its motive or reason, so if done for the wrong reason, it is a different and a wrong act; hence it is impossible to get people to do the right things by threatening punishment.)

The Role of God

Pufendorf is not squeamish about punishment and making the law effective. For him, God, as punisher and upholder of the natural law, is not a problem. The problem is rather whether any of his account is possible without God. For Pufendorf understands by law the command of a superior. So when it doesn't come from human command (from a human sovereign), it emanates from the divine sovereign. As we saw before, it is for him because God, as our superior, commands the natural law that we are under obligations. But now the problem starts. For, as we also saw, both Grotius and Pufendorf want their new natural law to be discoverable independently of all particular knowledge of God or the divine plan. However, given what has just been said, the relationship of God to this (supposed new) natural law does not disappear that easily. Furthermore, both Grotius and Pufendorf also think that it can be known by reason that God exists (even if it needs particular revelations, or sacred texts, to know in detail what he wants). And if we have a God who creates everything and gives it a purpose, this should give content to natural law. In other words, the nature of natural law is meant to follow from reason, from right reason. But if right reason shows that there is a purposive God, this is a theorem that can be used in its deduction.

I think that it may here be useful to separate three aspects of the way in which God can appear in the argument. He may appear in the *ontology*, as part of the explanation of why the natural law exists at all (that is, that it is created and upheld by God). He may appear in the *epistemology*, as part of our discovery of the content of natural law (that is, knowing God's purposes, we can deduce its nature). Or he may appear as the *explanation of the law's motivating force* (that is, we ought to obey because God will punish us if we don't). I take it that the central question of interest here is epistemological. We want to know the content of the natural law so that it can be used in argument about politics. We want to know what states may do, what relations they have to individuals, whether we should obey the municipal law, and so on, all the questions that can't be answered just on the basis of the municipal law itself. So we do not need to understand more about the ontology than is needed to deduce this content.

For Pufendorf, where 'God is as much the author of natural laws as of His own positive laws' (EJU 1.13.6), God is ineliminable, but the crucial question is what effect this doctrine has on the content of natural law. If natural law flows from God's will, it might seem that we would have to know God's will to know the law. However, this depends upon whether God could have willed otherwise, and what would happen if he did. In late Medieval accounts such as Ockham, the law depends upon God's will, and God might very well have willed something else. Hence we need revelation to discover (for example, by reading the Bible) that God has willed us not to murder each other rather than kill the fifth person we meet each day.

This, however, is not the way Pufendorf goes. God could have done otherwise and not created any human beings (or, indeed, any world at all). But given that he has created human beings, he has willed the law that is suitable for this kind of creature. (He not only created them male and female, telling them to go forth and multiply; he also created them rational, and hence limited how they should do it.) So, knowledge of reason, knowledge of the central nature of people (knowledge of the minimum of what is needed to live sociably) is needed to derive the natural law. We don't need special revelation.

With this, we are in effect back with Grotius's *etiamsi* clause. We need to understand human nature and rationality to discover natural law's content. Yet we could do this even if there were no God. Analogously, we might think that God was needed to give nature a purpose, but what the purpose was could only be discovered by studying nature. The results we reached might then be the same as a resolutely secular ethics, such as evolutionary ethics (which supposes an evolutionary purpose for nature, but then bases its conclusions on observation).

We get our natural law without God, but this still leaves the question as to why we should obey it, and here, perhaps, we do need God. In a state of nature (as between separate countries), the natural right to punish is meant to make it effective. In states, these requirements of natural law become part of a properly constructed civil law, so adding the sanctions of the punishment apparatus of the state. Then, as seen, God will also punish breaches.

So I do have a reason to observe the natural law – fear of punishment. Yet if fear of punishment is the only reason, then it would seem that we do need God, as punisher or effector of the law, to fill in when states and state of nature punishment fails. Yet both Grotius and Pufendorf also rely on something else. With respect to why we should keep our contracts, Pufendorf talks of a double 'weight' pushing us to do so. There is partly the fear of punishment. But there is also the contract itself (DJN 7.2.5). Like Grotius, he is concerned to show how obeying it is in our interests (as well as the sanctions listed, he is concerned also to list 'natural' punishments, such as how things tend to go badly for us in other ways when we do not follow it). However, as well as this, there has to be another source. In the end, the motivation has to be (and was taken by them) to be internal. That is, in taking something to be natural law, we also take it to be naturally obligatory. Once we understand that it is the law, we need no more to understand why we have a reason to do what it says. The motivation is internal, intrinsic.

Our reason for following natural law, therefore, is because it is right (however this rightness is explained in terms of the rightness of God). It is not, or at least not just, because we will be punished by God if we don't. This is certainly how it must be understood in Grotius, because of the way in which he understands punishment. If our only reason for following the law is that we will be punished if we don't, then punishment is necessarily connected to law; it would make no sense to suppose that something was part of the law if breaches were not punished. Yet Grotius says that it is civil law rather than natural law that determines the right quantity of punishment (DJBP 2.8.20). Holding that 'people should not do each other harm, except for the sake of some good to be attained' (DJBP 2.20.4), he holds that punishment should serve public utility. In other words, it should only be applied when it has a deterrent or reformatory effect, and he is all in favour of pardons. (Pufendorf – DJN 2.5.16 – also thinks that the degree of punishment should be determined by the public good.) All of this only makes sense on the supposition that offences and punishment are not necessarily connected. If there is a breach of the law, then punishment is permissible. But whether there should actually be punishment, and how much, is a matter of policy.

Why then should we obey the natural law? How can we argue about war, about international relations, about all cases where there is no political sovereign, no one with a Hobbesian sword? How can we criticise what our and other states do to their citizens? To what can Grotius appeal when he is trying to put considerations of natural law before his enemy, the King of Spain? One way to answer this is to see to what in fact he actually does appeal. He tells us in the Preface to the *Mare Liberum*. As regards people, his appeal is 'to the rulers and to the free and independent nations of Christendom'. He says that 'the law by which our case must be decided is not difficult to find, seeing that it is the same among all nations, and it is easy to understand, seeing that it is innate in every individual'. So much (hopefully) for natural law. This shows that there is a law that applies also to the kings to which he is appealing. Why should they observe it? The first (and best) answer is just because it is the law, and Grotius ends the Preface by talking about the happiness of good deeds. He does, however, also talk of 'two tribunals (*tribunalia*) open to those who are debarred from all others, 'conscience' and 'public opinion' (*famam*). In the last chapter of his great work *De Jure Belli ac Pacis*, Grotius again makes particular reference to precisely these two – conscience and opinion.

The force of conscience is in the end the force of the law itself. It is the force of one's own understanding of the law. But the power of public opinion or reputation is independent. It is the force of others' understanding of the law. Someone may follow the natural law to stand well with others, others who know the natural law. It might be asked what political purchase this has, politics being concerned with real power. To which the answer is that public opinion has power. In any case, appeals to fame, reputation, opinion, correctness, fit perfectly into the philosophical study of politics, however they may fare in real power (or in altering the situation on the ground). For in this study, we seek what is correct, and in terms of this correctness we criticise government and its operations.

In Grotius and Pufendorf, we have as proposals for such correctness that valid human authority depends upon the will of the governed, but that once it is in place we should obey and not resist the governors. We have it that there is a natural law that everyone's property should be preserved, without any particular holding of property being dictated by this natural law. In the next chapter, starting with the same natural law framework, we shall see what alternative conclusions are possible.

6

Locke's Law

Locke was important in his own day, is important now, and has been important in the interval. He is also important for more than his political philosophy. The two greatest philosophers for our purposes in the seventeenth century are Hobbes and Locke. Hobbes's greatest work was in political philosophy. Locke's was not. Both then and subsequently, Locke has been best known for his great work of epistemology, the *Essay Concerning Human Understanding*. Born in 1632, the same year as Pufendorf, Locke was already in his late fifties when the *Essay* was published, and for the rest of his life he was the famous writer of the *Essay*, which bore his name on the title page.

On this title page also is the date 1690, although the work was in fact published at the end of 1689. Almost simultaneously, Locke published his main work of political philosophy, *The Two Treatises on Government*. This is also dated 1690 on the title page, but it also in fact appeared in 1689. Here, however, the resemblance ends. The *Two Treatises* appeared anonymously, and Locke kept his authorship of them a fairly closely guarded secret for the rest of his life. He was not the famous author of the *Two Treatises*. Also in 1689, and also anonymously, Locke's other main work of political philosophy, the *Epistola de Tolerantia* appeared. This was rapidly translated into English (although not by Locke himself) as *A Letter Concerning Toleration*.

Early in 1689, the year in which all of these works of Locke were published, he returned to England from Holland. It was the time of the 'Glorious Revolution'. At the end of 1688, William, a Protestant Dutchman married to the elder daughter of a former king, invaded England. James II, the Roman Catholic king, ran away. William, with his wife Mary, became joint rulers of England. Sometimes called the 'bloodless revolution', this was all very satisfactory. Or at least it was in England. There was plenty of blood in Ireland. In 1690, William went and defeated James there in a proper battle, establishing a Protestant ascendancy also in Ireland. Today, the remains of this battle linger only in the North of the country. There people are still invoked to 'Remember 1690' by the writing on the walls. A Protestant Northern Irishman attending the Brussels International Exhibition in the mid-twentieth century found a machine that offered to tell him the greatest event in the world for any given year. He remembered 1690, as written on the walls at home. He typed in 1690, expecting to get the famous battle. The answer he got was 'The publication of John Locke's *Essay Concerning Human Understanding*'.

So Locke's *Essay* is a great event, framing eighteenth-century intellectual perspectives. Less known, less thought about, and unacknowledged by its author is the political work, the *Two Treatises*. It has naturally been connected with the stirring events of the time, being read as a justification of the takeover by William, whom Locke had followed from Holland. However, the reason Locke was in Holland was that earlier he had had to flee from England. He had been in danger of his life from the old regime, not just from James II but also from his brother and predecessor, Charles II. He had been involved in plots; even in Holland, Locke deemed it prudent to hide and adopt assumed names. It is now generally agreed that the *Two Treatises* was in fact written nearly a decade before its publication. Rather than being a post hoc justification of William's successful invasion, it was meant instead to rationalise a dangerous and desperate attempt to remove an earlier absolutist king, Charles II. The story, either way, came out well in the end. Locke returned with William, not just to England, but also to power and influence. He had government positions, he was on the side of the winners. But if things had gone differently, he could have been executed, as others were, some years before. Then we would have heard of neither him nor his philosophy.

Toleration

Religious conflict, religious war, toleration. William wished to introduce toleration into his new country, and there was a modest Act to that effect, somewhat less than he wanted. Locke's *Letter Concerning Toleration* was an influential appeal, written just at the time when opinion was turning away from the idea of forcing everyone into a single, established church (although for long afterward the established church in England continued to hold all the prizes, a monopoly of all state offices and positions of influence). In the *Letter*, Locke argued that the state should not force its citizens to attend any particular church or adopt any particular kind of religious worship. A church, for Locke, is a voluntary association, its membership being composed of those who choose to belong. This was radical for the time, even if from our current perspective we are more likely to recognise the limits of Lockean toleration, such as that it was not to be extended to atheists or Roman Catholics.

Locke's view was radical for the time in that it had previously been thought that a united state needed a united church. By contrast, Locke argues that the state can only benefit by not making religion a bone of contention with some of its citizens; indeed, the more sects there are, the less threatening any particular sect is either to the state or to its individual members. The way to win dissenters over was not by force but, rather, by persuasion and kindness. This, in fact, turned out to be a correct empirical prediction: once toleration was granted to the dissenters in England, they grew weaker, not stronger.

Locke's chief argument, at least on the surface, is that the understanding cannot be compelled to belief by force. By 'cannot' here, Locke does not mean that it is morally impermissible. He means that it is impossible. The nature of belief is such that we cannot choose to believe something just because it is in our interest. Since the goal of forcing belief is impossible, it is impractical for anyone, including the state, to try. Locke attempts to defend this position in his subsequent *Second* and *Third Letters Concerning Toleration*. However, in these he has to admit that force might sometimes be successful in directing people's attention, or getting them to consider things, and change of attention may lead to change of belief. Hence, even if we agree that people can't just choose to have beliefs, it may after all be possible for people's beliefs to change as a result of force. So it looks as if Locke needs another argument than the sheer claim that it is impossible to force belief. Another, and probably better, epistemological argument he uses is that there is nothing to suppose that the state that enforces belief has got it right. He points out the great variety of religious beliefs, most of which accordingly must be wrong. What I am forced to believe in Paris is different from what I am forced to believe in London. There is no obvious reason why the magistrate in one place is more likely to be right than in another, and there is no obvious reason why the magistrates should be right any more than any other individuals thinking for themselves.

Epistemology is here doing political work, and Locke's chief work of epistemology is the *Essay Concerning Human Understanding*. Although I started with the contrast between Locke's acknowledged and famous epistemological *Essay* and his anonymous political philosophy, the two are in fact connected. The *Essay* originally grew out of discussions about how difficult it is to find the right answers in morality and religion. The two quotations on the title page – one from Cicero, one from the Bible – both declare that we should respect our ignorance about God. Locke added a chapter to a later edition criticising enthusiasm – that is, the claim people make to a divinely inspired access to the truth. Epistemology is important in Locke's attempt to ward off the powerful and potentially destructive force of religious belief. It is important to be sceptical, cautious, not assuming that we know more than we do.

However, even if we accept all these points about belief, this will still not take Locke all the way to toleration. For the problem is not one of belief but one of practice. The prevailing established church in England did not want to enforce belief as much as it wanted to enforce behaviour. It held that there should be uniformity in the outward practice of religion. Locke's reply is that religion is none of the state's business. Religion represents people's bets about happiness in the next world, whereas government should be concerned about people's happiness in this world. The former only concerns the person themselves, and so they should take their own risks; the latter also concerns others, and so the state can interfere. This is impeccably liberal, but it does depend upon assumptions about the point of the state, and so upon arguments yet to be considered.

Indeed, even Locke himself, as a young man, had taken a different line. As a young teacher of moral philosophy at the University of Oxford, he too had held that uniformity should be enforced. The most vigorous disputes in England were not in fact about central issues of doctrine but rather about apparently trivial variations in how people behaved in church, such as taking communion standing up or kneeling, bowing at the name of Jesus, or the use of the cross in baptism. Such practices were generally held to be 'indifferent' – that is, not part of the fundamental essentials of faith. The problem is what power the state rightfully has over indifferent things. Locke's first position, which was the standard established church view, is that, precisely because they were indifferent, they can therefore be enforced by law. The claim is that if they are indifferent, then no one can be religiously or morally damaged by being forced to do them. Hence, because uniformity is a value, a single practice should be enforced. The contemporary church rules (or 'canons'), for example, expend considerable vehemence and energy demonstrating that the use of the cross in baptism is of no importance in the sacrament. It does not, that is, as the Roman Catholics thought, have any sacramental efficacy. From this, one might expect the canons to conclude that it does not matter whether it is used. However, that is not the temper of the time. Just because it is indifferent, the canons say, it therefore has to be enforced.

Early on, Locke changed his mind about this. Since religion is a person's own concern, and people here take their own risks, everyone should be allowed to judge what is indifferent. If someone thinks that kneeling is important, then it is important. As Locke wrote in 1667 in an essay about toleration, 'in religious worship nothing is indifferent' [PE p. 139]. It is a shift from an objective test to a subjective test: what matters is what people think, how it looks to them. And, throughout, Locke held that deciding things for oneself is both an epistemological duty and also, particularly, a religious duty.

So how it looks to people is important. But this does not mean that there is nothing but looks, merely subjectivity. Locke also believes that there is an objectively right answer about which things are indifferent, and this is that nearly every part of Christian belief and practice is indifferent. In his late *The Reasonableness of Christianity*, he takes Christianity to involve just one single belief – namely, that Jesus was the Messiah. Everything else is indifferent, inessential. People can disagree about it and still be Christians. What Locke here comes up with is in fact strikingly similar to what Hobbes had earlier proposed in *Leviathan*, the minimal belief that Jesus was the Messiah. However, Hobbes uses this to move from indifference to enforcement. It is just because nearly everything is indifferent for Hobbes that Leviathan has such power over religion. Locke also thinks that in fact nearly everything is indifferent. But, by contrast, he also thinks everyone should be allowed to judge for themselves whether or not this is so. It may not be indifferent for them. So we should not enforce religious practice.

Hobbes, Locke, and Filmer

In their treatments of toleration, Locke and Hobbes end up in different positions, although much of the material they use is the same. Hobbes argues for the right of the state to control, and the duty of people to obey. Locke argues for the right of people not to be controlled, and the duty of the state to be tolerant. More generally, Locke looks as if he is striking a blow for modernity. At the end of a confessionally riven century, he seems to be arguing for rolling back religion to leave room for the modern, secular, state. For too long, it would seem, the right thing to do or to think was taken to depend upon religious assumptions. First, get God right, then philosophy and action follow. Instead, Locke seems to be arguing for the privatisation of religion. Getting God right is to be a purely personal affair, so that the only business of the state in this area is to hold the ring between competing sects. However, as I shall argue in this chapter, this general impression is misleading with respect to Locke's political philosophy as a whole. It may be modern. It may have influenced many moderns. But it is not a political philosophy in which God has moved out of the way.

We also have to be careful about the relationship in thought between Hobbes and Locke. Locke rarely mentions or alludes to Hobbes. However, this is unsurprising given that Hobbes was taken to be such a notorious heretic. Hence, at a time when most of the angry noise still came from religion, any mention of Hobbes unaccompanied by a demolition was unhelpful in persuasion. So Hobbes is not mentioned. Yet, at least at first sight, the general shape of Locke's political thought with respect to Hobbes seems the same as in the particular example of toleration: different conclusions but much of the same material.

Here again, as in Hobbes but also in Grotius and Pufendorf, we start with a state of nature without government. Here again, it is assumed that people are in a condition of original freedom and equality. It is not just churches but also states that are voluntary associations. As in Hobbes and the others, the state is explained by Locke as a constructed or artificial entity, produced by contract or agreement in the state of nature. The agreement is again to relinquish private rights (or liberties) of protection, punishment, or vengeance, transferring them to the state. Hence the state is 'authorised' by its citizens to do this protection and punishing for them. 'I authorise and give up my right of governing myself', said Hobbes about the original social contract; Locke says of it that 'hereby he authorizes the Society, or which is all one, the Legislative thereof to make laws for him' [*Second Treatise*, Sec. 89].

So far, so similar. Yet there are important differences at nearly every level. As we have seen, both *Leviathan* and the *Two Treatises* were written in particular contexts. This influenced what they particularly wish to promote, and what they promote are precisely opposite conclusions. Hobbes wrote in and after a civil war. The known political world had fallen apart: Hobbes in reaction makes a plea for unity, strong government, absolute authority. Locke wrote in a period of strong government, absolute authority that he thought was taking England in the wrong direction. It is in reaction to this a plea for resistance, rebellion, war, for things (temporarily) falling apart.

Locke also differs importantly from Hobbes in the general principles on which he draws, particularly in his understanding of the law of nature. Here he is much more like Grotius and Pufendorf than Hobbes. Although, as we saw, Hobbes talks of a 'law of nature', he did not think that it was a real law but merely advice; he took its content to be prudential. By contrast, both Grotius and Pufendorf think that the law of nature is a real law, and that it produces real obligation. Here, Locke is like them rather than Hobbes. He also has a real law, offering obligatory commands rather than prudential advice.

Locke also differs importantly from Hobbes in style. Hobbes tries to produce much of his argument without referring to authority. Indeed, where people have gone wrong, Hobbes thinks, is to read books and cite them, particularly Aristotle, as authorities. Locke also criticises (in the *Essay*) the Aristotelian, scholastic, style of argument. However, much more than Hobbes, he writes in a particular context of books. He wants to persuade people who believe in the mistakenness in all circumstances of any resistance to political authority. So he uses the books they use. When the books cannot be given any other interpretation, such as the work of Filmer, he relentlessly criticises them. However, when he can use authors they respect for his own different purposes (such as King James I, Barclay, Hooker), he tries to turn them round. On the grand stage of political thought, these writers are small part players, minor figures of only local significance. However, they, and particularly Filmer and Hooker, frame Locke's thought in a way that no contemporary authors frame that of Hobbes.

This not only differentiates Locke from Hobbes. It also means that we should be careful when comparing them. They are for us the two great figures of that century. But this should not lead us to think that Locke is always consciously replying to Hobbes, or that this is the best way of understanding what he is trying to do. Secret agendas are always attractive, and Locke lived in an age made for secrecy. It was an age in which works propounding views like Locke's were publicly and officially burned, an age when people who plotted with him were executed, an age when discretion and dissimulation were the necessary means to stay alive. Locke explains at length in *The Reasonableness of Christianity* how Jesus had to disguise who he was to stay alive as long as he did. This shows insight; but however attractive it may be to try and uncode Locke's own Messianic secret, it is also worth trying to understand what he explicitly says he is doing. And what he is doing explicitly is not answering Hobbes. Instead, he is answering a quite different defender of absolute government, someone who was born in the same year and wrote at the same time as Hobbes, Sir Robert Filmer.

Filmer argues that the legitimate political power of kings is absolute – that is, he claims that it is not subject to control or question by parliament, citizens, or any other element in the polity. He bases this on an interpretation of the Christian Bible in which God is taken to have given complete power over everything to the first man, Adam, a dominion that Filmer thinks to have been inherited by Adam's successors. In the *First Treatise*, Locke specifically examines Filmer's argument. Many biblical texts are cited, and Filmer's interpretation queried. However, some of his strongest points do not depend upon the niceties of scriptural interpretation, and hence are independent of this particular Christian context. For example, Locke argues that even if Filmer were right about God and Adam, this would not help with respect to whom we were currently meant to be subservient. On Filmer's view, this is whoever is now the legitimate heir of Adam. But, as Locke points out, this is completely unknowable. It can't be all Adam's descendants for (on the Biblical beliefs they share) that would be everyone. Yet not everyone can be king. Hence, instead, it has to be the principal heir of the principal heir in an unknowable genealogy of well over a hundred generations.

The central point here has a much wider significance. It is that if legitimacy depends upon some particular historical happening, and upon a particular contingent connection between this happening and the present, then legitimacy is at the mercy of the specific historical facts. We could only then be sure about the right thing to do if we are sure about these facts. As Locke shows, the particular facts on which Filmer relies are now beyond recall. Yet the same sort of objection can be made to Locke's own preferred alternative system of justification. Here, instead of everything starting with subjection to Adam, we start with free and equal people who contract into government. However, this is again a historical story. If we are bound by contract, we are bound by the actual agreement that was made. Present legitimacy depends upon past facts. So, again, to know where we legitimately are, we have to know how things actually were.

Locke's government is meant to result from human will rather than from Divine command. The source is different, but both justifications depend upon the facts. Interestingly enough, Filmer himself objects to Grotius on these lines. Grotius (as we saw) gets absolute government by supposing that people contract into, and so create by their will, absolute government, in just the same way as people can contract into slavery. Having similar contractual machinery, Locke (as we will see at the end of the chapter) has to avoid this use of it, blocking the possibility of people contracting into either absolute government or into slavery. But the objection Filmer makes applies to the machinery itself. As he puts it in his *Observations upon H Grotius*, 'the most that is proved . . . is this, *that the people may grant away their power without retaining any part.* But what is this to what the people *have* done?' [223]. In other words, even if we give Grotius his assumptions and the original contractual machinery, the most it will show is what is possible. Yet to show what is possible does not show what actually happened. Yet it is only what actually happened that is important in establishing current legitimacy. Thus Filmer, writing in the 1650s against Grotius's work of 1625. But what he said then also poses a threat against Locke's position in the 1680s (and, come to that, the historically based property account of Locke's admirer, Robert Nozick, in the 1970s).

Locke's use of such original contract arguments, and his main political philosophy, occur not in the *First Treatise* (the one specifically against Filmer) but in the *Second*. The *Second Treatise on Government* is a relatively free-standing work, often known by its subtitle as the *Essay on Civil Government*. (For example, it appeared without its companion in the contemporary French translation.) However, although Filmer is mentioned by name much less frequently in the *Second Treatise*, the desire to refute him still dictates some of its structure. It explains, for example, why Locke is so concerned to distinguish between different kinds of power, in particular between paternal power and governmental power. Filmer claims that government had been granted to Adam as a father. It is as a father that Adam is held to have complete power over his children, and this paternal/kingly power is then supposed to have descended to his heirs. Kings are like fathers and fathers are like kings. Everyone is born into subjection. The political dependence in which everyone after Adam starts is explained in the same way as the physical dependence in which everyone after Adam starts. Babies depend upon adults. Children depend upon their fathers.

Or mothers. One of Locke's points against Filmer is that he seems to have left out the women. (Another, unacknowledged, echo of Hobbes.) For example, Filmer gives what Locke calls 'half a reason' in citing the Ten Commandments about honouring parents. Filmer quotes the commandment as 'honour thy father'; Locke notes that the actual commandment is 'honour thy father and thy mother'. Somehow Filmer has worked the women into a dependent position. Yet Eve, coming from Adam's rib, does not seem so obviously to entail dependence as a baby coming from the mother. As we saw, Hobbes had earlier observed that in the state of nature, children should be in subjection to their mothers rather than their fathers; it is a good deal easier to say who the mother is.

These are (yet more) problems for Filmer's paternal/patriarchal authority. However, Locke also has (yet more) problems with his alternative account whereby everyone starts free and equal. For, as Filmer brings out, people actually start life physically and emotionally dependent on others. Whoever brings them up thereby, at least initially, takes control of them. We might, just possibly, suppose that there was an original contract in some distant past agreed on between fully grown people. As Hobbes suggests in *De Cive* in an engaging metaphor, we can suppose for these purposes that they just sprung up fully grown like mushrooms. However, that is not what actually happens; people, unlike mushrooms, need care from birth. Also, even if we allow a distant past contract between fully grown people, this will not explain how it binds current people, who are born into already existing states as dependent and non-rational infants. Even if fully grown original ancestors contracted, why should this bind their children and their children's children? This is another of Filmer's objections. However, this one does not touch Locke. For Locke denies that the contracts of parents bind their children (*Second Treatise*, Sec. 116). However, in avoiding this problem, Locke needs some other method of getting these unbound children obligated to government by their own individual will or consent.

Locke therefore needs to distinguish sharply between paternal and political power. He can then allow that children are born dependent, he can endorse parental power, and he can allow that children have a duty to honour their parents. Yet none of this will then have any consequences with respect to political power. Children for Locke are born subject to parents but not born subject to states. Against the actual assumptions of states, both then and now, Locke holds that people are not born citizens of any particular country. 'British subject by birth' may be stamped on modern passports, but for Locke this is an error. People are only subject when they subject themselves. That is, they have to will themselves into this position. This can only happen when they have a sufficiently mature will, and so Locke holds that it is '*the consent of free-men born under government, which only makes them members of it*, being given separately in their turns, as each comes to be of age' [*Second Treatise* Sec 117]. Before then they are citizens of no country. For Locke, 'a child is born a subject of no country or

government' [Sec. 118]. This looks like a fairly drastic course to take
to avoid Filmer, if only because the contrary assumption is so widely
held. Yet the other way in which he could have avoided Filmer seems
even more drastic. This would have been to allow that infant children
do actually possess will and rational choice, and that they consent to
be looked after and controlled by their parents or guardians. We saw
this implausible claim in both Hobbes and Grotius, so strong is their
desire to base all subjection on consent.

So Locke here has no easy route. With children, we seem to have subjection, obligation to authority, not based upon original agreement.
And if we think that subjection to parental authority comes from birth
rather than consent, why not also subjection to political authority?
Much more is at stake here than the correctness of the views of one
obscure seventeenth-century thinker, or the niceties of Biblical interpretation. It is the question of whether the fact that people are developed inside a context of family or community means that it makes no
sense to think of their individually contracting into a particular society or government, or whether, instead, they should be regarded, as in
Filmer, as being by birth members of particular peoples, or subject to
particular governments.

Nature

Locke returns to the question of distinguishing political from parental
power in the *Second Treatise*, devoting quite a long chapter to it. Having
at the start of the work said that the essence of political power is the
power of life and death ('political power then I take to be a right of
making laws with penalties of death' [Sec. 3]), he tries to show that
parents do not have the power to kill their children. This may seem
obvious, both in Locke's time and our own, in England. Yet it did not
seem so to the Romans, who gave such complete power to the father. So
we cannot just take this as obvious. What Locke needs is an argument
from first principles showing parents not to have such power, and what
we need is to examine what first principles are available to Locke. We
need, that is, to turn now to the main line of Locke's account and to
examine its possible foundations. Suppose, that is, we could solve these
problems about Filmer and parents. Suppose that, as Locke assumes,
sometimes in the past fully grown people have contracted together to

produce new states. Suppose that what happens today is that people contract into already existing states when they come of age. Even if we allow all of this, we still have a whole string of unanswered fundamental questions such as why people should want to do this; whether they are allowed to, what their position is in the state of nature before they contract; and how this position alters when they agree to enter civil society. To answer such questions, Locke needs an account of the state of nature, and it is indeed with such an account that he begins the *Second Treatise*. So let us now turn to this account and this work, and so turn to the fundamental basis of Locke's political philosophy.

In Hobbes, the state of nature is a state of war, the war of all against all. Whether specifically because of this or otherwise, one of Locke's first main concerns is to distinguish between the state of nature and the state of war. After a short introductory chapter referring back to the *First Treatise*, Locke's next two chapters are called 'On the state of nature' and 'On the state of war', distinguishing the two conditions by describing them in different chapters. The state of nature is in effect an analytical device in Locke, a way of understanding certain kinds of situations rather than any sort of historical or more generally descriptive device. It is understood by definition: if a situation fulfils certain conditions, then it is dubbed a 'state of nature'. Similarly, Locke understands a state of war definitionally. Then, having different understandings or definitions of each of them, it is simple for him to distinguish between them and show that they do not necessarily coincide.

Locke starts Chapter 2, his state of nature chapter, by saying that it is the state people 'are naturally in'. So far this is not much help, given the many things that are supposed to be natural. However, Locke then goes on more specifically to say that it is 'a state of perfect freedom' in which people can order things 'without...depending on the will of any other man'. This last is the crucial bit. We can take it that what Locke means by the 'state of nature' is a situation in which everyone is independent; no one is subject to the will of another, a condition without political authority. This can be taken as definitional, and in the next chapter, Locke gives it as a sort of definition when he declares 'want of a common judge with authority puts all men in a state of nature' (Sec. 19).

'War' is a less slippery term than 'nature', and so war is simpler to understand. However, again, it is worth thinking of it as having a specific

and semi-technical sense in Locke, if only because it is centrally important to his over-all argument legitimising resistance to government. So,
just as with the 'state of nature', we should think of it in at least a semi-
definitional manner. Indeed, just after the definition quoted earlier of
the state of nature, Locke gives what looks like another definition. He
says 'force without right, upon a man's person, makes a state of war'
[Sec. 19]. So 'war' here is both wider and also narrower than our common understanding. It is wider because it is not only something that
happens between established states, involving soldiers, weapons, and
such like. It can also happen between individual people. It is narrower
because not every attempt by one person to apply force to another
counts as a state of war. For it to be war in Locke's sense, the force
has to be without right. Hence a state or individual exacting rightful
punishment may well be forcing someone, but since they are not using
force without right, they are not thereby in a state of war. Taking 'war'
in its normal sense, we can have just wars, but these will not be 'states
of war' in Locke's special sense.

Given these definitions, it is easy for Locke to distinguish between
the two states. For it does not necessarily follow that people living
together without a common judge are using force without right on
each other. Hence we can have a state of nature without its being
thereby a state of war. Conversely, even where there is a common judge
and political authority, we may have people using force without right.
So we may have a state of war without its being thereby a state of nature.
If a highwayman (to take an example of Locke's) threatens my life in
order to get my money, he thereby puts himself into a state of war with
me, and I can (according to Locke) legitimately kill him, whether or
not we are in a settled, political, state with law, common judges, and
authority.

This separation of the question of whether right is observed and
whether we are in a state without a common judge is possible for
Locke because for him the question of right is independent of the
existence of such a judge. That is, unlike Hobbes, the judge is not
needed to make things right and wrong. In other words, there is a
law of nature, a law that obliges us and lays down what is right and
wrong quite independently of the positive institution or commands of
human law-makers. Again, we are in the world of Grotius or Pufendorf
rather than (at least on my account) the world of Hobbes. 'The *state of*

nature has a law of nature to govern it, which obliges every one', is how Locke puts it, and he immediately goes on, 'and reason, which is that law, teaches all mankind who will but consult it, that being all equal and independent, no one ought to harm another in his life, health, liberty, or possessions' [Sec. 6]. So, in familiar fashion, the law of nature is the law of right reason, knowable by universal human reason, and that binds human beings as such. We are not to harm each other, not because the magistrate says so, nor because it is prudential good advice if we desire peace, but because it is right, correct, true.

So far so good; or at least it would be good if we could be sure that this was the universal deliverance of reason. Locke has to show that there is an objective, true, universal law. Furthermore, and importantly, he has to show that this universal law is also knowable. It has not just got to be true, but everyone has also to be able to tell that it is true. For, as Locke says, and as would seem to be a correct principle of natural justice, people may only properly be judged by laws that have been promulgated to them. 'Nobody', says Locke, 'can be under a law which is not promulgated to him' (*Second Treatise*, Sec. 57). That is, unless there is the possibility of knowledge of a law, it is wrong that people should be judged by it and suffer for not following it. All this is familiar from before, and produces (by now) familiar problems, but we still have to see how or whether Locke can solve them.

He adds another element, also familiar from before – that the law of nature is the law of God. Yet, since the law of nature has to be knowable to all, and since Locke thinks that the law of nature is the law of God, it follows that he has to show that it has to be possible for all people, anywhere and at any time, to know the law of God. Now, of course, and particularly for thinkers of this period, the law of God is supposed to be knowable because of his particular revelations of it. It is, for example, in the Bible. However, we again run into a familiar problem. For the Bible describes a revelation to particular people at particular times. So the problem is how this can be supposed to be a promulgation of God's law to people who did not believe in the Christian Bible, and might never have heard about it. Even in Locke's day, there was the problem of all those Chinese. They had a sort of moral law, but they did not have access to the (right sort of) sacred texts. ('I fear the *Chineses*, a very great and civil people', comments Locke, 'trouble not themselves much about this matter' [*First Treatise*, Sec. 141].)

The official answer to this, which is the one that Locke generally adopted, is that the law of nature is knowable by reason alone and does not depend upon any special revelation. As he puts it in the *Essay*, 'there is a law, knowable by the light of nature; i.e. without the help of positive revelation' [1.3.13]. Hence all human beings as such, having the universal human property of reason, may use it to discover the moral law. However, this still, as we have seen, leaves us with problems. Even if we turn from revelation to reason, we still seem to get different results at different periods and different places. The spectre of the enormous variability of human custom noted by Montaigne and Charron still hangs over the rationalist feast, and Locke himself was an avid collector of travellers' tales. We want more content from the rational, natural law than we can gain from universal agreement. On the other hand, universal agreement by itself will not show that something is part of the rational, natural law. It may just be part of the agreed law of the peoples, *jus gentium* rather than *jus naturae*. Pufendorf pointed out the Christian 'golden rule' – that you should do unto others as you would that they do unto you – appears in many widely varying cultures; he cites not only Confucius but also the Incas [DJN 2.3.13]. Here the Chinese and the Bible agree, but this is not enough by itself to make it a dictate of reason.

Furthermore, if reason alone (pure practical reason) is meant to deliver the truths of the law, there is the problem of how exactly it is meant to do it and so of what these truths are. This is particularly pertinent for Locke, who does not believe in innate ideas. So moral truths (for him) cannot just be intuitive, or read off from the innate contents of our minds. There has, therefore, to be a rational method whereby they may be discovered. Locke, that is, needs a proof procedure, an account of right reasoning that will lead us to the truths of right reason. However, he thinks that this is just what he can provide. Even if moral truths are not intuitive, he claims, 'morality is capable of demonstration as well as mathematics' [*Essay* 3.11.16]. So the law of nature is taken to be like Euclidean geometry: people may not all know the truth, but anyone prepared to use their reason to follow the demonstration will come up with the right (and the same) answer. Hence, as Locke puts it, 'moral knowledge is as capable of real certainty as mathematics' [*Essay* 4.4.7]. This demonstrable, objective, truth, which

Locke thinks is available in morality, means that for him morality is much more certain than most of our beliefs.

Although this sounds implausible, Locke does have sufficient apparatus in his theory of knowledge for this distinction to be possible. In the technical language and thought of the *Essay Concerning Human Understanding*, moral terms refer to what Locke calls 'mixed modes', and with mixed modes he holds that we may have true knowledge of the 'archetypes'. This is his jargon, but the basic idea is that mixed modes are a species of complex idea, analysable in terms of their constituent simple ideas. So far this makes them like what Locke calls 'substances'. However, an important difference for Locke between the two is that in the case of what he calls mixed modes, we ourselves put the bits of the complex idea together. Therefore, for Locke, we can know the real nature of, for example, murder (a mixed mode) in the way that we cannot know the real nature of, for example, gold (a substance). So we may achieve demonstrable knowledge about murder in a way we cannot about gold (where we have to rely on experience of things independent of us). However, although the theory leaves room for the possibility of a demonstrable knowledge of moral truths, it is another thing to achieve it in practice. We can all see what Euclid has done, yet there are no comparable demonstrations in either the *Second Treatise* or in the *Essay*. When he was encouraged to produce such a demonstration, Locke seemed constantly to get the equivalent of a diplomatic tooth ache. His correspondent Molyneux urged him to do it. The first thing he would look at and produce, Locke replied. Many years and works later, the promised demonstration of moral truths was still an unrealised possibility.

Locke indeed does give some examples in the *Essay*, but these are not very helpful. One example he gives, that *gratitude is justice*, is of the kind Locke himself calls 'trifling'. It is listed in the chapter entitled 'Trifling Propositions' [4.8.12]. More significant, perhaps, are the two examples he gives when explicitly claiming that moral proposition are 'as certain as any demonstration in Euclid' [4.3.18]. One is that *no government allows absolute liberty*. At first sight this is hopeful; it sounds like an important political truth, which Locke claims can be demonstrated with geometrical certainty. However, at second sight, it turns out to be merely definitional, trifling, since he understands here by 'liberty' that anyone can do 'whatever he pleases'. He understands 'liberty' differently elsewhere. With such different meaning, the claim would become more interesting, but it ceases to be demonstrable, and indeed might well be false.

The same applies to the other example given here, which is that *where there is no property, there is no injustice*. Again, we have what looks like a significant claim in political philosophy, which is held to be as certain as a theorem of Euclidean geometry. However, again, further inspection reveals it to be either trivial or false. On the most natural understanding of 'property', as Leibniz pointed out, it is false, since people could still be unjustly impeded in their rights even if all things were in common and there were no private, exclusive, property. Not all rights are property rights. Alternatively, if 'property' just means any right at all, then it becomes trivial, trifling ('where there is not a right, there is no violation of a right'). For the great political and moral concourses of the world, where kings were to be overthrown, countries invaded, and force applied to individual people, all in the name of the law of nature, something more substantial than all this is needed.

Even if these truths were demonstrable, there would still be a problem about promulgation. For if people are to be punished for not knowing the moral law, then it has to be something knowable by people at large, and not just something possibly demonstrable by a once-a-century genius who is even smarter than John Locke (Immanuel Kant?). It has to be knowable to everyone at all times and places. As Locke puts it, we have to explain how the law is known by the dairymaids and ploughmen, people who work for a living and have neither the time nor the background education required for abstract demonstration. It is not sufficient to say that they can read it off the (supposedly easily knowable) positive laws of their particular countries, for what we are talking about here is the moral law, the law by which the laws and governments of particular countries may be called into question. In the *Essay*, Locke talks of 'the *divine* law, whereby I mean that law which God has set to the actions of men, whether promulgated to them by the light of nature or the voice of revelation' [2.28.8]. We have tried promulgation by reason, by the 'light of nature'. But in the end, Locke falls back, after all, on revelation. His late work, *The Reasonableness of Christianity*, is devoted to showing why Christianity is good for you. But this is to be discovered simply by reading the Bible. Commentators, theologians, and philosophers are excluded (apart, presumably, from Locke himself). Study of the plain words of the Bible alone, he thinks, can reduce Christianity to the single truth noted earlier, belief in which is demonstrated by practice. So for Locke, the Christian message is basically a moral message. It tells people how to live. This is the answer for the dairymaids. They just have to read the Bible.

Here we seem to have a loss of confidence towards the end of Locke's life. Locke's explicit point is that these truths have to be available to simple people with no time for study. But on the route to this, he says that 'it should seem, by the little that has hitherto been done in it, that it is too hard a task for unassisted reason to establish morality in all its parts, upon its true foundation, in a clear and convincing light' [p. 139]. On the next page, he comments that 'it is plain, in fact, that human reason unassisted failed men in its great and proper business of morality'. Reason has failed. The power of reason unaided by revelation is insufficient. It is a little tragedy. The whole point of the reach to natural law, as we saw with Hobbes, Grotius, and Pufendorf, is to appeal to an independent arbiter, which holds true across the variations of custom that produce skepticism, and that, more particularly, works as a common standard in a confessionally fragmented Europe. This is meant to provide the true, absolute, standard by which the rights of taking land from native peoples in the Americas, or ships from the Portuguese in the Far East, can be determined; true for wildly varying cultures, true for both Protestants and Catholics, true for people who have no Bible, and true for people who cannot agree how to read the Bible. If, instead of this, we are told, as by the late Locke, that the way to discover the natural law is to read the Bible, then we are back to the original problem. Why should what we discover in this way hold good against people who have no Bible? Why should we do any better in the future than we have done so far in discovering what to do, even if we do read the Bible?

The Law Maker

When Locke was nearly seventeen (and after Hobbes had made good his escape to Paris), his king was executed by a sort of judicial process. The charge against him was treason to his country, even though one

of his country's laws was that the king could do no wrong. These un-
precedented events produced a rich flock of pamphlet literature as
well as a multiplication of sects. The pamphlets cited the Bible. The
sects disagreed. The Bible says that the powers that be should be obeyed
and that complete obedience is required to all authorities. The Bible
says that God should be obeyed rather than man. When Adam delved
and Eve span, who was then the gentleman?, they asked. The most
radical and the most conservative views were all founded on the Bible.
All the old stuff, as we have seen. Also, as we saw, Hobbes joined in
saying that preachers who preached sedition were not to be believed.
The Bible won't work as a base, and Locke, like Hobbes, particularly
wants to limit the power of the religious professionals to law down law
for others; this is part of the point for both of them of limiting the
certain content of Christianity to a single, minimal, claim. Therefore,
no Bible. Or so it would (have to) seem. However, not only does the
late Locke resign himself to the Bible for milkmaids and others; I shall
now show why, in terms of his own central presuppositions, he has to
use it.

Let us go back to definitions of words. In a draft called 'Ethics in
General', which he had originally designed for the *Essay*, Locke writes
that the scholastic and classical moral philosophy comes out as a series
of definitions, merely telling us what to call things. All that happens
is that we are taught 'to speak properly according to the fashion of
the country we are in' [PE p. 300]. Instead of this, what is needed are
laws that really obligate. We don't need definitions; we may not need
deductions. What we need is the power to create obligations. The
moral law is a real, obliging, law for Locke because it has a law-maker.
We now get to the key (and, again, it is not one that distinguishes
Locke from Hobbes). Real laws need real law-makers. This is constantly asserted by Locke, both in his early and his late work. Laws need
law-makers, and for the law of nature the law-maker is God.

We saw something similar in Pufendorf, when the imputed nature
of moral properties needs imputation by someone, which, for the law
of nature, turns out to be God. However, in Locke, the role of God
does not depend upon the metaphysical nature of law but rather on
the need for punishment. This is the other, vital, part of the account. A
law for Looke has no point without sanctions. As he puts it in the *Essay*,
'what duty is cannot be understood without a law; nor a law be known,

or supposed without a law-maker, or without reward and punishment' [1.3.12]. Here we get the complete package: for duty (obligation), we need law; for law we need law-makers; and why laws need law-makers is that someone is needed to punish in cases of breach.

With this we get away from mere definitions. For as Locke puts it in the 'Ethics in General' note, 'that is morally good or evil which, by the intervention of the will of an intelligent free agent, draws pleasure and pain after it, not by any natural consequence, but by the intervention of that power' [PE 301]. In other words, just as something may be naturally evil by causing pain, it becomes morally evil when someone like God who has the power to do so threatens its performance with pains. No sanctions, no law; no law-giver, no law; the law of nature is the positive commands of God. Incidentally, this also solves the problem of correct definition of terms and hence knowledge of what Locke calls 'mixed modes'. For law-makers can fully define, and hence know, their own laws. So the problem for us boils down to knowing what God has willed.

In taking this route, Locke has incorporated a psychology whereby people are motivated by the desire to avoid pain and seek pleasure. This also is constant throughout Locke's writings, which on several occasions deploy the whole psychological hedonist kit. For example, he says in a long 1676 note on pains and pleasures that pleasure and pain 'are the two roots out of which all passions spring' [PE 238]. In a note written a little later on 'morality', Locke starts by saying 'morality is the rule of man's actions for the attaining happiness' [PE 267], which he then defines as consisting in pleasure and pain. Here he propounds two axioms, that 'all men desire the enjoyment of happiness', and that 'men act only for what they desire'. So happiness explains action, and laws are explained if it is shown how keeping the law leads to happiness.

So although the central framework of Locke's thought, being based on a real law of nature, looks very unlike Hobbes's, nevertheless in both of them psychological hedonism explains. Both hold human beings to be creatures who seek happiness and avoid pain. People for both are rational in the sense of being interest maximisers. The difference is that Locke thinks that he can bring God into the equation and allow us sufficient knowledge of God to know which actions God punishes. The immortal god (that is, God himself) acts as a law-maker as well as Hobbes's 'mortal god' (that is, Leviathan). Hell fire is superior to the punishments of mere terrestrial magistrates. Or, at least, it would be superior if only we knew what we had to do to avoid it and if only we could keep it properly in our minds. This is the point of the Bible for the milkmaid and ploughman for Locke: reading it we discover what we should do and also the point of doing it.

In one of his rare references to Hobbes, Locke gives three different accounts in the *Essay* of why people should keep their agreements. The 'old heathen philosophers', he says, would have said that 'it was dishonest, below the dignity of man to do otherwise'. However, as we have seen, this is what Locke takes to be a merely definitional route. This is just how we happen to use words like 'honesty' and 'dignity'. Before this, Locke mentions the 'Hobbist'. He, says Locke, will 'answer: because the public requires it and the *Leviathan* will punish you if you do not'. The first account Locke describes is the 'Christian' who says that 'God, who has the power of eternal life and death, requires it of us' [1.3.5]. So far, this may seem like a stand-off, explaining, as he puts it in the next section, 'the great variety of opinions, concerning moral rules'. However, after noting the variety, Locke himself comes down firmly on the truth of the Christian view. 'The true ground of morality', he says 'can only be the will and law of a God, who sees men in the dark, has in his hand rewards and punishments, and power enough to call to account the proudest offender'. So the Divine avenger again does the trick. And although Locke also thinks that it can be proved a priori by pure reason alone that God exists (and gives a proof in the *Essay*), this proof (of the first-cause kind) will not show God to be a punisher, let alone what he will punish. So, back with the milkmaids to the Bible.

It may have been noticed that Locke said the Hobbist did not only have Leviathan to rely on (a mere mortal god, an inferior punisher who cannot see in the dark) but also what the 'public' required. This reminds us that Locke himself has in fact another way out. As was observed in the last chapter, just as Pufendorf, Locke thinks that the 'executive power' of the law of nature exists in the state of nature. There is a natural right to punish, independently of state or government, and since in those conditions there is no one special to have it, it is a right that there everyone has. So as well as the punishments by God and Leviathan, we can add the punishments imposed by ordinary people.

Most of Locke's chapter about the state of nature in the *Second Treatise* is in fact about such punishment. People who break the law of nature, says Locke, declare themselves to live by another law. Hence they can be treated like noxious beasts, 'destroyed as a lion or a tiger' (Sec. 11), and so on. Locke mixes a powerful cocktail of different theories of punishment. In Section 8 alone, he mentions 'retribute', 'reparation', 'restraint', 'deter him, and by his example others', certainly sufficient to lay waste offenders and uphold the law of nature, certainly sufficient punishing power. It seems therefore as if we do not need to wait for the official hell; we can produce our own hell here on earth. However, this returns us to the problem of knowledge of the moral law. We have the force of sanctions without God, but we have also to know that these sanctions are enforcing the right thing.

We could, of course, attempt to be purely positivist about the idea of a right thing. What is right is just what the person with punishing power wills. God's will makes the law of nature (he might have willed us to murder each other but, as it happens, he didn't). Our own arbitrary wills make the rest of the law. What is right is merely what in fact we choose to punish. However, on this route, what is right again varies for us and the Chinese, and there is no way in which we can reach standards that we are entitled to enforce universally, or in the so-called state of nature. Our sanctions may be powerful, but they will not uphold a natural law that does the job wanted by Grotius, Pufendorf, or Locke.

The Content of the Law

In any case, this is not actually the tack that Locke himself takes. His law may depend upon a law-making punisher, but he is not purely voluntarist about its content. To discover this content, we do not have just to wait for the hidden and terrible commands of God, gleaned at night from our Bibles. The light of nature (the 'candle of the Lord') may not produce much comfort in the *Essay*, but if we turn to the *Two Treatises*, we find that Locke does actually manage to deduce quite a lot of the content of the law of nature. The first hint about how to do it in fact comes in the *Essay* when he talks about the deducibility of the moral law. He talks there of 'the idea of a supreme being, infinite in power, goodness, and wisdom, whose workmanship we are' [4.3.18]. We need this idea, the idea of God, to deduce the law. But this is not because God orders us. Rather the key idea is that God creates us. We are his creatures. We are his 'workmanship'. As Locke puts it in the *Second Treatise*, we are 'the workmanship of one omnipotent, and infinitely wise maker'. Hence we are his 'servants', his 'property' [Sec. 6]. It follows directly from this, thinks Locke, that 'everyone is *bound to preserve himself*' and also 'as much as he can, *to preserve the rest of mankind*'. So the central point of the law of nature is preservation, preservation of ourselves and others, and the central reason for this is that we are God's property. We are not our own to destroy; if we destroy others then we are laying waste the property of God. So here we have a clear content, discoverable by reason, or at least discoverable on two assumptions. The first is that we are all created by God. The second is that creators have property rights in their creations.

If we can assume these (and property will be looked at later), then we can start deducing a content to the natural law. Take, for example, the obligation to bring up one's children. Parents, for Locke, are under 'an obligation to preserve, nourish, and educate the children . . . not as their own workmanship but as the workmanship of their own maker' (Sec. 56). Here we have a quite specific, and familiar, obligation, but in Locke it is drawn from God as creator. Furthermore, he wants it that it is really God who creates the child, not the parents. 'What father of a thousand when he begets a child', asks Locke, 'thinks farther than the satisfying his present appetite?' (*First Treatise*, Sec. 54). Fathers are not creating children; they are having a good time. (What mothers do is not here recorded.) Since fathers do not create children, they do not have creator's rights. Hence Locke blocks Filmer's argument that children are subservient to their parents because they are made by them.

Another example is slavery. For Locke, I cannot contract to enslave myself. 'For man', as he puts it 'not having the power of his own life, cannot, by compact, or his own consent, *enslave himself* to anyone' (Sec. 23). This is from the chapter on slavery, Chapter 4. The same points apply to suicide. Because we are made by God, not ourselves, we are the property of God, and cannot be destroyed without God's permission. Everyone, according to Locke, is 'bound to preserve himself and not to quit his station wilfully' [Sec. 6]. Hence, and now comes the political payoff, we cannot put ourselves into the arbitrary power of another, to be destroyed at someone else's will or whim. For this is not a power we have over ourselves, and, as Locke puts it, 'no body can give more power than he has himself' (Sec. 23). According to Locke, this prevents people from contracting themselves into absolute government. For that would be to give these others a power of absolute life and death over them. But this is a power they do not possess over themselves; hence they cannot transfer it to another. This blocks the Grotian arguments designed to get from original contract to absolute government. We saw that Filmer objects that even if it were possible, Grotius can't show that it actually happened. Locke objects that it could not have happened because it is not even possible. We cannot transfer what we do not have.

So we get, after all, a considerable content to natural law, and we will see in the next two chapters how this works out in detail. However, we can already see that we here have clearly different results from the earlier uses we looked at of the device of a social contract. These different results depend upon the specific content of Locke's natural law. In particular, they depend upon his assumption that we are all created by God. This raises the question of how much of this content would need to be changed if God were left out. There are many modern admirers of Locke, particular of his account of property. Yet this account, as we shall see, depends on our being here to serve God's purposes. However, these modern admirers of Locke do not normally have Locke's presuppositions about God.

In fact, denying the position of God changes the whole of the theory. First, it changes epistemologically. I have wallowed in Locke's problems. He has not given himself an epistemologically easy life. We are supposed to be able to deduce like Euclid, yet the moral Euclid never appears. Instead, we get Jesus Christ. We seem to have a retreat, a 'failure' at the end, even though in this very work (the *Reasonableness*) Locke himself also recognises that unless the moral law is knowable by reason, this is unfair on the heathen. So, even with God, things are epistemologically hard. However, without God they are even harder. Or even if they are not harder, they are certainly very different. Locke, as we have seen, manages to use God to get some content into the natural law. It also allows him varying suppositions about how we can know it. With no God, even this somewhat precarious route to knowledge is blocked. Also, relatedly, Locke's account explains both the universal objective truth of the law of nature and also why it is a law rather than mere advice. It explains why people may be punished for disregarding it. Without God, we need another explanation of how it can be supposed that there are natural rights whose truth is independent of us and that also place real obligations on us.

Furthermore, in Locke, the relationship between right and duty is different from his modern admirers. In modern thought, it is frequently supposed that rights are the ultimate basis, and that duties can then be explained in terms of them. However, Locke instead starts with duty. He starts with God's creation and God's purposes. As God's creatures, God has a purpose for us, as for all of his creatures. This purpose imposes duties on us. We have a duty to preserve God's creatures, including ourselves, as much as we possibly can. Locke also thinks that we have a duty to labour and to increase value. We have a duty not to waste or let things spoil. From these duties, rights follow: we have a right to things that are necessary for the performance of our duties. Duties imposed on some people will also give others rights as the benefit of our duties. Rights follow, but the point is that they follow. The account has a quite different logical shape from one that starts with the rights.

It might be objected that rights and duties are correlative in all accounts, that we therefore have both wherever we start, and that the start does not therefore matter. We have duties in modern accounts. We have the duty not to harm others, not to interfere with their rights. So it might be argued that, past or present, we may if we wish start with the duties. Alternatively, it might be objected that we could just start with the rights that Locke reaches while eluding the provenance he gives them. However, either way, the resulting patchwork would not make sense without Locke's purpose. Take, for example, suicide or contracting oneself voluntary to slavery. We have seen why Locke, starting from a duty to God to preserve ourselves, forbids these. However, these restrictions are not obvious or plausible if we just start with rights, or if we just start from a duty not to harm others. This is even more obvious if, with many moderns, we think of rights as fundamental areas of personal control rather than, as in Locke, things that we are permitted to do in order to fulfil our duties. For if we suppose that the fundamental right is that we have full control over ourselves (as long as we do not harm others), then it seems that we should have the right to kill or enslave ourselves. This, for example, is claimed by

Robert Nozick in his book *Anarchy, State and Utopia*, a book that starts with rights but also attempts to follow many of the contours of Locke's account.

This is what happens when we start with bare rights and Locke's own purposes are left out. Alternatively, we might try to keep the purposes but lose God. We might, that is, try to naturalise the purpose, supposing that nature itself has a purpose rather than one imposed on it externally by God. We might, for example, suppose that everything (or at least everything organic) has the natural purpose of survival. Everything organic naturally aims to preserve itself. However, this would not produce the same content as we get in Locke. For much of the content of Locke's natural law depends upon our being responsible for the survival not just of ourselves but also of others. In this way, he captures that important and traditional part of the law of nature (as in Grotius and Pufendorf) that others should not be harmed.

Alternatively, we might say that the natural purpose is not that everything (organic) should preserve itself but, rather, that it should be preserved. Everything is under an obligation to preserve everything. This sounds more like Locke, even if harder to naturalise convincingly. However, again, we will not reach the same content as in Locke himself. Here we run into the converse difficulty. If the natural purpose of the organism is to preserve itself, this won't explain why it should also preserve others. If, alternatively, its natural purpose is to preserve everything, this won't explain what happens when we get conflicts. Not every organic thing can be preserved. Here, Locke's God provides some answers. Inferior species are (on Biblical evidence) granted to human beings to be used for human purposes. So, with a conflict between person and germ, the germ has got to go. Also the cow that becomes human food. God's purposes for the world are human purposes. Humans rightfully exploit the natural world for their own purposes. Of course, on a green philosophy, it is just this to which objection might be taken. However, this only illustrates that the same rights doing the same job cannot be captured if we leave God out of Locke's account. God makes a difference in Locke, and the law of Locke is ancient lore.

7

Disobedient Locke

First, natural law, state of nature, the objective, correct, moral law governing all things and all peoples. Then, government, political societies, particular authorities that can create positive law. Starting with one, we are meant to reach the other. Whether we do, and how we do, depends, of course, on our understanding of both natural law and government. We have seen the somewhat uncertain basis Locke gives himself in natural law. Now we have to see what he can erect on this by way of government. We have to examine how or whether he can use the law that he has propounded in order to provide a legitimate basis for states, governments, political authorities.

This is one problem, the problem of political obligation. In fact, Locke has a double problem. As well as the problem of obedience, he also has the problem of disobedience. Both have to be justified. Yet the two problems are not only contrasting but also potentially conflicting. The general structure of the answer to the first problem – the problem of why we should obey – is to make use of the idea of a social contract or agreement. As with the earlier users of this device we have examined, the answer to why we are subject to government is that we subject ourselves. By consent or agreement, we construct a political society and bind ourselves to obey its government.

However, this is only the first of Locke's problems. This much is roughly similar to Hobbes (and Grotius and Pufendorf). For them, as we have seen, the result of subjecting ourselves is liable to be absolute government. We create a terrifying Leviathan we cannot subsequently avoid. However, as we also noted, Locke's overall project is in fact the converse of Hobbes's project. Hobbes wants to show why we have to obey. Locke also wants this, but he wants as well to show why and when we have to disobey. Leviathan is to be controlled; these natural law and social contract materials have also to provide an argument for the limits of government. Yet an argument that successfully grounds obedience may find disobedience difficult, while one that secures disobedience may find obedience a problem.

Locke therefore has to produce an account of political obligation that also displays its limits. In doing so, he has to show why people would ever want to subject themselves to political authority, what counts as such subjection, and what the limits of such subjection are. Obviously, in terms of what counts as subjection, he wishes to use the idea of contract – that is of an act of subjection. However, we have to look at what counts as such an act, and whether or how it exists in the modern state. As we saw in the last chapter, justification by contract is justification by particular historical facts, and so precisely what is justified by such facts or acts depends upon the precise nature of the facts or acts themselves. This is difficult enough, but it is still not the whole of the problem. An act of subjection cannot be the end as well as the beginning of the matter. Somewhere, Locke also has to find a way out – that is, an explanation of where subjection ends. For this, we need to understand what is implied by subjection, what sorts of subjection are possible. There are not only acts but also meanings. There is not only what people have done but also whether they were entitled to try. Again, this involves examining the point, nature, and conditions of the original subjection.

Consent

Consent is obviously central, and so it is with consent we start. 'When any number of men have so consented to make one community or government', says Locke, 'they are thereby presently incorporated and make one body politic' [*Second Treatise*, Sec. 95]. 'Presently' here means immediately. The act of consent in itself constructs a single corporation or political body. 'For', as Locke goes on, 'when any number of men have, by the consent of every individual, made a community, they have thereby made that community one body with a power to act as one body'. So, just as with Hobbes, we get here a unified, artificial, entity created by agreement. Notice that it has to be the agreement of every single person. So for each particular person, unless he or she individually agrees they are not bound to this body. 'And thus', Locke concludes, 'every man by consenting with others to make one body politic under one government puts himself under an obligation' [Sec. 97]. So here is the obligation, which, as before, is constructed by consent.

When making these remarks, Locke also says that each person has also consented to the idea that the decisions of this political society should be made by majority of its members. For him, what the majority decides has to be taken as the decision of the whole body. Otherwise the body would not be able to make any decisions unless all were unanimous, which, as Locke says, 'is next impossible ever to be had' [Sec. 98]. So there are actually two stages in the account, one in which unanimous consent is required and one not. To construct the political society in the first place, we need unanimous consent. No one can be bound to a society to which they did not individually consent. However, once we have the society to which the individual has consented, its decisions can then be decided by the majority. At the second stage, you can be bound by decisions to which you did not yourself agree, but this is only because you did agree to be bound to a society in which that was the inevitable decision procedure. Or, to put it another way, there is unanimous consent to be bound by majority decision.

This, if Locke is right, is only one of the hidden meanings or implications of consent. Others will follow. However, let us start with the consent itself, which Locke proposes as a necessary condition of legitimate government. 'The consent of any number of freemen', he says, 'is that, and that only, which did, or could give beginning to any lawful government in the world' [Sec. 99]. So it is clear that for Locke, no one can be 'subjected to the political power of another without his own consent' [Sec. 95]. However, the first problem is where this leaves us with respect to the natural law. We saw in the last chapter that for Locke, this is a law, but also that for him there is only a law if there is a law-maker. So far, so good. The maker of the natural law is God. Now, we are subject to the natural law (or to God, its law-maker). We have to do what it (or he) says, and we are rightfully subject to punishment if we don't. So we are subject. But did we subject ourselves? Or is God's government not legitimate? It existed before we were born, and is true whether we like it or not. We seem to have here in Locke a case of legitimate subjection, by birth and independent of our consent.

One way to meet this problem would be to understand Locke as limiting his remarks to government on earth. Different rules apply for God and heaven. However, if God's creation of us is taken to give him legitimate authority over us, from birth and independently of our consent, then Locke needs to be careful how he resists Filmer's claim that parents have political authority over their children. As we saw, he does this by denying that parents create children. However, he would be more secure in resisting this and other arguments aligning political and filial obligation (such as that in both cases we have benefited from care and support) if he could maintain his claim that legitimate government always depends upon mature consent. Yet, since this is a universal claim, it should work for divine as well as merely terrestrial government.

The alternative way to resist the problem would be to claim that God does not have political authority, and so although the law of nature comes from a divine law-maker, this should not be thought of as divine government. In fact, at least in the *Reasonableness of Christianity*, Locke may just have enough wriggle room for this. Here he talks both about God's natural law, true at all times and places, and also the kingdom of Christ. This kingdom, admittedly a kingdom more prominent for Locke than it is for us, is also one in which we become subjects by subjecting ourselves. Faith for Locke is the acceptance of the kingdom of Christ. Locke says here that the point of Christ's coming 'was to be a king, and, as such, to be received by those who would be his subjects' [p. 113].

The old problem of God and the natural law is whether it is true because of its content or because of its source. Does God will it because it is good, or is it good because God wills it? Locke, like Pufendorf, takes a middle position. It is true because its content follows from the eternal nature of God, but God's will gives it its power. What does revelation add to this? Well, if by faith we accept Christ, then we accept him as a law-maker. He reveals to us a law, which we are then commanded to follow. We believe this is the right thing to do, not because it seems right to us in its content (we have failed to find the right content by our unaided reason) but rather because we accept him as a God and

ruler of a divine kingdom. In fact, for Locke, what Christ commands
is the same as the natural law, which we could reach by our unaided
reason. But this is not why we accept it. So here is the difference between the Christians and the heathen: same law, different grounds for
acceptance.

This makes the rule of Christ political. As we have seen, the char-
acteristic of political authority is that things are accepted because of
their source rather than their content. If we are politically obliged,
then we are obliged to do whatever the authority says, independently
of its content. The source is sufficient. So Locke's claim could be put in
general terms as that whenever I have a reason for action that derives
from a source, this is because I have already chosen or consented to
subject myself to this source. I have many reasons for action. Sometimes actions are good for me; sometimes actions are the right thing
to do (the eternal, immutable, natural law). However, as well as these,
I sometimes have the reason that I am commanded by political authority. This command will only provide a reason if the authority is
legitimate, and for Locke it is only legitimate if I have consented to it.
This is true for him for all kingdoms on earth, but may also be true of
the kingdom of Christ. It legitimately provides me with reasons only if
I accept, by faith, Christ as a law-maker.

The Need for Government

So that is how we get ourselves obliged (or, at least, how we get obliged
to earthly authorities). The next question is why anyone would wish
to do this. And here also Locke has a clear and repeated answer. It
is to protect our property. As he puts it, someone 'seeks out, and is
willing to join in society with others who are already united, or have
a mind to unite for the mutual preservation of their lives, liberties
and estates, which I call by the general name *property*' [Sec. 123]. Or,
more succinctly, 'the chief and great end therefore of men's uniting
into commonwealths and putting themselves under government is the
preservation of their property' [Sec. 124]. It is clear from the first
of these remarks that Locke, at least sometimes, uses 'property' in
a rather wider sense than the standard one. However, the point for
him, unlike some other political philosophers, cannot be that we need
government in order to have property at all (in either the wider or

the more standard sense). This is a reason for Hobbes, who thinks that since there are no real rights without government, there are no property rights and hence no property. The same is true later for Bentham, on the same basis. However, Locke thinks that there are natural rights, independent and antecedent to government. Among these are property rights. So Locke, having a natural right to property, does not need government in order to give us property. The claim is not that without government we would have no property but rather that we need government to 'preserve' it.

In fact, if we remember Locke's state of nature, as briefly described in the last chapter, it becomes a serious question (which Locke asks himself) why people should wish to leave it and subject themselves to government. It is not to get rights or property. Also, as we have seen, among the rights we have without a state is the right to punish. So we don't need government to enforce our rights or render them secure. Furthermore, Locke distinguishes the state of nature from the state of war. So his state of nature is not necessarily one of continually unpleasant, Hobbesian, warfare.

So when Locke starts Chapter II of the *Second Treatise* with the question, 'if man in the state of nature be so free as has been said … why will he part with his freedom?' (Sec. 123), this is a real and important question for him. Even if, unlike Hobbes, it is not to get his rights, Locke might nevertheless suggest that life without government has a nasty tendency to be both brutish and short. It is true that Locke does here talk of 'inconveniences' in the state of nature whereby people 'are quickly driven' into political society (Sec. 127). But this is not just general inconvenience, or Hobbesian discomfort. Rather, Locke has here a quite specific and interesting account of the inconvenience of even his un-Hobbesian state of nature. In this account, Locke makes three claims as to why government is to be preferred to the state of nature – that is, three reasons for consenting to government. The first is that the state of nature lacks 'an established, settled, known, law' (Sec. 124). This takes us back to the problem, much discussed in the last chapter, of the knowability of the law of nature. If it can be known, then the state of nature is not defective in this way. However, perhaps it cannot. Locke wavers on knowability. In Chapter 2 of the *Second Treatise*, the state of nature chapter, he bravely declares of the law of nature 'that it is certain there is such a law, and that too as intelligible and plain to a rational creature and a studier of that law as the positive laws of commonwealths, nay possibly plainer' [Sec. 12]. There are conditions: a creature has to be rational and also has to study it. Nevertheless, Locke does here explicitly claim that (under these conditions) the law of nature is at least as clear and intelligible as the positive laws of particular countries. If this is so, we will not improve the problem of knowledge by getting into government and so gaining such positive laws.

Yet, in the chapter we are presently considering (Chapter 9), Locke seems to make the converse claim, saying that in the state of nature, we 'lack a common measure to decide all controversies'. This latter claim also seems to be the more plausible one. With a particular commonwealth (state), we get an agreed source of law, (normally) an agreed written code that can be consulted, and an agreed adjudication procedure for handling problematic cases. However, the question is not just whether positive, state, law is more obvious than natural law. For Locke thinks that 'the obligations of the law of nature cease not in society' [Sec. 135]. He talks of the 'municipal laws of countries, which are only so far right as they are founded on the law of nature, by which they are to be regulated and interpreted' [Sec. 12]. In other words, natural law binds positive law. So, however clear a particular positive law seems to be, our duty will not be 'plain' unless we can also clearly see that it is not in conflict with natural law, and for this natural law also has to be clear. So if the right thing to do is more 'plain' with government, this cannot be for Locke because government clarifies natural law for us. Locke thinks that there is a natural law that we can know. So the point for him about government and knowledge of the law cannot be, as it is in Hobbes, that there is no way in which we can know God's law, and that we only reach knowledge with human commands. It therefore remains an open question as to whether more knowledge is available with states and governments. There is more clarity about what the law is, but there may be equal uncertainty about whether this law properly promulgates the law of nature, and if it does not, its greater clarity is pointless.

Locke, however, adds a specific reason why people are not good at knowing the law of nature. He first mentions this in the second, state of nature, chapter, and it also occurs in one of the passages of Hooker that he quotes. He repeats it here. It is that people have interests that bias their thoughts. He says that 'though the law of nature be plain and intelligible to all rational creatures, yet men being biased by their interest, as well as ignorant for want of study of it, are not apt to allow of it as a law binding to them in the application of it to their particular cases' [Sec. 124]. Here again, he mentions lack of study, but it is interest that is the real killer to the possibility of knowledge. It is another scene in the continuing Lockean tragedy: another example of the constant affirmation of how the law can be known by reason alone to everyone, balanced with an explanation why, as a matter of fact, this possibility is not realised. People could know, but in fact they do not know. Being interested, biased, creatures they are not competent judges in cases that particularly affect them. Whenever they think that they have dealt with unjustly by others, they will not judge correctly.

This runs into the second problem about the state of nature that Locke puts in this chapter. He says that it lacks 'a known and indifferent judge' – that is, one who is impartial between parties. In the state of nature, everyone is, as he puts it, 'both judge and executioner' of the law, so people act as judges in their own cases. Yet to judge in your own case is something standardly taken to be against natural justice. We might put the point as that although there are right answers in the state of nature, it lacks a proper procedure for reaching them. It lacks due process, or procedural natural justice. This is another version of the point that interest biases outcome. People with an interest should not be the judges of the outcome.

According to Locke, 'known and indifferent' judges only come with states. However, again, there seems to be a bit of a shuffle here about the importance of God. After all, the law of nature is supposed by Locke to come from God, and so God sits as a judge over the state of nature. Yet God is a known and indifferent judge. So it would seem that Locke does not need the state in order to acquire a known and indifferent judge. He has God. Presumably the reason that this is not good enough for him is the same as the reason that God's execution of the law of nature is not good enough for him. As we saw, Locke thinks that terrestrial punishment has to be added to divine punishment if the law of nature is to be effective. So here the claim presumably is that without the state, this terrestrial punishment will not be administered by a known and indifferent judge.

States can certainly provide such impartial judges. However, having a state is neither necessary nor sufficient for their terrestrial provision.

Independent arbitrators may be employed by disagreeing parties without having or resorting to states. This can be seen from the relations between independent, sovereign states themselves. These were standardly taken at the time (for example, by both Hobbes and Locke) to be an example of relations between parties in a state of nature. Yet states do not necessarily lack impartial arbitration of their disputes. Even though in the state of nature (or, at least, in a condition analogous to it), they can appeal to third parties or to mutually agreed arbitrators. If states can do this, so may private persons.

Even ignoring God, therefore, it is not necessary to have political society in order to gain what Locke calls a 'known and indifferent' judge. Nor is it sufficient. We may have people incorporated in a political society and yet have a judicial or punishing system that is anything but impartial. It may, for example, favour the groups that happen to have political power, such as members of particular classes or races. So, even if we have government, the argument has to go on. The impartial administration of justice is an obvious advantage. It may be a reason for having states. However, insofar as it is a reason, it is also a reason for having particular kinds of states. Again, in effect, this is part of Locke's hidden message of consent. We will be deemed only to have consented to states that provide this. We wish to be impartially ruled according to known law; for Locke, this rules out rule by an absolute king on the basis that we have not consented to arbitrary rule.

Locke puts his points about impartiality more precisely in terms of achieving the just quantity of punishment for offences. He claims that everyone in the state of nature, 'being both judge and executioner of the law of nature, men being partial to themselves, passion and revenge is very apt to carry them too far, and with too much heat, in their own cases; as well as negligence and unconcernedness to make them too remiss in other men's' [Sec. 125]. So, again, passion and self-interest leads us astray. We are too hot in our own causes. When our interests are attacked, we over-punish in reply. Alternatively, when we are not involved ourselves, we are liable to be negligent. It might have seemed a good idea to back up the sanctions of God by placing the 'executive power' of the law of nature in everyone. However, the trouble with this is that it is liable to lead to either over-supply or else under-supply of punishment. When we are personally involved, we are liable to be partial, and we get over-supply. Alternatively, if we are not involved, we are liable to be negligent, and we get under supply.

This possibility of under-supply is an application of public goods problems to the case of punishment. We all benefit, we may suppose, from the proper provision of punishment. Yet in cases where we are not personally involved, it can seen that we are putting more effort into the provision of this good than we are getting out of it. So the cases in which we would achieve impartial justice in the state of nature – that is, the cases where people disinterestedly take it upon themselves to punish on behalf of third parties – are precisely the cases in which this impartial justice may well not be provided. For disinterested punishers are liable also to be uninterested ones. It is in no one's particular interest to provide the public good of the right levels of punishment, and hence it is not provided. In the state of nature, relying on the uncoordinated actions of independent people, we get under-supply. The answer, as with similar public goods problems, is to have a state that not only co-ordinates actions but also provides officials – that is, provides people who, being paid to do the job, have an interest in the disinterested provision of justice.

Locke's third and last reason for having a state in Chapter II is that 'in the state of nature there often wants power to back and support the sentence when right and to give it due execution' [Sec. 126]. But this again depends upon how serious we take the public goods problem to be. As long as the individual punishing power of people can be co-ordinated and applied, there is certainly power enough. A mob engaged in lynch law may fall foul of Locke's second supposed problem, about whether they are sufficiently impartial to be just. They do not, however, fall foul of Locke's third supposed problem, about lack of power. Individuals in a state of nature, acting together but not under common authority, have sufficient power to retribute or deter. A mob bent on vengeance is quite terrifying enough without its powers being monopolised in, or organised by, a state. Conversely, a state that has not solved the knack of getting people to do what it wants may lack adequate punishing power.

Sometimes there is a lack of power. In particular, weak people who lack the power to punish their injuries by themselves are not likely to be helped by others. However, the general problem is not lack of power but its correct direction and application. Here we do get reasons, based on justice, for having states. People and property are to be preserved. Such is the requirement of the natural law. So we want a situation in which this law is properly respected and enforced – that is we want a just situation. Locke's argument is that we are more likely to be in this situation if we are in a state (because of better knowledge, greater impartiality, and more power). Notice that the argument in Locke for the state is not a straightforward prudential one, as in Hobbes. It is not that life is too painful in the state of nature. It is, instead, an argument in terms of justice. With states we get more justice; we get better justice. It is a moral argument, an argument based on natural law. Even if it has a consequentialist flavour, the good being maximised is not pleasure and pain, but justice.

Social Contract

We now have a reason for having states. So we can return to the question of how, or when, these states oblige us. It might seem that we have also solved this – that reasons for having states are also automatically reasons why we are obliged. States are good for us; they give us more justice. Also, once these states exist, they assume that we are obliged. However, for Locke, neither of these is sufficient. For Locke, good reasons for having states do not give us the grounds of our obligation to them. For Locke, as we have seen, we are only obliged if we choose to make ourselves so. So we return to consent and the social contract – that is, to the only legitimate way for Locke in which states can be constructed or in which we can become a member of an already existent state. States are good for us, but this only obliges us if we choose to submit to them. That they are good gives us a reason for such submission, but unless we follow this reason and actually submit, we are not obliged. The advantages in justice that states provide flow from the monopoly of their punishing power. For Locke, this monopoly can only arise if each person alienates their natural right to punish, transferring it to society. This is what is signified by the social contract; it is to this that we consent.

Now, as we have seen, any such consent only obliges insofar as it is an actual historical event. Yet, surveying the current scene, we seem to see political obligation without any such events. We see people and governments and we see the people obeying the governments. But what we don't see are contracts being signed, or any other actions in which people are explicitly transferring their natural rights to punish to the state. Indeed, in the next century after Locke, David Hume wrote a brilliant essay called 'Of the original contract', in which he says that 'it is strange that an act of mind, which every individual is supposed to have formed, and after he came to the use of reason . . . should be so much unknown to all of them, that, over the face, of the whole earth, there scarcely remain any traces or memory of it' [*Essays* p. 470].

The central question, both when Locke wrote and also today, is the obligation of people, born into settled states, to the governments of these states. There may have been occasional situations or historically distant happenings in which states were created by agreement between independent adults. Locke provides empirical evidence for this, as also for the contemporary existence for collections of individuals still in the state of nature. However, all of this, true or false, is irrelevant to the actual obligation of nearly all current people to current governments. These people have been born into settled states. Whatever happened in the past, the contracts of the parents cannot bind their descendants. So if consent is the source of obligation, people must consent for themselves as adults, at an age of full rationality. These consents have to be actual, particular, historical facts, something that happens in the adult lifetime of each consenting person. In which case, as Hume says, it is surprising that so much consent has been forgotten.

Locke realises that he has to explain what 'shall be understood to be a sufficient declaration of a man's consent, to make him subject to the laws of any government', and here he distinguishes between 'an express and a tacit consent' [Sec. 119]. Perhaps we are on the wrong track by looking for explicit declarations of transfer of rights, all of which seem somehow mysteriously to have been forgotten. Such explicit declarations, if we could find them, would be 'express' declarations of consent. However, perhaps instead we should have been looking for 'tacit' consent. Tacit consent also has to be a particular historical act (or situation, or series of acts). Something has actually to have happened that is understood to imply tacit consent. However, what this is may be much more subtle than what is involved in explicit consent. We may all have been engaged in these tacitly consenting acts and yet have not been aware of them. Sometimes, for example, we may be deemed to have tacitly consented by what we did not do, rather than what we did. We saw earlier how Locke reads an agreement to majority decision-making into consent to political society. It is not explicit but it is implied; I am deemed to have tacitly consented to it. Similarly, other acts may be deemed to imply tacit consent to government. If this is so, I may not have mysteriously forgotten consenting, as Hume ironically suggests. Rather, it may be that at no time have I been aware that consenting was what I was doing. I thought that I was just minding my own business, or just doing something else, but it turns out that as well I was tacitly consenting to government.

The problem now therefore becomes which other such acts may be properly deemed to be such signs of tacit consent. The weakest sign would be that we don't actively protest. But if this were sufficient for tacit consent, political obligation would come rather easily. At any point I am not actively protesting, I would be deemed to have consented, and so held to be obliged. If this were enough, any would-be political authority would become legitimate whenever we do not have the energy or nerve to oppose it. Several different political authorities might all simultaneously lay claim to me. On this argument, if I don't object explicitly to any of them, then I am obliged to all of them. Obligation comes easily, but so also does disobedience. For, presumably, on the same basis, if I do object, then I am not obliged. So if I want to stop being obliged to a supposed political authority, I merely have to start objecting. Obligation here puffs round like a feather and has no greater value. The central problem of political obligation arises from the fact that if I really am obliged, then I am also obliged at the times when I wish to object and at the times when I am being asked to do things with which I do not agree. We therefore need a more substantial obligation than passive acceptance can provide. In any case, Locke himself distinguishes clearly between 'common practice' and 'common consent' in the *First Treatise* [Sec. 88]; merely going along with things is not sufficient sign of consent.

In the *Second Treatise*, Locke also uses and gives much more explicit signs of tacit consent than merely going along with things, or not objecting to them. In these examples, I am taken to consent tacitly to a political authority if I derive benefit from it. 'Every man that hath any possession of enjoyment or any part of the dominions of any government', he says, 'doth thereby give his tacit consent and is so far forth obliged to obedience to the laws of that government'. The chief example here is ownership of land in the area controlled by the government, but he also includes 'lodging only for a week' and 'travelling freely on the highway' [Sec. 119]. Receipt of benefits are often thought to put people under obligations. So, at least at first sight, it would seem to be the receipt of the benefit here that has created the obligation. I benefit from being able to travel freely on the highway. This highway has been constructed and maintained, otherwise I would not be able to use it at all. It is guarded so that I can travel on it in (relative) safety without fear of being stopped or robbed. This benefit has been derived by me from the work or expenditure of others, and so it is plausible to suppose that my taking the benefit puts me under obligations. Similarly I benefit from the government's protection of my land. So it might seem that the core argument here is one in which my receipt of benefits from a government puts me under an obligation. However, if this is the core argument, then the obligation is not created by consent.

In fact, Locke does not say enough here to place his account among more specific attempts to relate obligation to benefits, in particular the benefits derived from the existence of regular, rule governed, practices. However, he is right to think that the examples he does discuss relate to consent as well as to benefit. For in Locke's supposed tacit consent cases of enjoying land or the highway, we choose (or consent to) the enjoyment, and Locke thinks that the obligation only lasts as long as this chosen enjoyment. If, for example, I give up land in a country or cease to travel on its highways, then for Locke I am no longer obliged to that country. This means that I am only under the obligation if I choose to have land in that country or travel on its highways. Yet if choice is involved, so also is consent. In choosing to enter a country and travel on its highways, I may be deemed to have tacitly consented to obey the laws of that country until I choose to leave it. So it is not just the benefit that puts me under the obligation; it is that I have freely chosen to enjoy it.

This may work for visiting what we think of as other countries – that is, for example, travelling along the roads of a foreign country on holiday, or buying a holiday property abroad. Here it is plausible to suppose that if I do such things, I have thereby agreed to abide by at least as much of the laws of those countries that relate to roads and property. I may think that the laws are silly, but if France, say, has a national speed limit, I cannot reasonably object if I get fined by French political authorities for exceeding it. I did not have to go to, or drive in, France; if I choose to do so, I am then reasonably deemed to be subject to its speed limits, however silly I might find them.

However, even if we can make something of tacit consent with respect to such passing obligations, this is very different from the prime example of political obligation in which people are committed in a particular way to one country of which they are a subject or citizen. With this government, I am committed in a special way to obey, and this government may well be thought entitled to impose special burdens on me, such as requiring military or jury service, taxing me in special ways, and otherwise organising my life. Furthermore, Locke himself clearly wants this kind of particular obligation. For the question at which he is aiming in the *Second Treatise* is the point at which such special allegiance ends, and he therefore needs an account of when, if ever, rebellion is permitted with your own country, government, or political society. For this, an account of your obligation to obey the laws of foreign countries while travelling in their lands will not be sufficient.

Locke, that is, needs to discuss more than one kind of obligation. There is obligation to the laws of places we are passing through and there is obligation to our own government. These are different commitments, and hence need different bases. And, at least at first sight, this is just what Locke seems to have. For he has a clear distinction between two kinds of consent, and also holds that they lead to very different commitments. For tacit consent, we have seen that the obligation only lasts as long as the enjoyment. This fits foreign countries, and is very different for Locke from what I am committed to by express consent. Express consent binds someone for ever to a particular political community. It cannot be revoked. As Locke puts it, 'he that has once by actual agreement and any express declaration given his consent to be of any commonweal is perpetually and indispensably obliged to be and remain unalterably a subject to it' [Sec. 121]. As we saw, for Locke I am not a citizen of any particular country by birth. However, if when I come of age, I declare myself, say, to be English, then I cannot subsequently decide that I'd prefer to be American or French. I have done it as irrevocably as if I'd sold myself into slavery.

So we have two kinds of consent with two quite different kinds of consequences. If I am just enjoying or travelling, any transfer of a right to punish that this implies is strictly temporary. I can elude any obligation by selling up and leaving. Compared with this is the once-and-for all transfer of rights achieved by explicit declaration, after which I can never regain the state of nature. We have two sorts of consent and two sorts of consequences. So far, so good. However, the trouble is that the combination will not do the work that Locke wants. We can get evidence of tacit consent, but it does not create the strong sort of obligation in which Locke is particularly interested. Express consent would create this strong sort of obligation, but it is something for which we do not seem to be able to find evidence. As Hume suggests, it is something that does not (normally) happen. All that is left therefore is countries that we are merely passing through, which would make the problems of rebellion rather too easy (as easy as coming home from holiday).

Oaths of Allegiance

This objection depends upon following Hume's claim that explicit consent is something that rarely seems to happen, and discovering that the attempt to elude the claim by switching to tacit consent will not produce enough. However, perhaps this is too fast. Perhaps we should not have accepted the force of Hume's objection. We may not swear an explicit once-and-for all oath of allegiance to particular governments when we come of age (repeated performances with a national flag by school children are something different). However, if we go back to Locke's world, we find that in fact it was a world of oaths. Among these were oaths of allegiance – that is, explicit agreements to obey the government. Both Grotius and Pufendorf discuss oaths. Contract, agreement, is important to all of these thinkers, but oaths are special. They are agreements before God. With oaths, people pledge their faith in a way that explicitly invokes the possibility of divine sanctions if they defect. This is why atheists do not get the benefit of toleration on Locke's proposals. Anyone who does not believe in God cannot usefully be put to an oath, and hence for Locke cannot be a reliable member of civil society. Of course, the validity of this, just like other parts of

Locke's God-backed natural law, depends upon people's apprehension of the consequences. If no one believes in God then oaths are no more special than any other kind of agreement.

This is one problem with oaths. Another can be seen if we look at the oaths actually used in Locke's day. At the beginning of the century, after the Roman Catholic attempt to blow up king and parliament known as the Gunpowder Plot, the government came up with an oath. This could be administered to anyone in the country over eighteen who missed a certain number of church services – that is, it was designed to test the loyalty of Catholics (and led to an exchange of arguments about political authority between King James I and Catholic writers). The person taking the oath declared in his 'conscience before God and the world, that our sovereign Lord King James is lawful and rightful king of this realm'; that he will 'bear faith and true allegiance'; that he will make known any conspiracies; and so on.

This, no doubt, is all to be expected. But then, even on the face of the document, the problems start. This long oath ends with the declaration that it is sworn 'without any equivocation or mental evasion or secret reservation whatsoever'. But this threatens an infinite regress. If, when I am swearing, I can make a mental reservation about what I am saying, then I can make a mental reservation when I say that I am making no mental reservations. In other words, just as in other contractual situations, the obligation has to come from the supposed meaning of the performance, from these words in this context. The oath does not work like a magic potion: if it commits, it depends upon the assumption that oath-takers are rightly committed to what they are commonly supposed to be committed to by such performances.

More, then, than the oath is needed. This, however, is only the start. There is a worse problem with the position of the head of the Roman Catholic Church on earth, the Pope. Obviously, given the oath's aim, it has to deny that the Pope has any power, either directly or indirectly, to depose the king. So the luckless oath-taker was required to swear 'that I do from my heart abhor, detest, and abjure, as impious and heretical, this damnable doctrine and position, that princes which be excommunicated or deprived by the Pope may be disposed or murdered by their subjects'. So far, again, only to be expected. The problem is that if the Pope really does have greater authority than the king, there is not much that the oath itself (or the king) can do about it. The oath tries,

making the person taking it swear that 'I do believe and in my conscience am resolved that neither the Pope nor any person whatsoever
hath power to absolve me of this oath or any part thereof'. However,
if the Pope really has power to absolve, he will not lose it because the
person so swears, and if he has power to absolve, he will absolve the
oath-taker from this bit as well.

In other words, these oaths have to depend upon already existing
authority, and so do not create it. If kings really are superior, absolute
monarchs who have to be obeyed, then they have the authority to
administer such oaths, but this authority does not come from the oaths.
Alternatively, if they have no authority to administer the oath, the oath
itself is not going to give it to them. We can see an example of this
in oaths administered later in the century. During the period of the
Commonwealth, after the king was executed, people were required
to take oaths of loyalty to the new government that had replaced the
king. However, later still, as we saw, the kings were restored again. So
what happens when the restored king, Charles II, comes back from
his 'travels'? Again we have an oath, here as part of the 1662 Act of
Uniformity (and to be taken by anyone, as Locke was at that time,
teaching in an Oxford college). Apart from the declaration that 'it
is not lawful upon any pretence whatsoever to take arms against the
king', the swearer was also obliged to 'declare that I do hold there lies
no obligation upon me or any other person from the oath commonly
called the Solemn League and Covenant'. In other words, the oaths
taken during the period without the king are held to be void. By my
mere declaration (or oath), I can will these former oaths away. But
how may I will them away if oaths are binding? This is explained in
the oath itself, for in it I explicitly declare that the former oath I took
'was in itself an unlawful oath'. In other words, just as before, if the
authority already exists, the oath is lawful, but then the lawfulness of the
authority does not come from the oath. Alternatively, if the authority
is unlawful, then so is the oath, and so, again, the oath does not make
the authority lawful. This time it is not the English government that is
possibly trumped by the Pope; the English government trumps itself.

However, it might reasonably be objected, all this misses the point.
The point is that persons making oaths in good faith are bound by
them. Both a punishing God and disapproving people will hold them
to their express declarations. Once declared, they are bound, and no

one can absolve them. If they swore in good faith to the Commonwealth, they cannot then subsequently swear to the King. However,
whether or not this works with kings, it does not work with the Pope.
For this is where the Pope's power of absolution comes in. Roman
Catholicism is a religion in which a specific institution or person is
given the keys of heaven as God's minister on earth. This person has
God's dispensing power. I am of course normally to be held to my
oaths; I am normally bound in conscience before God. However, this
does not apply if God himself, or his minister on earth, dispenses me.
So James I and his government can make Catholics take the oath. Then
the Pope can nullify its effect, even in conscience before God. So we
are back where we are. (In this particular case, what actually happened
was that the Pope declared that it was unlawful for Catholics to take
the oath.) This is why Locke does not extend toleration to Catholics.
Just like atheists (as he sees it), there is nothing to require them to
keep their word. The atheists think that God is not there to do the
work; the Catholics think that his representative can let them off.

Locke's defence of political obligation in consent does not therefore seem to fare too well. Tacit consent is too unspecific and too
weak to be the foundation for the consent he wants and needs; express (or explicit) consent is neither sufficiently available nor, even
if it were, would it work straightforwardly. The limitations to what
can be achieved even by explicit consent are the inevitable result of
there being an independent source of validation or authority. This
source might be particular, as when a political authority stops its citizens consenting to other authorities or swearing oaths to them. The
independent authority prohibits consent. However, the same consequences ensue if the independent source is more abstract. If the law
of nature has independent authority, then it also may well declare that
there are certain things or governments to which we are not allowed
to consent. However, if the law of nature prohibits us consenting to
certain kinds of governments, then we have an argument against the
validity of these kinds of governments quite independently of the fact
of whether anyone consented to them, or indeed of anything to do
with consent.

Locke himself at one point in the *Second Treatise* mentions the kinds
of oaths of allegiance we have just been discussing. He is considering
an 'oath of allegiance' to a single, supreme, person, and claims that this

allegiance is to the person 'not as supreme legislator but as supreme executor of the law'. For, he says, 'allegiance being nothing but obedience according to law' it cannot be owed to a person acting by 'his own private will' but only when he represents the 'public will' [Sec. 151]. This comes as a consequence of Locke's argument against the legitimacy of an absolute, arbitrary, authority. The point to notice, however, is that the question is not, and cannot for Locke, be settled by the explicit terms of the oath. If someone, in explicit terms, declares allegiance to a dictator or absolute king as legislator, then Locke simply says that this is an oath that he may not legitimately make. But if oaths may be set aside in this way, it shows again that we need not get too excited trying to trace the historical record of exactly what was agreed, or how particular actions may be construed as exhibiting tacit consent. We may instead move directly from natural law and these purposes to the legitimacy or illegitimacy of certain kinds of government.

Limits to Consent

Locke's own understanding of the law of nature, as we saw in the last chapter, takes it to have a purposive character. Our rights are not areas of protected decision-making but powers granted to us to enable us to fulfil God's purposes. Hence we may not contract ourselves into slavery or commit suicide. So this places limits on our legitimate consent. I may not, for example, consent to someone's killing or maiming me. The same applies, both in general theory and also in the details of Locke's own account, to consent to the state. There are certain kinds of government to which I may not legitimately consent since they are against God's purposes. In fact, there are not just analogies in Locke between the prohibition of consenting to slavery and consenting to absolute, arbitrary, government; they are part of the same argument. For Locke's central claim, working with the consent idea, is that such consent involves a transfer of our rights, yet we can not transfer what we do not have. Hence, since we do not have an arbitrary power over our own persons, we cannot transfer such a power to another. This is why we cannot by consent (contract, agreement) make ourselves the slave of another individual. We don't own ourselves in this way, and so cannot transfer such ownership to another person. However, exactly the same argument shows that we cannot make ourselves slaves to government either. So we may give no one arbitrary power over us. As Locke puts it, 'nobody can transfer to another more power than he has in himself and nobody has an absolute arbitrary power over himself' [Sec. 135].

We saw that Locke defines political power as a power of life and death. Yet if we have not such power over ourselves, and hence cannot transfer it, it might seem that political power could not exist. However, this is to forget what is transferred, which is the state of nature right to punish. Such punishment, at least for Locke, involves power of life and death. If someone declares that they live by a law other than the law of reason, then they drop out of normal human respect. I am exempted from my duty to preserve God's creatures, and they may be destroyed as noxious beasts. So I do have power over other people's lives in the state of nature. The point is that it has to be exercised according to the law of nature. I cannot decide arbitrarily whom to punish, what for, and how much. I may only do it in accordance with fixed, standing, law. This is the power that is transferred. Hence states also have a life and death power over their citizens only according to fixed, standing, law.

Locke puts this argument in terms of the possibility of legitimate consent, but it can be seen that its force comes from the principles of legitimacy rather than from the consent. It is the law of nature that says that I may not treat people arbitrarily in the state of nature (when I have the power to punish) and it is the same law that says that the state may not treat people arbitrarily (when it has the power to punish). We do not need consent for this result. This becomes even clearer when we look at the occasions on which Locke gives a more substantive role to consent. For sometimes, instead of the argument that I cannot (legitimately) consent to absolute, arbitrary, government, he uses the argument that this is something that I would not consent to. He says that this is something that people 'would not quit the freedom of the state of nature for' [Sec. 137], or that 'a rational creature cannot be supposed, when free, to put himself into subjection to another for his own harm' [Sec. 164]. There is clearly a valid point here in terms of the relative goodness of states of affairs. If an arbitrary government is something that no rational person would choose in preference to the state of nature, then this shows that it has less goodness or utility. This is an argument against it; indeed, a conclusive argument if the facts are correct and if maximising utility is the proper end of action.

However, this conclusion follows directly from the utilities, and any claims about what people would have chosen is merely an indirect way of establishing the utilities.

Alternatively, this might be taken as a claim about what actually happened. Since this is what no rational person would have done, we may infer that this is not what actually happened. However, this is at best a probabilistic argument. Just because it seems irrational does not mean that it did not happen. For people are irrational. People do explicitly subject themselves to absolute authority. So if Locke's argument is meant to be a retrodictive argument about what actually happened, it is very weak. However, neither we nor Locke need worry too much about this. For any arguments about what might have happened are in fact trumped by the arguments about what could not have happened. If it is not possible for people to consent properly to absolute government, then it does not matter what actually happened, and we can stop trying to make guesses about what people may or may not have been trying to do.

So much for absolute government (although the weight of the argument now rests completely on the arbitrary use of punishing power's being forbidden by the law of nature). The next question is how and when exactly Locke permits resistance to such government, and here we do have to enter a bit further into the details of the supposed consensual structure. I noted earlier that consent is supposed to have two stages in Locke: a first stage in which everyone consents, and then a second stage in which the majority decides. This does not mean, however, that Locke thinks that only democratic governments are legitimate. There is in fact a third stage. The people consenting together form 'society' – that is, political society – a single body that moves with a single will. This will is inevitably (or so Locke thinks) that of the majority. However, what this society then does is to use this majority decision to establish a government. And this government might be of any form – a constitutional monarchy, an oligarchy, a representative or direct democracy, or something else. All we know (from the argument just given) is that it cannot be mere wilful, arbitrary rule. In Locke's frequently used quasi-historical terms, this is because that is not what the majority in fact did decide. In Locke's better argument, this is because it is something that no majority could legitimately decide.

Either way, we can see that Locke has more pieces in play, as in
Pufendorf but not as in Hobbes. As well as individuals and government, there is an intervening entity, society (or 'political society').
Individuals do not submit themselves directly to government. They
incorporate, and then the corporation (the people as a whole) gets
government. This (more traditional) account gives Locke room for
a double contractual operation, unlike Hobbes. People contract with
each other in order to have 'society', and then this 'society' (the people
as a whole) decides to have a government, a government it constructs
on conditions. Leviathan in Hobbes is not contractually bound; it is
the result of contracts (or something like contracts) between individual people. However, government in Locke is bound by its method of
creation, and so there are reasons (unlike with Leviathan) for calling
it to account. As well as arguments for obedience, based on the contracting structure and transfer of rights, there are also arguments for
disobedience, based on the fact that government also has obligations,
obligations that it may not meet.

Trust and Discretion

With Locke, we get this double account, except that the second stage is
more accurately thought of as a trust rather than a contract. The term
'trust' appears all over the end of the *Second Treatise*. Governments
are entrusted bodies; they have fiduciary powers. Trust is of the same
family as contract in that they are both creations by will of obligations
between separate parties. However, the difference with trust is that the
trustee is given a goal rather than making a more specific promise,
and has discretion on how this goal is to be reached. For example,
a trustee holding the goods of a child has discretion with respect to
how these goods are used, but has the task, or goal, of preserving the
child's interests. Similarly, for Locke, governments have discretion but
are entrusted with using their power for the public good. (It is the
public good either because, weakly and hypothetically, that is what the
people can be understood to have chosen, or, strongly and straightforwardly, because the preservation of its people is the natural purpose
of government.)

The considerable discretion that Locke allows governments can be
seen in his treatment of prerogative power, on which he has a chapter

in the *Second Treatise*. Here he claims that 'tis fit that the laws themselves should in some cases give way to the executive power' [Sec. 159] – that is, when the executive is using this power in order to promote the 'fundamental law of nature and government, that as much as may be, all the members of the society are to be preserved'. In other words, government in its executive branch has the goal of the preservation or good of society, but discretion about how to achieve this goal, and, as Locke puts it, 'this power to act according to discretion for the public good . . . is that which is called *prerogative*' [Sec. 160].

Some of the things Locke mentions here as uses of prerogative power are things that most people might allow to government: mercy (the prerogative of mercy) and equity (where laws are not interpreted according to the letter in order to serve the wider purposes of justice). Yet any such discretionary power is liable to be dangerous, and Locke himself is bound to have a problem distinguishing such discretion from the arbitrary government of which he disapproves. The problem is how he supports this prerogative power at the same time as he attacks arbitrary power. If governmental discretion is a good, then perhaps we should just contract ourselves into absolute power, allowing it to get on with it. But it is just such a contract that Locke thinks the law of nature forbids. So, instead, it would seem that we should tie power down by rules, preventing it from being arbitrary. Then we have Locke's desired government by 'settled, standing, laws' [Sec. 137]. However, in this case, it is a problem how he can grant government prerogative powers that, as he says here, is a power to act 'without the prescription of the law and sometimes even against it'.

Here is a particular example of this problem, as it arises in the text of the *Second Treatise* itself. It concerns the question as to whether the executive can change the terms of election to the legislature. At separate points in the *Second Treatise*, Locke gives two, potentially conflicting, answers. On the first occasion, just before the prerogative chapter, his attention is on the inequity of the representation system of his day when, because of the variable growth and decline of populations, widely different sizes of constituency were all equally represented in parliament. Here he thinks that it would be appropriate for the executive, by use of prerogative power, to change the electoral system. The government is to aim at public good, and this is public good, 'it being the interest, as well as intention of the people, to have a fair and equal representative' [Sec. 158].

On the other occasion, when at the end of the work Locke is justifying resistance to tyranny, he lays out a series of hypothetical actions
by an executive that would, in his opinion, so alter the legislature
that 'dissolution of government' might be 'imputed to the prince'
[Sec. 218]. Although these are presented as hypothetical cases in a
possible country, they are in fact, at least as Locke sees it, the actual actions taken by King Charles II of England, which therefore, in his opinion, justify armed resistance against him. Among these (hypothetical
or actual) actions he lists are that 'the electors or ways of election are
altered without the consent and contrary to the common interest of
the people' [Sec. 216]. So Charles II has been using his prerogative
power to alter the franchise, and this time, Locke criticises such use of
prerogative power.

These two positions are not necessarily opposed to each other. For
Locke, 'prerogative is nothing but the power of doing public good
without a rule' [Sec. 166]. So Locke could say that the common theme
is that discretion has to be used for the public good. The two cases
of alteration of the franchise by prerogative are therefore different.
The first case is aimed at the public good, whereas the second is not.
However, this just takes us to the heart of the problem, which these
particular examples illustrate. For the fundamental question is who is
to be the judge of the public good. No doubt, any executive making a
change in the franchise – for example, Charles II if asked the question –
would say that he was acting for the public good. If discretionary power
is granted, this is a power to act, but it is also a power to judge.

The question of the independence or merging of judgement is at
the heart of the question of government, particularly in the social-
contract tradition. In Hobbes, we make government by merging our
wills. So when there is government, 'private' judgement is excluded;
instead, judgement is to be governmental, public. So also in Locke.
What we are doing in creating political society by transferring our right
to punish is transferring also our right to judge when punishment is
appropriate. We have seen how, even at the initial stage, our individual
judgements are meant to be subservient to majority judgement. When
this majority creates a government, then, in recognising obedience to
it, we are suppressing our private judgements. We only get the 'known,
indifferent' judge and all the other benefits that Locke outlines for
states if we relinquish any attempt to second guess this common judge.
So Hobbes; so Locke; so government.

The central problem with respect to discretionary power is not with respect to its object. This, the public good, is relatively uncontentious. It is with respect to who is to be entitled to judge the public good. In the *Second Treatise*, Locke quotes King James I, a king from the beginning of the century, when there was considerable public discussion about the extent of the king's prerogative. In the speech Locke quotes, King James claims that he aims at the public good and that he had promised in his coronation oath to devote his power to that end. Hence he is not a tyrant. 'Thus the learned king who well understood the notions of things' comments Locke sagely, 'makes the difference betwixt a king and a tyrant consist only' in that the king 'makes the laws the bounds of his power and the good of his public the end of his government', whereas the tyrant just follows 'his own will and appetite' [Sec. 200]. Hence Locke quotes the learned king, as if James were on Locke's side. They are both against arbitrary power. However, being against arbitrary power, or even having made a kind of contract with the people in a coronation oath, is neither the centre nor the end of the question. It is who is entitled to decide what is the public good. The King of England, unlike some Eastern potentate, thinks that he has to govern for the public good, but the king of England also thinks that it is he who is entitled to decide what is for the public good.

It is not that there are not sanctions or controls on what the king does. The king has promised in a coronation oath, promised before God. Hence he has to answer before God. As James puts it in part of the speech not quoted by Locke, 'yet doth God never leave kings unpunished when they transgress these limits' [p. 183]. It is a severe test, as James thinks of it; 'the higher we are placed, the greater shall our fall be', he says. But the point is that it is God who will be judge. The king answers to heaven; he has no judge on earth. As James puts it here, it is 'sedition in subjects to dispute what a king may do in the height of his power'.

For Locke also, 'princes... owe subjection to the laws of God and nature' [Sec. 195]. For Locke also, princes have to aim at the public good. The difference is with respect to who is entitled to judge whether this is what they are doing. The aim is the same, but the means are different. For both Locke and the kings he opposed, princely prerogative power rightly permits the king to act for the public good in an emergency – for example, seizing and demolishing houses to stop the spread of fire, or putting soldiers in private houses to stop an invasion.

For both Locke and James, this is subject to natural law. It is supposed that there is a right answer with respect to the question of the public good, and the king does wrong if he acts arbitrarily not for this good. So much is common. The difference is with respect to the question as to who shall be judge of whether the king has acted wrongly. For James I (and the other kings of the time), the answer is God. This is where Locke differs. His answer is that 'the people shall be judge' [Sec. 240].

Rebellion

So it is the people who are supposed to judge. And if they judge that the government (executive, king) has not acted in the public good, then they judge that it has exceeded its trust. Hence, as in other cases of trust, the trustee can be dismissed for exceeding its powers. This is another example in which the relationship is better thought of as trust than contract in Locke. In a contract, if one party performs, the other is bound, and the judgement as to whether this has happened must depend upon independent arbitration. However, with trust, the body entrusting retains the power of deciding whether the trust is properly being performed. The people trusted – the trustees – are in this sense agents of whoever is trusting them – the trustors. As such, they can be recalled or dismissed. So if we think of it like Locke, rather than the king's having a kind of contract with the people of which only God can be judge (as in James I), we have the people entrusting power to government and retaining the judgement whether this trust is being properly used. 'The people shall be judge', says Locke, 'for who shall be judge whether his trustee or deputy acts well and according to the trust reposed in him, but he who deputes him . . . ?' [Sec. 240].

Hence we get a justification of rebellion. Strictly speaking, it is not a justification of rebellion against an existing government. Rather, if the government acts beyond its powers (as judged by the people), then this government is held to be 'dissolved'. That is, it attempted to do what no government was entitled to do, and hence ceases to be government. If dissolved, then power reverts to whatever gave it power in the first place. Here, the details of Locke's apparently unnecessarily complex story about origin come into place. For in this many-staged story, as we saw, power does not flow immediately from individuals to government, as in Hobbes. Instead, first we get an incorporated 'people', and this people sets up a government. Hence, if government is dissolved, power returns to the preceding stage – that is, to the people, but the people incorporated and as a whole. We do not get back to a state of nature with only separate individuals. Individual people are still bound inexorably to this 'society' by their supposed express consents. However, this intervening body – that is, the people as a whole – now has the chance to create a new government. It also has the chance to create a new form of government – for example, changing from kings to a more democratically controlled executive.

We saw before how Locke's supposed historical stories can be recast as more abstract argument. Here again, for much of its scope, this argument does not need the specific historical story about entrustment that Locke gives it. It could work directly from natural law. In natural law, at least for Locke, the point of government is to preserve God's creatures and enforce the law of nature. Therefore, anything arbitrary, particularly anything arbitrary that risks the lives of people, is wrong, and to be condemned. The problematic step, however, is whether we are entitled to move from this to either active or passive resistance. Here, natural law by itself (God's commands) are less clear in their consequence, and the additional mechanisms of trust and supposed historical events may be needed.

Several times in the *Second Treatise*, Locke talks of an 'appeal to heaven'. This is a rather coded expression that needs disentangling. For King James I can also say that the appeal is to heaven. He has God as the judge. For someone like King James, this means that subjects should leave kings alone. God will be judge, and if you, a subject, happen to be unlucky enough to fall in with a bad or incompetent king, you have to leave the amendment of this to God. You appeal to heaven, and then you wait. That would seem to be the most natural understanding of the expression 'appeal to heaven'. However it is not, it would seem, what Locke means by it. He starts his story of appeals to heaven (in the 'state of war' chapter) by invoking a Biblical hero prior to a battle. The actual Biblical story is a bit less obvious than Locke allows (as far as the given story goes, this hero could have first appealed to God and then subsequently set out on battle as a separate act). However, as Locke understands it, this hero, Jephtha, appeals to heaven by seeking battle. It is in trial by battle by which the judgement of God is sought; to appeal to heaven is to take to war. So when, towards the end of the work, Locke wants to invoke a similar trial by battle with a recalcitrant king, he talks of this as appealing 'to the supreme judge, as Jephtha did' [Sec. 241].

However, we do not particularly need battle in this story. The point is that government is dissolved (in the judgement of the people). So, although the people are not in a state of nature with respect to each other, they are in a state of nature with the old government or king. This king is now just like a highwayman. He is someone who has declared himself to live by another law, can be punished, is a noxious beast, may be destroyed, loses his normal natural right not to be attacked, and so on. He is 'justly to be esteemed the common enemy and pest of mankind; and is to be treated accordingly' [Sec. 230]. Just another pest to be destroyed. Just another legitimate object of punishment by war. In other words, just as with Grotius's different examples, war works as a justified punishment in the state of nature. Again, we may appeal to whomever we like, but we do the hard work ourselves.

8

The Key to Locke's Property

Although Locke kept his authorship of the *Second Treatise* secret in his lifetime, he did recommend the anonymous work as the best modern treatment of property. He was particularly proud of this part of it. Not only that, but much recent philosophical argument about property consists of an argument between a basically Lockean view on the one side against a basically utilitarian view on the other. So Locke's chapter on property (Chapter V of the *Second Treatise*) is important, and its importance is independent of the value of Locke's thoughts about the foundation and dissolution of government that were discussed in the last chapter.

The central point for which Locke wishes to argue in this chapter is that there are natural rights to property. Property is normally thought of as a bundle of rights, and different treatments of property will include different items in the bundle. At a minimum, the 'private right' with which Locke says he is dealing includes an exclusive right to use. That is, people having property in something have both the right to use it themselves and also the right to control its use by others. Other rights are often included in the bundle, such as the right to destroy or the right to alienate by sale, gift, or other transfer. However, we can start with the right to control use. If this is a natural right, as Locke wishes to argue, then people have such rights, independently of, and antecedently to, government. Other people are similarly under duties, quite independent of government or positive law, not to impede this use. Particular people have the exclusive use of particular pieces of land and other objects, and other people must not use these without their consent.

Given, as Locke wishes to establish, that there is such a natural right to property, then, as we saw in the last chapter, this gives a purpose to government. The reason for government is the preservation of property. In fact, two consequences follow from this account of property for the theory of government. First, property gives government its point. Second, it places conditions on how the government may handle private property. If property is the point of government, then government must respect property in ways that do not interfere with this point. So, in Locke, we have both that people subject themselves to government in order to secure their already existing property and also that this government has to show particular respect to this property.

Taxation

This is what happens when we have a natural right to property, independent of government, and that frames the point and possibilities of government. The rival view is that there are no such natural rights to property and that, instead, property comes from government. In this rival view, the bundle of rights that constitutes property are created by the positive laws of particular governments. Governments create rights, and in so doing create property. On this rival view (as, for example, in Hobbes or Bentham), there is no great conceptual difficulty about the government that creates the property also controlling it and taxing it. On this view, we have property as a benefit of government, and so there would seem to be no principled objection (although of course there may be practical or prudential ones) to the government's removing some of this property from individuals by means of taxation. The taxation is designed to support the system of government and law that gives the property in the first place. However, if, as in Locke, we have natural rights to property, then things are different. Taxation by government now looks more like theft. It is a taking of something that rightfully belongs to someone else.

On Locke's account, taxation therefore needs a special justification. The easiest one is that it is not theft because it is a gift. Rather than being taken by the nasty government, it is a freely willed transfer by the owner. So as well as Locke's general reliance on consent, he particularly stresses the importance of consent where taxation is involved. 'The supreme power cannot take from any man any part of his property without his own consent', he says [Sec. 138], adding two sections later that 'if any one shall claim a power to lay and levy taxes on the people, by his own authority and without such consent of the people, he thereby invades the fundamental law of property and subverts the end of government'. Property sets the end, or point, of government, and in so doing constrains its activity.

It sounds fine to say that we only give money to governments if we want to. Nothing could be wrong with that. The trouble is that it does not seem to match taxation in the real world, where governments are continually taking things from us without first soliciting our personal consent. In this real world (the one in which we happen to live), people do not individually agree to taxation. We cannot just treat taxation like a gift to government. In no modern state do people just pay as much as they feel like, on the analogy to their contributions to charity. If people merely paid what they liked, the expensive operations of modern governments would no doubt be impossible. A purely voluntary taxation system would also be thought by many to be unfair, since there would be great inequality of contributions bearing no relation to people's ability to pay. Some people could give nothing, free-riding on the voluntary contributions of others.

The cure for these problems is to maintain that the basis of taxation is consent, but, instead of having people consenting individually, allowing representatives to consent for them. This consent by their representatives then binds the choices of individuals. This is Locke's solution. Governments 'must not raise taxes on the property of the people without the consent of the people, given by themselves, or their deputies', he says [Sec. 142]. Earlier he immediately glosses a claim that taxation must be with consent as 'the consent of the majority, giving it either by themselves, or their representatives chosen by them' [Sec. 140]. These remarks allow an individual consent, but the only practicable course is the alternatives they mention, consent by representatives and majorities. The people decide as a whole, rather than individually, and this joint decision is made by the representatives of the people. So here the consent is doubly, or perhaps trebly, removed from what any particular individual desires. First, it is not the individual who decides but the majority. A particular individual in the minority hence loses effective consent at this, the first stage. Then the majority does not decide directly but (typically) works through elected representatives. These representatives, once elected, may not happen to agree on a particular matter of taxation with some or all of the majority that elected them. So even an individual member of the electing majority may lose effective consent at this, the second stage. Then, typically, these representatives themselves will decide by majority vote rather than by unanimous decision. So, since their representative may be in the minority, even an individual who agrees with their representative may lose effective consent at this, the third stage. Locke does not mention all these complexities. In particular, he does not enlarge on representation, the filtering process through which our explicit consent is made to pass. However, as we saw, he is prepared to take majority decision as being the decision of a people as a whole. Indeed, he thinks that this is what we have implicitly agreed to when we signed up for political society. So no doubt he could say that we have also consented to our consent's being attenuated in these various ways. However, if so, and just as in the last chapter, we are liable to find that we have been consenting to more than we thought we had.

We get in Locke no taxation without representation, but not the needed account of representation. That is, if the consent is explicit. But, perhaps, we could also press Locke's other kind of consent, tacit consent, into service. As we have seen, this is another useful device for deeming us to consent to more than we thought we had. When we travel freely on the highway, we may be tacitly consenting to the highway laws, but are we also consenting thereby to the highway taxes? If I start across a toll bridge, I can't reasonably object to paying when I reach the toll barrier; this is deemed to be an implicit contract just the same as boarding a bus or eating a meal in a restaurant. I have tacitly consented to pay when the appropriate time comes. Perhaps this can be extended to road tax. One wheel on the road, and I have tacitly consented to pay. Perhaps it can be extended to sales tax. Here it may depend upon how much choice I have. If I have free choice about whether or not to buy, then the tax may be just something involved in the choice, just like my free choice about whether to drive in France can involve knowledge of their speed-limits or motorway tolls. (I might, as in Switzerland, pay a tax for motorways at the border of the country rather than on the roads.) Here, perhaps, the free choice means that

I am properly taxed without representation. (No representative of mine decided the Swiss motorway toll.) On the other hand, if I have no choice about the items, such as the basic necessities of life at the place I do, or have to, live, then I seem to be taxed without even indirect choice. With no choice there is no tacit consent; hence representation has presumably to be wheeled back into play. Changing the rates by executive prerogative would be an arbitrary attack on the citizens' property of the kind that, as we saw in the last chapter, would be regarded by Locke as an example of dissolution of government. Taxing tea by prerogative power leads to legitimate colonial revolt.

So whichever way we take consent, the bold claim that government cannot take the property of people without their consent is liable to be attenuated. Natural property rights will not in fact place as much constraint on the operation of government as it seemed that at first they would. Locke here is liable to be in the same kind of double squeeze, as we saw in the last chapter, with obedience to government. If we justify obedience, then we are liable to foreclose rebellion; if we allow people to think for themselves, then government dissolves into anarchy. In the present case, we can introduce the dilemma by asking whether the consent to governmental use of our property has to be fully individual or not. If our individual rights to property gives each of us individually a blocking vote on whether the government may tax this property, then it seems that government will not be able to raise sufficient taxation, and so risks dissolving into anarchy. So, again, the theoretically justified respect for the individual voice threatens the emergence of the common voice that is government. To prevent this and make government possible, we reduce the respect given to individual consent. We remove each individual's veto; we attenuate what is to count as consent. So we say that the people will consent as a whole rather than individually, that they will consent by their representatives, that they will consent tacitly by being in the country and drawing benefits from government rather than expressly, and so on. This gets government back into business, but it results in consent meaning much less than we first thought. Effective government means that it has effective control of property, and the final position on property and taxation on this account may not in the end be so different from in the rival account in which property is made by government and hence properly controlled by it.

The Origins of Property

The way that natural property rights are meant to frame and control government operation therefore seems to be problematic, and, so far, we have only been looking at consequences, at matters downstream. The source of these ideas or difficulties is the very idea of natural property rights. Somehow Locke has to justify this to give point and meaning to his general account of government, whatever particular problems this may produce for taxation. Whatever problems follow, and whether or not they can be solved, Locke wants to show that we have a natural right to property. So it must now be seen whether there could be any such rights. One way in which it seems that I legitimately acquire private property is by trade. I freely exchange something, thereby acquiring property by mutual agreement. However, I can only acquire property by agreement with someone else if it was their property to give to me in the first place. A mere movement of an object or land into my proximity or into my de facto control will not make it my property. I must as well have an exclusive right to control its use, which means that others must be under a duty to respect my control. When someone transfers an object to me by agreement, other people will be under no such duty to respect my control unless they were formally under this duty to the person who transferred it to me. If, for example, that person had stolen it, then he or she would not have been under this duty to the others, and therefore whatever I gained by the transfer, it would not be property.

So before property can be legitimately acquired by transfer, there must be another way in which someone can legitimately acquire property. There has to be a proper start to the process. Perhaps we could try birth, so that people start life and property together. People are born into property, they acquire natural rights to it by birth, and they may then subsequently trade it. However, this again cannot be a complete explanation. Even if we think that there is a natural right to inheritance from ancestors, the ancestors will not go on for ever. Somewhere or other there has to be another explanation of how the first ancestor legitimately held the property. People can only pass property to their descendants if it is legitimately their property in the first place. Again, we need another account of original acquisition. Acquisition by transfer, whether by trade, inheritance, or gift, has to depend on some other mode of legitimate acquisition. Before people can transfer property, they have to have it.

So there has to be an account of original natural property rights. We need a start. In the world in which Locke wrote, where the Bible was taken to provide a true history of the early life of human beings, the Bible was taken to give an authoritative account of origins. So perhaps the Bible can show how the whole process of property started. After our daily labour as ploughmen or milkmaids, we can read the Bible (or have it read to us). If we start at the beginning, we discover that there was a first man called Adam. This first man got his property from God. So that is how it started. However, this bit of (supposed) history would not help to explain how some people now have particular pieces of property. For, on this story, we are all descendants from Adam. So if God gave it to Adam, and if descendants legitimately inherit, then property is something shared by everyone. God, in effect, gave the world to everyone in common. However, this will not explain why individual people now have individual pieces of private property; in fact it puts the whole question of individual private property in question. The land is given by God to everyone.

Alternatively, we might think (as with Filmer) that Adam only had one legitimate heir, who in turn had a heir, and so on. Or we might think that Adam and his successors had free choice about bequests. However, either way, we are back with the same problems as Locke brought out with Filmer's account of patriarchs and kings. However true this story might be, it is quite pointless in practical terms. For it is quite impossible for us now to trace these transfers all the way back to Adam and to see in fact who has entitlement. A present just entitlement requires a just original acquisition and also a continuous chain of just transfers from this original acquisition to the present entitlement. Even if we believe the Bible enough to secure the first step, and so see how the whole process of property started, we have no chance in establishing the continuous chain of just transfer. This is a historical story, and, as we have seen, historical stories stand and fall on the facts, and facts beyond knowledge yield results beyond use.

Furthermore, most of what we now call property did not exist in the beginning. It was not around at the time of the actual or mythical Adam. The ploughman might read the Bible, but Bibles did not exist in the garden of Eden about which he reads. In the beginning there were only natural plants and animals. Like the ploughman's house and tools, Bibles did not exist. All these are part of the artificial or improved rather than the natural world. So some story has to be told about these things, things that were created by people rather than by God, and therefore things that cannot be supposed to be just given to us by either God or Nature. This Locke's account does.

Furthermore, even if Adam (or anyone else) got his property by direct grant of God, this would not explain how God himself had the property in the first place (or, alternatively, why he was entitled to grant it). Even with God, we need an explanation of how property may be originally created, and in fact Locke's account does this as well. As we saw in the last chapter, the way the law of nature works in Locke is that we are all God's workmanship, and that it follows from this that our control of ourselves and others is circumscribed. We are all, in fact, as Locke himself puts it, God's property. To repeat a remark quoted in the last chapter, people are God's 'property, whose workmanship they are, made to last during his, not one another's pleasure' [Sec. 6]. Repeating the remark reminds us why we are all God's property. It is because we are made by him. God has maker's rights. So here is how property can be created. Objects are made, and by being made become the property of their makers. Someone who makes something produces something new. And by making this new thing, or so at least Locke thinks, they thereby acquire rights of use and control over it. They acquire property rights.

We now come to the centre of Locke's account, for this is the story he tells, not just for God but also for us. This is how, for him, we have legitimate, natural, property rights. However, let us first go back a step, and see exactly what Locke is trying to do in this chapter, his chapter explicitly on property. I said earlier that his central aim was to show how there are natural rights to property. However, he says himself at the start of his recommended chapter on property that he has an even more specific aim. He wants to show how there can be natural property rights without explicit agreement. As Locke puts it in the first section of this chapter, 'I shall endeavour to show how men might come to have property in several parts of that which God gave to mankind in common, and that without any express compact of all the commoners'. Starting with all given in common to Adam and his successors, one way we could get private property would be if this common possession were divided up into individual portions by explicit and universal agreement. This is, after all, the way in which (as Locke himself recognises) we are used to dividing up joint property. However, Locke's aim is quite explicitly to give a different account. It is to get from the universal common to the individual private without any explicit (or 'express') agreement at all.

Either way, we start with the common. We begin with no one's having any property, and everything being for common use. This may be taken as the proper reading of the Bible, in which wild animals and other natural objects are given to mankind as a whole – that is, in common. It may be taken as the natural understanding of the state of nature idea in which all are equally free (which would seem to preclude different amounts of property). It is also what is in fact assumed by Grotius and Pufendorf. So we start with the assumption that everything is initially in common and that property has to be created. The natural things that exist do not belong to anyone in particular, and something has to be done to them to make them property. Other things have to be created as property out of these natural materials. So somehow it has to be explained how some individuals get rights over particular things that are not possessed by others. It has to be explained how we get from a common use right to particular private rights of exclusion.

We need creation, artifice, production. In the accounts we have been looking at, in Grotius, Hobbes and Pufendorf, we have seen how strong is the inclination to explain such creation as being by human will and agreement. We do not start with a state. It is an artificial creation, created by agreement or social contract. Together, we willed it into existence. Such construction by agreement would also explain property, if property is not natural but is created by government. In this rival account to Locke's, property is not there at the start, but once the government has been willed into existence, this government can create property by laying down rules that assign to particular people control over particular things. This will not do for Locke, who wants natural property rights, property rights antecedent to government. However, perhaps, or so it might seem, we could construct such natural property rights by an analogous procedure. Just as government can be created by agreement, so may property. We start from a situation without private property, and then, by common agreement or will, construct the property. We start with everything in common, and then we agree how to divide it up so that individual people acquire individual property rights. This would give us property independently of and prior to government, property that we might subsequently agree to have government to secure.

This, it seems, is a possible account. It is, in fact, the account provided by Grotius and Pufendorf. Agreement gets us to private property from an original common use. It is difficult to suppose that there was an actual historical explicit agreement, dividing up the earth. But the capacious resources of tacit agreement can be deployed instead. It can be taken to be tacitly agreed by everyone, just in the same way as for them the use of language is tacitly agreed by everyone. We did not all get together, like an enormous French Academy, and decide that in English we would use the word 'chair' to mean chair; however, Pufendorf thinks that our use of 'chair' for chair represents a tacit agreement on use of the name. Similarly for property. An old example they use is the possession of places at the theatre. At the start no one owns anything. But when someone sits at a place, then it becomes theirs. A better example for modern life would be parts of a beach: at the start of the day, the sands are open to all, but families and groups, by placing their impedimenta in particular places, make those places theirs for the day. For Grotius and Pufendorf, it is tacit agreement that makes this place at the theatre or beach the person's who occupies it. It is their property not just because they occupy it but also because it is a custom tacitly agreed by everyone that this sort of action will give someone that sort of rights.

Labour and Self-ownership

This cannot, however, be Locke's way. He wants to do it without agreement. It is true that tacit agreement is a capaciously slippery concept, and that in any case what Locke says he is doing without is not tacit but explicit agreement. However, he would not want tacit agreement either. For evolution of private property by human custom, which is a sort of tacit agreement, will not do for his purposes. Custom changes, custom varies from place to place. Yet the property that Locke wants is a true, objective, right, an unalterable moral fact. The sitting on the seat by itself does the work of creating the property quite independently of custom or consent. Property cannot for him just arise from an explicit or tacit agreement, from something that might not happen, from something that might vary from time to time and place to place. Whatever it is that makes property has to make it really and truly, in an unvarying manner, at all times and places, and independently of explicit or implicit agreement.

In fact, in Locke, the work is done by work. What is true for God is true also for us. Property comes from workmanship. We being the 'workmanship' of God are his property; whatever is our workmanship is our property. Labour creates, and what it creates is property. Labour makes value, and the value is owned by the labourer. The people in the theatre or on the beach acquire ownership of the place by the work they do in pitching their camp or sitting on the seat. Of course, these actual examples are not the best ones, because the theatre, a result of other people's labour, may well thereby already be someone else's property; so how someone acquires a use of part of it may properly be controlled. Even the beach might be owned. However if we take the situation for which the theatre was only meant to be an analogy, a desert island beach, or (as Locke does) wild animals or plants in an unowned place, then for him the taking, the mixing of the labour, is sufficient to make the property. The wild mushrooms I pick are mine, and they are mine because of my work in picking them.

So Locke's main argument for property, in both land and moveables, is that we acquire property by mixing something with our labour. By labouring on something, we make it our own. When I make something, I make both it and also property. Similarly for land. I mix my labour with it, working on it, planting it, improving it. Someone doing this hence makes it their own, removing it out of the common stock and rendering it personal, exclusive, property. 'Whatsoever then he removes out of that state that nature hath provided, and left it in, he hath mixed his labour with, and joined to it something that is his own, and thereby makes it his property', says Locke, noting that this thereby 'excludes the common right of other men' [Sec. 27].

This argument inevitably runs into familiar objections. There is the problem of why the mixing means that the person acquires the property rather than just losing the labour. As Nozick remarks in *Anarchy, State, and Utopia*, 'If I own a can of tomato juice and spill it in the sea...do I thereby come to own the sea, or have I foolishly dissipated my tomato juice?' [p. 175]. This could be answered, perhaps, on proportional terms, but it does bring out that as well as the part attributable to labour, there is also another part to which the labour is applied. I start with the sea, or bare land, or raw materials. Matter is given form by labour, but without matter there would be no form. Therefore if this argument justifies anything, it justifies property in the added value rather than full property rights over objects. 'Labour', Locke says, 'makes the far greatest part of the value of things' [Sec. 42].

More fundamentally, there is still the question of why the mixing means that you acquire property. Locke has an answer in the remark just quoted; it is because when someone mixes something with their labour, they are joining it to something that is already their own. So the argument has to start with a presupposition that there is something that is already that person's own, their labour. In other words, whatever entitlement this argument gives to property, it only gives because it presupposes that there is already property to start with. People already have property in their labour, and so, by mixing things with the labour, they also get (some of) these things. This presupposition is quite explicit in Locke. He starts the argument just given with the claim that 'every man has a property in his own person', commenting that 'the labour of his body and the work of his hands, we may say, are properly his'.

Locke states this as if it is obvious, and then from this first axiom about self-ownership moves on to the private ownership of other things. Yet it is far from obvious. Of course, in one sense of 'his' and of 'property', someone's work is 'his' work just like his hair colour is 'his' hair colour; they are, in a grammatical sense, properties of him. But this is a mere pun, no more property in the sense being considered here (and by Locke) than someone's having the temporal property of being born in the same year as the Battle of Waterloo. 'In his time cavalry dominated battles', we might say. This is true. It is also true that it was his time, but this does not mean that he had an exclusive property right to the time. Other people were also having the time of their lives; his time was also their time. Once we have this pun out of the way, then it is a substantial, and still open question, why someone's person and labour are their exclusive private property.

Some of Locke's initial arguments in the chapter look as if they play on this trivial pun, or ambiguity. He starts with a native inhabitant in America taking fruit or killing deer, and says that when it nourishes him it 'must be his, and so his, i.e. a part of him that another can no longer have any right to it, before it can do him any good for the support of his life' [Sec. 26]. But surely this is the same confusion. Of course, to nourish him the food has (eventually) to be inside him, part of his body. In that sense it is 'his'. But this by itself says nothing about rights, about whether everyone else is under a duty not to interfere. In that sense, even if he eats it, it may not be 'his' – that is, his property. Apple thieves successfully swallow what they take, but do not thereby cancel the theft. A slightly later argument depends upon the same assumption, or ambiguity. When someone eats acorns he picks up, Locke says that 'nobody can deny but the nourishment is his' [Sec. 28]. Then, having gotten property at that point, as he thinks, he works back to its supposed origin, and finds it is when he picked up the acorns. This is the conclusion he wants; the labour makes the property. However, the premiss is questionable. Just because the acorns are inside him, it does not follow that they are 'his' in the property sense. Again, if he stole the acorns, then they are not his, even when inside him. Alternatively, if they were no-one's acorns, then he might be entitled to eat them, but this would not in itself show that had acquired private property in them.

So all this has to depend upon the first assumption that people own themselves and their labour, which cannot just be achieved by playing on the word 'his'. Even so, the assumption may seem to be securely enough grounded. For it might be said that it is fairer for people to belong to themselves than to anyone else. However, this still makes the questionable assumption that people have to belong to someone. The argument is meant to show why there is private property in a world when originally everything was in common. It cannot just assume it. Perhaps people should also be regarded as part of the original common. This in effect is what they are in Hobbes's state of nature when everyone has a right to everyone else's body. Of course, these are not full, exclusive, rights, but this is just another way of saying that there is no private property, not even in one's own body. Suppose we get over this by assuming that people have to be possessed by someone. We still don't automatically reach the result that people possess themselves. For even if creation makes property, people, just like other things, consist of raw material which they themselves did not create. If they were created by labour, then the people in labour were their mothers. Yet Locke does not give mothers property rights over their children. It is part of his argument against Filmer that parents are not entitled to eat their children; yet if they had property rights in them, it might seem that they were.

More importantly, as elsewhere in Locke, God has an ambiguous position. We are all God's creatures, according to Locke. This makes us his property, and this is why we may not destroy ourselves, transfer ourselves into slavery or absolute government, and so on. Yet if we are all God's property, it would seem to follow that we do not have property in ourselves. We are all the property of God, and it is precisely because of this that we do not have legitimate control over what we do with ourselves and our bodies. If we do not have control, then it would seem that we do not have an exclusive use right. Hence our persons are not our private property. Hence, whatever other problems there may be with mixing, it does not seem that mixing with the person could ever lead to acquisition of private property.

A way out for Locke here is to treat persons as being importantly different from bodies. God may create our bodies, but it is we who make them into persons. The distinction is one that Locke makes elsewhere in his work; it is important in his account of personal identity in the *Essay Concerning Human Understanding*, where he wants to distinguish between the continuing existence of a body (or a man) and the continuing existence of a person. So self-ownership should not be thought of as bodily ownership, and strictly speaking it is only their labour in which people have private property. A person's body is not theirs to use and destroy, but their labour is. In other words, it is just the added value in which we have exclusive, private, property. We ourselves, just like land, wood, or iron, are originally not owned. However, our labour is, and by labouring on ourselves as well as the land and iron, we eventually hack property out of the common. We make ourselves, and hence elude becoming the property of our parents. We work on plants and animals, and hence manage to take them over from God. We make things, and hence we legitimately control them.

The Provisos

One trouble with this is that labour is not presented by Locke as a free option, under individual control. We are sent into the world by God for a purpose. 'God', says Locke, 'when he gave the world in common to all mankind, commanded man also to labour' [Sec. 32]. So we have no options about labour. Labour is a duty, not something under our choice, not therefore obviously property. Hence I would prefer to develop instead another strand of the argument, a strand in which the natural right to property follows more directly from Locke's understanding of natural law, and one that by-passes assumptions about people having property in themselves or in their labour. Let us therefore start again with the great central purpose of preservation, such as Locke laid down in the natural law chapter as our duty with respect to God's creatures. Now, one of his arguments against having to wait for general agreement before constructing private property is that if we had to do this, we would all have starved before we were able to get it. This by itself is not conclusive. If agreement were the only legitimate way of acquiring natural property rights, and if such rights were needed before things could be legitimately eaten, then legitimate people would just have to starve. When the common is made private, people are dispossessed from common access. When this happens, as with the native Americans from use of the land, it might reasonably be thought that this could only be by their agreement. If this could not be achieved, this would just mean that there could not be any legitimate private property. If a result of this was starvation, then this would just mean that there was no legitimate way to prevent such starvation (people would just have to take their chances with the common).

If, alternatively, we start with the necessity of preventing starvation, then we are not starting with suppositions about property rights but with something else. In fact, we are starting with the Lockean duty that God's creatures be preserved. So we start with a duty. We may then discover, or so at least Locke thinks, that we cannot fulfill this duty that has been laid upon us unless we have exclusive rights to the particular use of land and objects; in short, private property. With private property, Locke's (economic) assumption is that we get much more product. With private control of land, for example, the assumption is that we get much more food. Locke makes enthusiastic calculations, taking the multiple into hundreds or even into thousands. In Devonshire (private property), ten acres of 'equally fertile land' yields as much as a thousand acres in America (no private property) [Sec. 37].

So private property does not come here as an original right (or as something that follows from our original rights in our persons or our labour). It comes instead as a right we possess because it is a necessary means of fulfilling our duty. Since, as Locke puts it, the earth and its fruits are 'given for the use of men, there must of necessity be a means to appropriate them some way or other before they can be of any use, or at all beneficial to any particular man' [Sec. 26]. So far this only establishes a use right, or a right to consume what is common. However, the point is that the right, whatever it is, comes in as a means to fulfil the duty that God has laid on his creatures. Once in this far, Locke only needs to add that private property in a full sense (an exclusive use right protected by duties on others) is also necessary to fulfil this original duty to preserve God's creatures. This is where the added value arising from private property comes in. More property, more preservation. More wheat, more people fed. Privately owned Devonshire fulfills God's purposes better than wild America. So we are entitled to enclose, improve, cultivate, and have exclusive access to bits of land.

This need to fulfill a duty explains what we are entitled to do. It also explains its limits. Because it has a goal, and so is merely a means to an end, this right has clear limits, limits that follow from the end. We only have the right so far as it is working as a means to this end. Hence, as Locke puts it, 'the same law of nature, that does by this means, give us this property, does also bound that property' [Sec. 31]. Our rights have bounds, limits. Someone must keep 'within the bounds, set by reason of what might serve for his use'. These bounds are the so-called Lockean 'provisos'. In fact, at least on the surface, there are two, although they may be inter-related in various ways. The first is a prohibition on spoliation. This is relatively straightforward, given the underlying natural law assumptions. Things were given for a purpose, for use, for survival. If they just waste and spoil, this is no part of the purpose. 'As much as any one can make use of to his own advantage before it spoils; so much he may by his labour fix a property in', says Locke [Sec. 31], noting that 'nothing was made by God for man to spoil or destroy'.

Since, then, its justification is use for a particular purpose, there is no property beyond this use. Locke is quite specific about this. In the state-of-nature conditions he is describing, he says that if anyone took too much fruit or venison (the same examples as he starts with) so that 'the fruits rotted or the venison putrefied', then he would have 'offended against the common law of nature and was liable to be punished' [Sec. 37]. Nothing could make clearer the difference between Locke's account of natural property rights and prevailing modern assumptions. Normal modern assumptions are that if there are private property rights at all, these include the right to use or abuse the property at will; a property right is an area of protected choice over something where the owner may do anything with it that does not interfere with the rights of others. However, Locke here, by contrast, thinks that letting property spoil would be an offence against the natural law. It is also clear why the difference arises. Locke starts, as always, with the duty, with the fact that things were not made by God to spoil or destroy. It is because property has a purpose that we are not entitled to do just what we like with what both Locke and we think of as our property.

This is the first 'proviso', or limit on our control of our own property. The second does not so obviously connect with the underlying law. It particularly concerns appropriation, and hence relates to the initial stages of property formation in the state of nature. It appears immediately after Locke talks of people gaining property by mixing things with their labour. 'For this labour being the unquestionable property of the labourer', he says, 'no man but he can have a right to what that is once joined to, at least where there is enough and as good left in common for others' [Sec. 27]. The first thing to notice is that a restriction is being applied. If labour on an object were sufficient to give property in it, then it would give this property whatever else might be happening in the woods. However, there does seem here to be an additional condition. Property will only come from the labour if 'enough and as good' is left for others. As before, the presence of this condition shows that the right is being controlled by an overarching purpose. The point of acquisition is to preserve mankind. Acquisition that makes the position of others worse is not fulfilling its point (or, at least, not obviously fulfilling it). Hence, what in other conditions would lead to private property, will not do so here (or, at least, will not obviously do so).

The question is why this proviso, or limitation, comes in. It is not just an accident, since Locke frequently repeats it and also gives a series of examples. I can drink from the common fountain, since my mug of water leaves as much for anyone else. Obviously I do not literally leave the same; some water has disappeared, but I do leave 'enough and as good'. The point is that I have not worsened anyone's position since everyone is still able to do what I have done. I drank; they may still drink. Locke thinks that the same applies to catching fish. I am entitled to the fish I catch in the open ocean ('that great and still remaining common of mankind' [Sec. 30]), since once I have fished, someone else can still come and catch fish. He cannot catch the same fish as I, but Locke thinks that he can catch the same amount of fish; he is supposing in this example that there remain relatively abundant natural resources.

The same applies to land, in two different ways. In the beginning when, as Locke puts it, 'all the world was America', he thinks that someone enclosing and improving a bit of land leaves as much and as good for others. Obviously (like the fish) he cannot have precisely that bit of land, but there is still (he thinks) land, roughly as good as the land already enclosed and enough for those that want it. However, as he recognises, the story has to change when we get to the position, as it will, when the land runs out. We may start with an open frontier in which anyone wanting land just travels a bit further West, but, eventually, the open frontier meets the Western ocean.

At this point, Locke makes a different move. Since, as he thinks, enclosure and private cultivation adds so much value to land, even if now not everyone can have land, those that do not are still doing better because the land is enclosed and improved. They are excluded from what was originally common, but since this has led to a great increase in product, this exclusion is in their interest. Two things at least would be necessary for this argument to work. First, it has to be the case that the 'enough and as good' requirement may be satisfied with general value rather than with particular kinds of object. That is, the claim has to be that I leave 'enough and as good' for someone as long as I have not diminished their utility; the argument will not work if I have to leave enough and as good land, or water, or fish, or whatever the particular product is that is being considered. If the assumption can be met in this general way, it amounts to the claim that I can enclose and improve as much as I like as long as no one is harmed (in the sense of having their utility reduced; not in the sense of having failed, relatively, to increase their utility). As such, the argument backs into one from tacit consent. For if something has happened, and is such that it has benefited everybody, then it is something for which we may suppose that there is general approval, or tacit consent.

However, all this has been on the supposition that everybody's position has been improved by the private ownership of the original common. The other assumption Locke needs for this is that the increase of value is in fact distributed to everyone. Otherwise it will not in fact be true that no one suffers. It is one thing to say that there is an increase in value (or in average value); it is quite another to say that everyone has improved. A distribution mechanism is needed as well as a production mechanism – for example, taxation of the added value achieved by private ownership of resources. Yet such taxation – for example a land tax for the benefit of the landless – is exactly the kind of thing that Locke himself would seem to be resisting in his no taxation without consent claims. For it is the consent of the landed he has in mind here – that is, the consent of the people who would lose by the tax rather than the consent of the people who would gain.

Since the landowners are not likely to approve of a tax that offers them no benefit, it does not seem that redistributive taxation can be used to meet the proviso. But, if not, at least when population presses, we seem to be stuck with a proviso that cannot be satisfied. Well before the last piece of vacant land is occupied, enough, and as good, is not being left for anyone who wants it. When the last piece of vacant land goes, no land is left at all, and after that, things are even worse. So, at least when we reach current conditions of scarcity and full occupation, we would seem to have a necessary condition for natural rights to land that cannot be satisfied. Hence, in current conditions, it seems that there can be no just acquisition. Original acquisitions long before this current condition of scarcity are too far back for the series of just transfers to be traced. So it seems that Locke loses any justification of private property that could be applied to current conditions.

Alternatively, these problems with the 'enough and as good' proviso could be met by denying that Locke's remarks were ever intended to be a proviso, or a necessary condition, on just acquisition. As I said, it does look like a necessary condition. However, if we examine his remarks again, we see that what Locke is claiming is rather that acquisition is clearly permitted when enough, and as good, is left for others. If this applies, the acquisition is just. However, this by itself says nothing about the justice of a situation in which it does not apply.

It is, that is, acting as a sufficient rather than a necessary condition. It says that when this happens, things are just; it does not say that they are just only when it happens. Locke thinks that when the condition is satisfied, the acquisition is just because no one is harmed by it. It is not like theft, or, as Locke puts it, 'he that leaves as much as another can make use of does as good as take nothing at all' [Sec. 33]. Nothing (morally significant) has happened. Locke also seems to be appealing to a primitive assumption of equity or fairness: it is fair to take the land or fish because anyone else may do exactly the same kind of thing; no special or different claims are being made on behalf of the person who takes. Finally, he claims there is greater production with private property, so this supposedly fair activity has advantages. These are a mixture of arguments whereby the acquisition may be justified. However none of them depends upon the 'enough and as good' being understood as a necessary condition on just acquisition.

Locke is talking about situations in which (he thinks) there is land, or water, or fish enough for all. In these cases, since anyone taking land (or water or fish) leaves enough and as good for others, the proviso is satisfied. Then, for him, we have justified acquisition of private property. However, just because property can be shown to be alright when the condition is satisfied does not mean by itself that property would not be alright if the condition were not satisfied. That needs another argument. Locke is trying to justify natural property rights. Hence he takes the best possible case. This is when acquisition of property does no harm to anyone, is fair between people, and improves everyone's utility. So he considers examples where the initial taking leaves 'as much and as good' for others. However, it does not follow from this that there could not be legitimate acquisition and natural property rights in less favourable conditions. Hence there is a careful way of reading Locke in which he just has one proviso, the spoliation one, and all the difficulties to which application of an 'enough and as good' proviso would lead may be ignored.

Property and Government

This chapter started with the downstream consequences of natural property rights: the constraints they provide for governments and taxation. Now that we have seen the shape of Locke's argument for natural property rights, we can return to the question of exactly what constraints the thing for which he has argued may provide for government. A prime problem here is that whatever may be the case in the pure state of nature, it is not clear from Locke's text exactly how much of these natural property rights are supposed by him to survive once we reach the stage of government. Several remarks he makes make it sound as if the transition to political society amounts to a new property deal. He tells a historical story that starts with acquisition in a primitive state of nature but, with increase in population and the invention of money, all has now been replaced by politics and agreement. A Biblical example (which we should remember that Locke takes as authoritative early history) is Abraham and Lot, who 'by consent . . . separated and enlarged their pasture, where it best liked them' [Sec. 38]. Earlier in the same section, he notes that when families increased enough to settle in cities, 'then, by consent, they came in time to set out the bounds of their distinct territories'.

So Locke's text seems to be ambiguous on this crucial matter. In the material just quoted, and other similar remarks, we seem to have a historical story where natural rights without consent only applies at an early stage, and later the division of property is by consent. However, on the other hand, the whole point of the account seems to be lost unless the natural rights to property limit what states may do to property, because, as will be remembered, it was precisely to protect this property that, according to Locke, people entered into government in the first place. Therefore the problem with Locke is to see how conditions that may work in a primitive or fictional state of original plenty are meant to apply in the actual contemporary situation with scarcity, money, and government. The natural law, as we have seen, applies universally. So it still applies in the later, contemporary, stages of the story. If no spoliation is a condition of natural law on the just ownership of property, then it also applies when there is scarcity, money, and government. However, as Locke wishes to bring out, even if this is so, the effect of the condition is greatly altered once money is in use. For with money, other goods can be exchanged into money, which stores value and does not spoil at all.

With money, we have a little gold thing ('a little piece of yellow metal', as Locke calls it [Sec. 37]), that being exchangeable for other goods, means that the spoliation provision can be eluded (or, more accurately, means that it ceases to provide any constraint on acquisition). Money lasts; as Locke puts it, 'money, some lasting thing that men may keep without spoiling' [Sec. 47]. So once we have money, instead of the extra fruits or venison rotting away uselessly, they can be sold, sold for gold, which can in turn be used to buy other things. The gold will not spoil, and is always tradeable. Therefore a potentially indefinite amount may be kept for a potentially indefinite time without anything being wasted. Hence, with money, nothing need spoil, and there is no limit to acquisition. Hence, in Locke's conjectural histories of the world, after the invention of money, we get much greater inequality. Locke also thinks that a purely natural society, such as he takes the society of the native Americans to be, cannot long survive the invention of money. This means that even if it is not the same process (we could in principle have political society without money, and money without political society), the two are liable to be tied very closely together in time.

It is not clear whether or not there is a new property deal with the advent of political society; nor how exactly this change is meant to be tied to other changes, such as the invention of money, which also alter the original acquisition story. However, either way, this is not of practical significance in providing constraints to current governments. That is, whether or not we think that there is a new property deal with political society, Locke's natural right to property will not in practice provide much constraint on the operation of government. If there is a new deal with the coming of political society, then Locke's account of natural property rights is just a picturesque piece of supposed history. It has analytical interest in being an argument for the very possibility of natural property rights. However, it has no other contemporary significance. For on this account, the property we now have comes with the political societies we now have. It is created by agreement, can be changed by agreement, and as such provides no constraint to the (agreed) operations of government.

The alternative (and, I think, more plausible) account of Locke is one in which people keep their natural property rights even after the advent of government. This account therefore provides constraints on government. However, these constraints only apply as long as people have such natural property. Therefore, even this alternative account lacks contemporary significance. It applies to a situation when people gather together with an original contract to found a political society. However, people living in contemporary societies have not done this. Instead, they are people who (according to Locke) agree in turn when they come of age to join already existing societies. The world is already saturated with government before they are born. These governments need only respect natural property rights if people can acquire them in such a government-saturated world. For this, people would have to possess property before agreeing to attach themselves to existing government. However, it is not clear how much property of this kind could be possessed by such people. Perhaps they inherit property. But this property does not come to them as natural property; it comes as already part of a government settlement.

Locke uses this as part of his argument that people are not born citizens of countries. For, he says, on inheriting, people can always give up the property, and hence avoid the political obligations that are already connected to this property. But whether or not this argument establishes its intended conclusion, the thing to note for our present purposes is its presupposition. This is that the property surrounding the growing child, waiting to be inherited, already comes with political connections. Locke says of children that 'if they will enjoy the inheritance of their ancestors, they must take it on the same terms their ancestors had it' [Sec. 73]. It is already property controlled by government. Of course, on coming of age, the child can go elsewhere, but then Locke makes it clear that 'he must also quit...the possessions there descending to him from his ancestors' [Sec. 191]. Therefore in the normal case where people stay and inherit property, this property does not place any effective constraints on what the government may do with it. By the time it is gained, it is already covered with governmental strings and benefits, and this means that, whatever other arguments there may be to regulate government taxation and interference, government is not here limited by natural property rights.

From Duty to Right

Whatever the right answer about whether government is constrained by natural property rights, we should note two other ways in which Locke himself thinks that private property is constrained. For they are again ways that make his account unlike most modern understandings of the subject. The normal modern understanding is that private property gives the property holder complete control, subject to respecting the rights of others and also, perhaps, the requirements of government. Yet, as we have seen in Locke, property is also subject to one or more provisos, constraining what may properly be done with it. This is because it is not so much a foundational right as a means of fulfilling a duty. However, also arising from this, there are in Locke two other ways whereby an individual's use of property is constrained. The first of these is that children are taken by Locke to have a legitimate rights to the property of their parents. Since parents, he thinks, have a duty to support their children, the property of the parents should be used in the first instance for such support. This is revealed in his typically English, but still strange, view that an attack on property is more serious than an attack on a person. One example is the only case in which Locke thinks that there legitimately can be slavery, which is when someone is taken as a captive in a just war. The person is in the wrong, and so loses rights to freedom. However, Locke does not think that in this case the person forfeits property. The conqueror, says Locke, 'has an absolute power over the lives... but he has not thereby a right and title to their possessions' [Sec. 180]. His reason is that 'the miscarriages of the father are no faults of the children' [Sec. 182]. For Locke, that is, the children are not treated unjustly if the conqueror kills their father before their eyes, but they are treated unjustly if the conqueror seizes one of his fields. They are treated unjustly in the latter case, it would seem, as they would lose a field through no fault of their own. However, this only applies if children have a natural right to the property of their parents. Otherwise it is just bad luck on me if my father does wrong and I don't inherit his possessions, just as it is my bad luck when my friend who was about to give me a big present suddenly loses all his money.

Locke's argument for thinking that children have such natural property rights is that parents are under a duty to support their children. This means that their property should be used, among other things, for the support of children. The parent has a duty to support the child; the child has a right of support. Again, the right comes in Locke as a consequence of the duty, as a means of fulfilment of the duty. Of course, this will only give a right to inherit, insofar as children still need support at the point of their parents' death, and it only gives a right to as much property as is needed to support. Furthermore, this (or any other) duty imposed on property is a double-edged weapon. It gives an individual property rights but also subjects these rights to certain controls. Here the parents' right of control of property in their lifetime is circumscribed by the use they are required to make of it for the benefit of their children. Their right to transfer or alienate it at will at death is circumscribed by the duty to bequeath it to their children.

This constraint on property in Locke comes from the needs of family members. But, at least in the *First Treatise*, Locke thinks that the needs of non-family members also provide constraints on people's control of property. People have a duty to help the starving, even if they are quite unrelated to them. According to Locke, at least in the *First Treatise*, 'God hath not left one man to the mercy of another, that he may starve him if he please'; hence he has given no one such property 'but that he has given his needy brother a right to the surplusage of his goods' [Sec. 42]. People who are starving have to be fed; cases of what Locke calls 'extreme want' make a claim on other people's property. This again follows from the general, overall, argument, which is driven by a need to preserve God's creatures, particularly human ones; 'the fundamental law of nature', as Locke says, 'being that all, as much as may be, should be preserved' [Sec. 183]. So as many as possible have to be saved. This is Locke's ultimate justification of private property; with it, more are saved from starvation. However, it also means that uses of property will not be justified when they lead to starvation. So I can't use my property (for example, bequeathing it to a cats' home), which may result in the starvation of my children, and, sitting on my property, I cannot refuse the desperate plight of the 'needy brother' at my gate. As much as may be, all have to be preserved. It is the same argument that leads to the no-spoliation condition. With spoliation, less than might be is preserved.

The final justification of private property in Locke is therefore that with it, more people survive. The landless 'day labourer' in private-property England 'feeds, lodges, and is clad' better than a 'king of a large and fruitful territory' in common-property America [Sec. 41]. But this private property must provide charity to those who are in desperate want. Locke's economic calculations are sufficiently optimistic that he does not think that there will be many such. However, any that there are have to be fed, and this forms a legitimate charge on private property. If is supposed that there is this kind of full duty of charity (as, on a certain reading of a few remarks of Locke in the *First Treatise*, it seems there is), then, again, any particular individual's bundle of property rights will be circumscribed. In the family case, it might be said that the property actually belongs to the family and not to the individuals. Each generation has certain rights of use, but their duty to other generations means that they cannot alienate the property. Similarly, if there are indeed duties of charity, then all property is still partly common property, property for common use. Private property is in Locke a restricted right of use. Particular individuals are granted use and control, but this is subject to restrictions. Just as we were sent into this world to work, so we were given property for a purpose. For Locke, God gave the world 'to the use of the industrious and rational (and labour was to be his title to it)' [Sec. 34]. Property is not something over which you have a free play of your fancy and which you may waste and use at whim. Rather, it was given for a purpose. You must grimly labour, you must grimly preserve, and grimly you must mind the needs of children and the destitute. Property for Locke is as much a compound of duties as of rights. All this makes the actual, historical, Locke a very different animal from the one displayed by modern admirers of Lockean property rights.

9

Why Utility Pleases

'The cause too, why utility pleases, has of late been assigned by an ingenious and agreeable philosopher, who joins the greatest depth of thought to the greatest elegance of expression'. This is a quotation from 1759, so we have moved on to the next century. It is in fact from Adam Smith [*Theory of Moral Sentiments* IV.1.2], and the ingenious and agreeable philosopher he is describing is his fellow Scot and friend David Hume. Elegance of expression, agreeable philosophers, admiration of utility – it all seems to be a new and different world, far from the blood- and Bible-stained conflicts we have been describing. So, or so at least the first superficial glance might suggest, we have moved into the modern world, the start of our own times. We have science rather than religion, enlightenment rather than confusion. However, what I shall show in this final chapter is that it is not that simple. I aim here to discuss continuity rather than difference; I aim to connect the people we have studied with these later elegant and agreeable admirers of utility.

I had originally thought of calling this chapter, 'What's the Use?' For I want also in this chapter to reflect more generally on the possibility of political philosophy and on the use for political philosophy of the historical philosophers I have been describing. Only if we can connect will this thought be of use. In fact, as can be seen, I have called it 'Why Utility Pleases' to mark, as well as these general questions of use, a particular concentration on the use of utility. The words of my title were used by Adam Smith to describe Hume, and they are in fact Hume's own title for Section V of his *Enquiry Concerning the Principles of Morals* of 1751 (which may explain why the title sounded vaguely familiar). Hume is not the centre of this chapter, but he forms a marker, a convenient conceptual and historical mid-point between the philosophers we have been examining and the fully fledged later utilitarians such as Bentham or J S Mill with whom I wish to compare them.

We have already seen one appearance of utility in this book. This is with respect to the moral scepticism that Grotius picks up at the start of *De Jure Belli ac Pacis*. Here, his sceptic, Carneades, arguing against justice, is taken to say that we have laws not for justice but for expediency (*pro utilitate*), because 'all creatures, men as well as animals, are impelled by nature toward ends advantageous to themselves (*ad utilitates suis*)' [DJBP Proleg 5]. Notice how *utilitas* appears in Grotius's Latin, but notice also that such utility is a sceptical position that Grotius is concerned to dismiss. Instead of the idea that 'nothing is unjust which is expedient (*utile*)' [3], Grotius is going to show that as well as utility, there is also justice. So, as well as the pragmatic reasons for action based on utility, we have a framework of natural law and natural rights, giving us right reasons (justice). The classically trained readers of the period also knew that they were meant to aim at the *honestum* as well as the *utile*.

This also seems to be the way in which political philosophy is organised in more modern times, where it is frequently presented as a competition between the rival bases of rights and utility. We might, for example, have a utilitarian treatment of property and other rights, whereby they are part of a system of legally established rights whose point is to maximise utility (nothing is unjust that is useful). Alternatively, we might have property rights resting on a natural-law foundation, based on theories about original acquisition and citing Locke in the process. So, or so it might seem, seventeenth-century natural law on the one side against the primrose paths of eighteenth- and nineteenth-century utilitarianism on the other. After all, all of the thinkers described in this book – Grotius, Hobbes, Pufendorf, and Locke – espoused some sort of natural law. Yet such natural law gets placed and dismissed by Hume and Bentham in the greater name of utility. Humanity, and the happiness of humanity, sets the goal rather than the impersonal will of God. (Bentham said that on reading Hume he had 'for the first time learnt to call the cause of the people the cause of virtue' [*Fragment* I 36n].) This all seems to fit together, and is the opposition we might expect. This book about the seventeenth century is a book about natural law and natural rights, whereas a book about the later eighteenth and early nineteenth century would bring out the great goal of utility. Like all such general statements, this is obviously partially correct. However, what I wish to show in this chapter is that nevertheless it is not as simple as that. There is more continuity than divergence between the people we have been studying and these later, more explicit, utilitarians. When Nietzsche said In the *Twilight of the Idols*, 'Man does *not* strive after happiness; only the Englishman does that', he had his contemporaries (such as the 'offensive clarity' of Mill) chiefly in his sights. However, what I wish to show is that the English disease he diagnosed was already endemic in the country two centuries before.

The Tasks of Political Philosophy

Let us start on this menu of inter-connected tasks by considering the possibility of political philosophy. As I see it, political philosophy has at least three tasks (three elements we can consider in assessing the masters of the genre). First, there is a task of explanation, or, better, promoting understanding of political aspects of our (social) world. It helps us to see and understand what these aspects (for example, democracy, equality, alienation) are; it shows us how and when they occur. Then, second, because this is philosophy rather than political science, there is a task of justification. As well as understanding it, we want to know why or whether we should have it, or in what way. These two tasks connect. In showing, for example, what political obligation is, we may thereby show why it is (or is not) desirable; by seeing what might be desirable about democracy, we may thereby understand better what it is or could be. So political philosophy is therefore in this respect a normative subject, a part of applied ethics. Yet if it is a part of ethics, then, at least given the central concerns of much recent writing about ethics, it also has a third task, that of explaining motivation. As well as showing why some things are justified, it also has to be explained why people are motivated to produce them. Political philosophy is a practical subject. So a story about the good is not by itself good enough; it also has to be explained how or why it comes about. It has to be explained how actual people are motivated in practice to provide it.

So that is a first list of three tasks for the subject, tasks with obvious internal connections. Returning to our first example of Hume, it can be argued that anyone successfully showing why utility pleases achieves all three of these tasks. In Hume, an aspect of our political world, justice, is explained by showing that it is an 'artificial' or 'social' virtue, whereby certain social rules are explained by their promotion of utility. This explanation now provides a justification: by seeing that justice promotes utility, and knowing that utility is a good, we thereby demonstrate the goodness of justice (or show on which occasions and in which applications it is justified). Finally, we pick up the question of motivation. Utility pleases. In this (Humean) account we are naturally constituted so that we are attracted by the idea of utility, and so once we have explained justice in terms of utility, this will not only explain it (show what it is) and justify it (show it to be good) but also show that we are motivated to produce it and make it part of our communal practice. As well as explaining what justice is, it also explains why we happen to have it.

I said that these three tasks had obvious internal connections. Indeed, it might be thought that the second and third tasks are so closely connected that they are not separable. That is, we might think that once we have shown why something is justified (desirable), we have thereby also shown why we are motivated to produce it (why it is desired). Showing something to be good or right is thereby to provide the motive for action. However, for two quite different kinds of reasons, I think that it is important to realise that these two tasks are separable in political philosophy, whatever may be the right answer for individual ethics. The first reason has to do with the special character of political agency, distinguishing it from normal individual private behaviour. Insofar as we have political entities (states, governments, parties) we can also talk of political agents. To the actions of, for example, a government, we can apply the three tasks. We can explain what the government is doing (for example, increasing inequality) and we can also decide whether this is right. We can then go on to the third task, explaining why it is doing this (its motive for action). Here it is implausible that the best, or at least the sole, explanation is that the government believes that the end is right (that the actions of the British government in Africa can be solely explained by its desire to pursue an ethical foreign policy). Of course, for individuals also, we don't explain all of their actions in terms of their desire to realise the good or the right, but there seems to be something special about political agents, so that purely moral motivation is even less applicable (they are expected to act 'realistically' rather than 'idealistically').

This is the first reason why, in political philosophy, the question of motive can be distinguished from the question of justification. The second reason is, I think, more important. This is that we not only have in politics different kinds of agents who act unlike normal individual people, we also continue to have the actions of normal, individual people. What happens politically is the product of the acts of many individuals. The justification we consider in political philosophy is justification of this political result, but the motivations of the individual people who happen to produce it may be quite different. It may be the completely unintended consequence of their actions. Yet if this is so, or so far as it is so, the question of explaining why something happens is quite separable from the question whether it is a good thing that it has. As Adam Smith memorably pointed out in his later work, it is not their concern for me that enables me to get my bread and meat from the butcher and baker. So I can consider both why it is a good thing (if it is) that bread and meat get provided in this way, and also why it actually happens. Defenders of the free market, citing Adam Smith for their cause, pick up both tasks, but it is two tasks they are picking up.

We can see this separation more clearly in utilitarianism of the classical period – that is, of the time after Hume (and Smith). In Bentham, we have a sharp separation between the question of value and the question of individual motivation. The criterion of value is general happiness. This shows what the government should attempt to effect. But the way it effects it is by acting on individuals, whose actions have to be explained on the basis of a particular theory of individual motivation, which is that (in general) individuals can be supposed to act in a ruthlessly self-interested (or what we now call an 'economically rational') manner. So the value theory (the answer to the second task) says something quite different from the explanation of motivation (the answer to the third task). This shows that they can be separated, once we distinguish individual from political agency. The two separated accounts are also consistent. Since utilitarianism is a consequentialist theory that looks at results rather than intentions, all that matters is which things get done, not why they are done. So the reason why they are done (the individual motivations) can be quite disjoint from the reason why they are of value.

Let me complete this survey of the tasks of political philosophy and later exemplifications by a sketch of how Bentham's account of law could be taken to fulfill them. Bentham gives three different accounts, corresponding to the three tasks with which I started. There is first an analysis, or explanation, of what law is (a command by someone to whom there is a habit of obedience, threatening punishment for non-performance). Then there is a justification of law, a theory of value that demonstrates that it is a good thing, or when it is. The value theory says that the greatest happiness is the sole measure of right or wrong, and the application of this to law is the empirical claim that law (that is, government) brings more happiness than anarchy does. More specifically, it can be shown of each law, why or whether it is a good law, and so a perfect code of laws that contains only laws that promote general happiness can be constructed. Third, it is explained why these laws motivate, how they work. By threatening pain (punishment), they move self-interested citizens into action. Just as we do not depend upon the altruism of the baker to keep us in bread, so Bentham does not depend upon people's moral sense to keep us free from theft; rather he depends upon their interest in avoiding what the state will do to them if they are caught stealing.

This is a sketch of the possibility of political philosophy, concentrating on later, specifically utilitarian, examples. We now have to try and apply it to the people examined in this book. No doubt what I have just said is disputable, and also, even if I am right about the aims of political philosophy, showing that various historical figures have attempted these three tasks shows nothing about whether they succeeded. It is not good enough for Hume or Bentham to think that something is justified; it really has to be so. So, in turning back to the seventeenth century, we not only have to try and discover corresponding accounts of explanation, justification, and motivation; we also have to see if they work. Particularly this is true of justification. It has to be shown what, if anything, beyond everyday political rant or moral preaching, political philosophy can provide, either in general or for the particular people being studied.

Since justification is the hardest problem, I shall concentrate on it and its relationship to motivation. There is explanation, or analysis, in our thinkers, but neither earlier nor here shall I give it the attention it deserves. In Hobbes, for example, before he justifies the state, he analyses and explains what it (state, commonwealth, government) is. It is for him a single will, so that there can be a single decisive voice in those matters where people disagree. So in his account of original contract, what is important is that a plurality of people 'reduce all their wills... unto one will' [*Lev* 17.13]. Some of the crucial analysis is conducted earlier – that of a 'person' – since for Hobbes the state is an artificial person. 'A multitude of men', he says in the previous chapter, 'are made *one* person, when they are by one man, or one person, represented' for, as he puts it 'it is the *unity* of the representer, not the *unity* of the represented, that maketh the person *one*' [*Lev* 16.13]. So far, so good, perhaps: we want unity, and here is a clever piece of analysis making the unity depend upon the unity of what Hobbes calls the 'sovereign' ('he that carrieth this person is called sovereign' [*Lev* 17.14]) rather than presupposing that a group of separate persons form a natural unity or entity (a 'people') or otherwise giving the state some other kind of disembodied, mystical, union.

A clever account. It may, of course, be wrong, but it is an analysis that connects with the possibility of justification. As we saw when studying him, justification in Hobbes is sometimes merely of the prudential, skin-saving, kind. However, he also has another story whereby justification flows from the will, and the only justified authority is what we ourselves authorise. This second justificatory story fits neatly with his analysis of the sovereign. Description and justification are different, but our will occurs in both. By will we make the sovereign (the unified representer), but the will that makes also justifies. The different analyses of Hobbes and Locke on this matter are also important in their different justifications of obedience and resistance. For, as we saw, the relationship between state and people is different in Hobbes and Locke. In Hobbes, there is nothing but the sovereign and the individuals (the single will and many individual wills); there is no intervening entity 'the people'. Therefore if the sovereign loses power, we are back to the disorganised multitude. Whereas in Locke, the 'people' also exists as an entity rather than as a mere collection of individuals. So, once power (as Locke sees it) is legitimately removed from the king, then it can be exercised by the people collectively. We have a different analysis of what 'the people' is, related to different justifications of what they may do.

Normativity

These are important analytical insights and differences. However, as I say, I shall concentrate on justification. The need for justification engendered by confusion and the masterpieces of justification produced in response to this need is the central reason for my concentration on the seventeenth century, and, in it, the possibility of fundamental justification is the most persistent topic I have worried about. The topic and problems of justification runs like a rich lode of ore through all these philosophers. They all think normatively; they all, that is, give what they take to be good reasons for action. Such is the explicit function of natural law in Grotius, Pufendorf, and Locke. However, it is also true, I think, for Hobbes. His new natural law tells us how it is rational for us to behave. Seeking peace and avoiding the war of all against all is a good thing to do (good for us to do). It is not natural or inevitable. People may well not follow good reasons. The theorems that the moral scientist Hobbes provides are not merely natural scientific accounts of human behaviour. They are not just an analysis, or explanation, of how people actually behave. Instead, they are recommendations (Hobbesian 'council'); they tell people what to do.

So even Hobbes, as I see him, is a normative thinker (as opposed, for example, to Spinoza who, similar as he is in many ways, nevertheless seems to me to be merely descriptive in intention all the way down). Of course, Hobbes also has a strong descriptive aim, and descriptions of how we are (of human nature) are meant to provide support for his account of how we should act (of natural law). Natural law is natural, and so for Hobbes it naturally has a naturalistic foundation. However, it also tells us what to do. Suppose we take Hobbes (over-simply and over-reductively) to be all about skin-saving. Suppose we take Hobbes to be all about power. Nevertheless, what power provides is justification for action. We can understand the motivation provided by threats to our skins, and so predict how people seeking to save their skins will act. However, this is because such threats give natural reasons for action. We can ask what these people under threat ought to do; we can evaluate their responses. Power, as we saw in Chapter 2, gives the reason for obedience, whether to God or Leviathan. However, what it gives is nevertheless a reason for obedience as well as a cause.

This is a fundamental, extremely basic, example of justification. It is so basic that it travels beyond its particular religiously saturated context. It can be used in a stripped down, naturalistic, way and applied to the problems of a merely secular age. Power gives reasons; threats give reasons. We must trace through this the right prudential course for people to preserve themselves. Then, if we follow Hobbes, we get an argument for the state, for the fundamental problem of political obedience. We also get a lot of more traditional natural law, showing that we have a reason to keep promises, and so on. So this is how Hobbes provides an answer to what I dubbed the second task of political philosophy, the task of justification. In this case, it is not really applied ethics (which is how I described it at the start of the chapter). Hobbes provides a form of justification, or reasons for action, more prudential than moral. His reasons are amoral reasons. However, this is just the point. If it is as difficult to found morality as it is to found politics, the more fundamental we can get the better. The foundation does not have to be moral; it simply has to provide justifying reasons. These reasons can then be applied to the state. Therefore the state is justified.

This is how, even in Hobbes, the normative task is fulfilled. With Locke, it looks easier. Locke is much more explicitly justificatory. We have a more substantive natural law. As he puts it, 'the state of nature has a law of nature to govern it, which obliges every one: and reason, which is that law, teaches all mankind . . . that . . . no one ought to harm another in his life, health, liberty, or possessions' [*Second Treatise* Sec. 6]. So we here have a firm basis showing which actions are justified and which unjustified, a basis on which we can found justification for the state or particular parts of state activity. In Locke, the law of nature is also more clearly than in Hobbes the law of God. (Hobbes says as clearly as Locke that it is the law of God, but it is not so clear that he needs God to make it work.) So, with stronger law and more God, it would seem that Locke has better justification. However, just because Locke is more connected than Hobbes to the prevailing contemporary theological context means that his thought travels less well to our secular age. Justification is more obviously provided than in Hobbes, but it is justification that less obviously travels out of its context.

An example of how such transport may shed justification can be seen in its more modern use by the twentieth-century political

philosopher Robert Nozick. Nozick, in his *Anarchy, State, and Utopia*
aims (just like Hobbes and Locke before him) to provide a fundamental justification of the state against the alternative of anarchy. In his
early methodological section, entitled 'Political Philosophy', Nozick
outlines what would be required to justify the state. It would be to show
that the state 'would be superior even to this most favoured situation of
anarchy' by arising from it 'by a process involving no morally impermissible steps' [5]. Obviously to do this we need to know what a 'morally
impermissible step' is, and so Nozick states that 'moral philosophy sets
the background for, and boundaries of, political philosophy' [6].

Here we have justification in political philosophy as quite explicitly
applied ethics. First we have moral philosophy, and then we subsequently apply it to politics. However, if we are after fundamental justification, the justification provided by this will only be as secure as
its basis. Nozick himself notoriously starts the book with a dogmatic
moral claim ('individuals have rights, and there are things no person
or group may do to them . . .'), which he presents as if it were the moral
truth. Throughout the text, he reaches for the thought of Locke. It is
Locke who describes for him the moral law that bounds the best possible form of the (non-state) 'state of nature'; it is Locke who lays down
those rights that will determine whether we can get from this state of
nature to a state by a series of morally permissible steps (including a
natural right to punish); it is Locke who provides a 'proviso' on property acquisition. So the question is how or whether this reach for a
seventeenth-century thinker endows Nozick's text with authority.

In fact, or so it seems to me, in this case it merely produces problems.
For, as we have seen, rights as used by Locke come from a different
intellectual and argumentative context than the one that we (and, I
presume, Nozick) naturally occupy. Lockean rights describe parts of a
moral law that is given to us by God, breach of which he will punish, and
that he is entitled to impose on us because we are his 'creatures' (that
is, created by him). Without God, the whole thing works differently,
has a different (if any) justification, and cannot just be plugged into a
modern system of ideas to give it the necessary authority.

This is the obvious difficulty about Nozick. The route is meant to
be from a certainty about morality to enlightenment about politics,
and the obvious problem we have just discussed is why we should
be certain of the truth of a morality produced in quite a different

intellectual context. However there is also, I think, a more subtle difficulty. Seventeenth-century morality tends to be founded on the idea of law, and it also tends to be assumed (as we have seen certainly was by Locke) that law needs a law-giver who both makes the law and threatens punishment. So Locke's natural law owes its law-like status to God's will and God's punishing power. However, this means that as well as the obvious problem of only convincing those who believe in this divine legislator, there is the more subtle problem that the morality only works on the presupposition of ideas more at home in a political, than an individually ethical, context, ideas such as authority, law, and punishing power. In other words, we already need a kind of political understanding to gain our moral truths with which we are to construct the politics. So the seventeenth century seems a bad period to pick for persuasive examples if we approach the task with the presupposition that morals bounds politics, and that we have to start justification of the political with wholly unpolitical justificatory material.

Motivation

Hobbes's justification runs beneath both morals and politics, and its worth comes from something (naturally, both then and now) understood to be a good reason. Such prudential reasons as self-preservation are seen to be naturally motivating. However, here we now run into the next problem, and approach the third of the tasks of political philosophy I outlined at the beginning of the chapter, the task of motivation. In doing so, we run again into the problem of disentangling descriptions of motivation and evaluation of good reasons. To seek the means of survival is obviously motivating. So, or so it would seem, we have an account that neatly ties together the question of justification and motivation: it gives people an obvious and understandable reason for action to say that something saves their skin. Yet just because it is so obvious, once it is known, we expect it also to motivate and explain what they actually do. So, or so it might seem, with this material what I called the second task of justification will also accomplish the third task of motivation. However, I do not think that it is quite that simple. Modern games-theory reconstructions of Hobbes explain, if they work, what happens when a set of self-interested individuals act together in the same public space. They model Hobbes's claim that without a powerful punishing superior, people will (in prisoners' dilemma fashion) arrive at a sub-optimal outcome. This gives a reason for having the powerful, punishing Leviathan. However, notoriously and as we have seen, it does not provide an actual route by which the separate individuals can get from a state of nature to a state. It is a transition that (in their terms) is justified, and which they would also be motivated to follow if they thought that they could successfully accomplish it. However, as we saw, the same problems that lead to the drift to war in the state of nature bedevil any such attempt to get out of it. So we here have a justificatory story that is not at the same time a motivational story. The difference, again, comes from the distinction between the motivations of separate individuals and the explanation of what happens when they act as a group.

As was explained earlier, in utilitarian thinkers of the classic period, this account of motivations is sharply distinct from an account of the good. Explanation is distinct from motivation. The good legislator, aiming at the good, produces a justified system of laws. However, these laws work because they are followed by people motivated only by their own interest. The goodness these people produce is a wholly unintended consequence of their self-interested actions. Here we have a sharp and clear split between justification and explanation, and the question is whether any such split is possible in the seventeenth-century thinkers we have been considering. More particularly, the question is whether their similar accounts of self-interested motivation go with anything similar to utilitarian value theory.

Let us start with the similar account of motivation. Hobbes says 'of the voluntary acts of every man the object is some *good to himself*' [*Lev* 14.8]. Bentham says 'self-regarding interest is predominant over all other interests put together' [*Constitutional Code Rationale*, 1.2]. People cannot help but aim at their own good, and so we have an account of motivation. However, this same account of motivation occurs also in Locke. All voluntary action, he says in the *Essay*, originates from desire, and 'if it be further asked', he says, 'what 'tis moves *desire?*, I answer happiness and that alone' [2.21.41]. 'The pursuit of happiness' may be a phrase rendered memorable by the American Declaration of Independence, but it occurs several times in Locke's *Essay* [for example, 2.21.51]. Humans are animals who pursue happiness, and happiness is to be explained in terms of pleasure and pain.

'All passions', he says, 'are moved by things, only as they appear to be causes of pleasure and pain' [2.20.14]. We are here on the high road to utilitarianism. This part of the classic synthesis is the utilitarian theory of motivation, psychological hedonism. Humans seek pleasure and avoid pain. The ideas of pleasure and pain Locke (like Bentham after him) calls 'simple ideas' – that is, they are the fundamental atomistic building blocks out of which the complexes can be constructed and make sense of them.

So here we get explanation. We get an account of motivation that explains how people act. Hence the central importance of punishment for Locke. As we saw, Locke thought that there was no law without a law-giver, and no operation of the law-giver without the threat of punishment. By giving people self-interested motivations, we oblige them to do what is right. So punishment here (in its motivational aspect) works just as it does in Bentham. We need sanctions because we need motives to right action. With Locke, it is the divine legislator who threatens punishment; with Bentham, concentrating on humanity, a human legislator has to serve. In this respect, Locke does not, after all, seem so different from Hobbes. In both cases, it is the overwhelming power of God that does the work. The difference is that Locke is more sanguine about our being able to tell, by either reason or revelation, what God intends. Threatened punishment is no spur to action unless we know what we are threatened with.

So Locke's divine legislator works like Bentham's human legislator, stimulating people into right action by adding additional incentives of self interest to make them do their duty. God has, for Locke, 'by an inseparable connection joined virtue and public happiness together' [*Essay* 1.3.6], just the juncture that the later human legislator of Helvetius or Bentham was supposed to achieve. The result, as Locke puts it here, is that 'he may, out of interest as well as conviction, cry up that for sacred'. Make it in someone's interest, and then you will get them to do what you want.

General Theory of Value

This gets the account of motivation (or explanation of action), and also places the need for a legislator. Politics occupies the centre of normative space, even if most of the work is done by a divine rather than a human legislator. Yet, as Locke also observed (in a note he wrote in 1693), 'there be two parts of ethics, the one is the rule which men are generally in the right in...the other is the true motives to practise them' [PE 319]. We have the account of motivation, but there is more than this to ethics. There is also the general theory of value. For the classical utilitarian it is the greatest happiness of the greatest number. The question is whether this extra part can be provided by Locke or Hobbes.

In fact in both we tend instead to get an anti-realism about value. They both say that different people find happiness in different things. Hence different people will value different things. This extends, particularly in Locke, to whole societies. Different societies will have different words enforcing different customs. So the ancient philosophers could cry up what was *honestum* as well as what was useful. However, this is all customary, conventional. If we cut beneath these appearances to real, underlying, value, then what we discover is happiness. Happiness is what different people find in different things. Happiness is what is associated by different societies with different things. So happiness gives us the real, justifying, reasons for action. We may think of obligation as quite different from the pursuit of happiness; but it is Locke who can write of people that 'the inclination and tendency of their nature to happiness is an obligation and motive to them to take care not to mistake or miss it' [*Essay* 2.21.52]. That's what people do when they are rational. That is what people ought to do; that is to where the ties of obligation motivate them.

So we have happiness as justification as well as explanation. What more might be needed? Well, what more can the later utilitarians provide? We have with them also happiness. Here also happiness is understood as pleasure and absence of pain. Happiness is the single ultimate motivation; and we have the similar political project of a legislator who uses threats in order to build a properly functioning society. However, with the classical utilitarians, the proper normative end is general or universal happiness rather than individual happiness.

Could a similar substitution of the general for individual happiness be achieved in the century here being studied? One way to do it is to change the naturalistic, or descriptive, base. This is what Grotius had tried, pointing out people's natural sociability. It was also later tried by the British moral philosophers of the early eighteenth century, wishing to respond to Hobbes. This is what Hume did, showing (as a natural fact) that utility pleases, utility in general – that is, whoever's utility it is. This is what a proper account of human nature would show, and Hume had earlier written *A Treatise of Human Nature*. Before Hume (and referred to by him) were Hutcheson and Butler. In a note to the first of his *Sermons Preached in the Rolls Chapel*, Butler takes to task the mistakes made by someone 'writing a grave book upon *Human Nature*' and failing to account for 'benevolence or good will'. He is, in fact, referring explicitly to Hobbes' book *Human Nature* (the 1640 manuscript that we considered, but Butler is referring to its later unauthorised printing). Such a matter, says Butler, 'is a mere question of fact or natural history, not provable immediately by reason' [I 339n]. These are all purely descriptive accounts of human nature, aiming to establish by empirical rather than a priori means that people act in non-self-interested manner. We find as part of an experimentally based account of human nature that utility pleases, but it is the utility (happiness) of others as well as our own.

This is a reply to Hobbes if all there is to Hobbes is a descriptive account of human motivation. If, however, there is also a value theory, giving good reasons for action, then this refutation falls short. For questions of fact (or actual empirical accounts of motivation) are not all there is, or should be. On the other hand, it would be too quick a reply to these counter-examples to psychological hedonism to claim that these apparent examples of altruistic behaviour occur because of the pleasure they give to the agent. Locke, for example, remarks how the happiness of giving one's dinner to a starving man is a lasting pleasure that is much greater than the merely transitory pleasure of eating it [PE 319]. Without trivialisation, such reduction cannot be complete. People do sometimes behave altruistically. We can, if we wish, put this as that, for them (other people's) utility pleases. However, it is misleading to suppose that they therefore do it for the pleasure they get for themselves and hence that all such apparently altruistic action is really egoistic.

We might try this, but we need more than such a naturalistic gesture to gain this independent value. It is similarly too reductionist to suppose that people gain personal pleasure from the pursuit of general utility. For sometimes there are bound to be cases where personal and general happiness unfortunately fail to coincide. So to make general

happiness the right end of action, and to distinguish this as a normative (or justificatory) truth from empirical claims about human motivation, we need in some way to reach, or underwrite, the impartiality
that is implied in classic utilitarianism. We have to be able to see it
from no particular point of view, in which one person's happiness is
no more or less important than anyone else's. In other words, some
parts of the required content are given by these seventeenth-century
thinkers. For they associate the good with happiness, and happiness
with pleasure and the absence of pain. So they agree on what alone
can give meaning to goodness. However, as well as this similar content,
we have differences about distribution. The classical utilitarian distribution will not be given by principles of goodness that concentrate
on the good to the individual in pursuit of happiness. We need an independent perspective that sees all agents impartially. However, here
also there are seventeenth-century resources. For such a perspective
is what, in the seventeenth-century context we have been examining,
God can provide. From a God's eye perspective, the happiness of one
of his creatures is neither more nor less important than the happiness
of any other. God for Locke needs to threaten punishment to motivate. So much for the psychological hedonism, shared by the later
utilitarians, delineating what they both called the 'springs of action'.
However (in Locke's other part of ethics), God can also provide the
content of the moral law that he so motivates. And this content can be
put independently of any question of motivation or descriptive human
psychology. It takes this good and looks at it impartially. Even if God
needs to threaten us into action, the action that he threatens us into
is right independently of such threats.

It is from such an impartial perspective, for example, that the Lockean theory of property described in the last chapter can be worked out.
Enclosure is a good because it produces more utility, so Devonshire
is much more valuable than America. That is, it is justified, because
more good or utility arises. So greater goodness justifies, independent
of whose goodness it is. Locke's 'proviso' more specifically brings in
matters of distribution. People may seize land if 'enough and as good'
is left for others. That is, the happiness of the people without the land
has to be considered as well as the people with the land. It could be
put as a theory of mutual bargaining (in a hypothetical manner, since
Locke's claim is that he can give an account of property rights that

involve no actual agreements). It is what everyone would agree on, or it is only right if everyone were able to agree. As such, it differs from a pure theory of utility maximisation, which would permit the happiness of some to be sacrificed for the greater happiness of others. However, it is similar in its concern for distribution: it is the happiness of everyone rather than just the happiness of the individual agent that is being considered. Locke's story could be run either as mutual bargaining or as increase in general utility. However, either way, it involves an impartial perspective in which the happiness of each person is treated equally. Either way the justificatory force provided is more than could be provided by a descriptive account of how individuals pursue their own happiness.

There is one thinker of the time who quite explicitly took general happiness as the proper, justifying, aim. This is Richard Cumberland, an Englishman who wrote a Latin treatise on the laws of nature, *De Legibus Naturae*, in 1672. Cumberland's aim is to reply to Hobbes, showing that the rational aim is universal rather than individual good, that the 'common good' [*commune bonum*] is the 'supreme law'. More precisely, he wishes to show that it is a 'necessary truth' that everyone's happiness is best promoted by being joined with the happiness of others. This, however, for him does not depend upon a mere empirically observed correlation between the two (whether put together by God or Nature), nor the supposition that being good to others is a strategic good bet in advancing one's own interests. Cumberland is after a more ambitious, a priori proof, even if he leaves the details rather obscure.

This being the century it is (and the writer being on his way to becoming a bishop), God and God's punishments inevitably enter. The law-like status of the law of nature depends upon God's sanctions. However, its content does not depend upon God. In his fifth chapter, specifically on the law of nature, Cumberland claims that 'reason does not allow' that the good of any one individual should be the ultimate end for 'then there will be truly good actions opposed to each other, which is impossible' [V xvi]. In other words, not all the goods will be consistent, as different people compete in aiming at different things. This is an ambitious attempt to reduce such competition to absurdity ('an obvious contradiction'). However, it would be easily met by anyone thinking that the good was indeed plural, and so potentially conflicting, contradictory. It would also be met by anyone claiming (in more modern language) that the good was agent-relative, so that good-for-A does not contradict good-for-B, even if they are not capable of joint realisation.

So this suggestion need not trouble the Hobbesian war of all against all in the state of nature (although it may require us to be careful about our understanding of the good in which it can be stated). However, another claim Cumberland makes some sections later is more pregnant with future possibilities. This is that the common good is the only end 'in the pursuit of which all can agree [*consentire*]' [V 46], and that it is therefore from 'common rational nature' that we should all seek the common good. At first this may look just like the social nature cited by Grotius or Butler. However, the addition here is that this comes from reason. As we have seen, throughout the century reason is taken to be the foundation of natural law. This reason is common reason – that is, reason that people use in discussion and in terms of which they have to agree. It is the reason by which they can reach common conclusions. The quite plausible suggestion Cumberland makes here is that there will only be such agreement about things whose goodness is general or common. We will agree only about those things where the goodness of one person is not purchased at the expense of harm for someone else.

We have here the beginnings of a contracturalist method (as it would now be called): we discover the good by discovering those things into which everyone could contract. We use the idea of possible agreement (consent, *consentire*) as a method of discovery of the good. And, as we have seen, the connection of obligation with will that is implied in consent, as well as the prevalence of the social contract justification of the state, have been prominent features of the century. Let us now therefore conclude this study by coming back to this for a final time, but now from the direction of the foundations of morals at which we have just been looking.

Take as an example the golden rule (do unto others as you would that they do unto you), which aims at the common, rather than individual, happiness, and yet which was centrally supported by Hobbes. It is also firmly held by Locke, 'a most unshakeable rule of morality and foundation of all social virtue' he calls it in the *Essay concerning human understanding* [1.3.4]. But why should we do it? We have, as we have seen, the possible punishments of God, whose rule it is. However, at times, Locke proposes it as a good rule of conduct, independently of God. In the note he wrote for himself in 1692 and called 'Ethica A', he observes 'if then happiness be our interest, end, and business, 'tis evident the way to it is to love our neighbour as ourself, for by that means we enlarge and secure our pleasures' [PE 319]. Locke adds some details (this is one of the appearances of his observation that we gain more pleasure giving our dinner to a starving man than eating it ourselves), but the general strategy is clear. We are prudential beings, whose 'business' it is to seek our own happiness; however, it turns out to be a strategic good bet to do so by also promoting the happiness of others. This may or may not be so, and showing that it is in our interests to be 'moral' has been attempted many times since the ancient world. However, put like this, it is an empirical proof that is at the mercy of the facts. Once people discover that they gain more pleasure from eating their own dinners rather than passing them on to the teeming underfed of the world, then there is nothing in such an argument that could touch them.

At first sight, this may seem also to have been Hobbes's answer. We have the same self-interested basis, which is taken to be stipulative as to what counts as 'rational'. Prudence is king, but an attempt is made to enlighten prudence and thereby deliver the 'laws of nature'. So these traditional laws, including the golden rule, will be shown by the great student of the theorems of practical reason, Thomas Hobbes, to follow from a proper study of such self-saving self-interest. Keep peace, if you wish to survive; follow the golden rule if you want to be smart about your own good.

So at first sight it may seem to be the same strategy. However, this forgets the hypothetical nature of Hobbes's law of nature when we are in the state of nature. For it is only rational for us to observe this law if we have reasonable expectation that others will as well. Of course, I ought to keep my promises (it is ultimately a good deal for me), but only if I can reasonably expect that others will as well (that I can rely on my payoff). Hence in Hobbes the need for the state, the need for a power that is sufficiently formidable to compel others to keep their agreements. In other words, we need politics (the *polis*, the state). It is a political solution to a moral problem. Recapping: we have a moral question or problem (why we should do good to others). We partly answer it by showing that it is in line with what we rationally do (doing good to ourselves), but we only get it in line by having a powerful, threatening, state (politics). The first self-interested thing we do is get ourselves out of the state of nature, and then once we have done that, the law of nature declares and enforces itself (for it now becomes the law of the resultant 'commonwealth' and its 'sovereign'). This is just the familiar story of the Hobbesian social contract, but the point is that a political move has here been added to reach a solution at which Locke was merely waving. This is, again, true of the content of the natural law. As we saw, Locke thought that it was 'plain and intelligible' in a non-state situation, but that nevertheless it takes the state for it to be 'established, settled, known' [*Second Treatise* Sec. 124]. Locke looks here as if he is trying to have it both ways. Hobbes again is much clearer: determinacy of content comes only with the commonwealth.

So what we get in Hobbes are political solutions to moral (that is, prudential) problems. Only with the state are we secure, yet security is our natural aim. Our natural, rational, aim. For, as I said, all these thinkers, including Hobbes, are concerned with justification. They are not only concerned with the descriptive facts about what actually happens; they are also concerned with how it ought to be. Here it is worth remembering again the two ways in which the social contract story can be told, at least as I gave it. We can try it as a story about an actual movement in which self-interested, individual, players reach a state. Here we are at the mercy of all the games-theoretic problems in such accounts (it may be a good play for them each to make agreements, but why should they keep them?). However, as I suggested, it can also be used as a justificatory account, showing what is good for people. For Hobbes, it is good for each person to be in a state. If they happen to be in a state (for example under the rule of good King Charles), then it would be a bad thing to get out of it (to fall into civil war). The good is shown by what all could contract into, a contracturalist account of the shape we have just seen. However, in this case, the contracturalist account does not deliver the good directly. Instead, it delivers the state, which in turn delivers the good. Hence it is a political solution to a moral problem.

In this way, political theory (political philosophy) is an essential part of general moral theory, not merely an adjunct or extension of it. We started the century I have been examining with confusion. This was partly political confusion, in a century of civil conflict and war. The removal of kings and other governors produced what was called in *Macbeth* (and my title) 'confusion's masterpiece'. However, as I showed, it was not only political confusion. The intellectual resources that could be used to explain, clarify, and (at least in intellectual terms) resolve these conflicts were themselves in a deeply confused condition. There was no text, sacred or otherwise, to which people could unproblematically reach in order to restore conceptual clarity and order. So we have, or need, the reach to reason itself. We need a natural law, which will speak to people's rationality as such, independently of book or Bible. However, in a deeply sceptical age, this basis of rational morality was itself confused, disordered, unavailable. Hence the construction of a new natural law by the intellectual giants of the period. Hence the masterpieces of foundation and clarification that we have been considering. And the greatest of these place politics as an essential part of the solution of these moral and intellectual conflicts.

Book Notes

Introduction

The writings and speeches of King James can be found in *King James VI and I: Political Writings*, edited by Johann Sommerville (Cambridge: Cambridge University Press, 1994).

Chapter 1

Grotius, Hobbes, and Locke are dealt with more fully later. Locke's early lectures have been published (with Latin text and facing English translation) by W von Leyden as *Essays on the Law of Nature* (Oxford: Oxford University Press, 1954). The English translation of this edition is included in the much more recent John Locke *Political Essays*, edited by Mark Goldie (Cambridge: Cambridge University Press, 1997).

John Ponet's *Short Treatise of Politic Power* is reprinted in a facsimile edition of the original 1556 edition in Winthrop Hudson, *John Ponet* (Chicago: University of Chicago Press, 1942). There are several editions of Hooker, but the chapter discussed is included in the extract from *Of the Laws of Ecclesiastical Polity*, edited by A S McGrade (Cambridge: Cambridge University Press, 1989). This is from the series of *Cambridge Texts in the History of Political Thought*, which includes the Locke just mentioned as well as the work of several other people touched in passing in this chapter – for example, Milton (John Milton

Political Writings 1991); Knox (John Knox *On Rebellion*, 1994); and Bodin (Jean Bodin *On Sovereignty: Four Chapters from the Six Books of the Commonwealth* 1992). Also in this series is a small volume with useful translations of both Luther and Calvin (*Luther and Calvin On Secular Authority*, edited by Harro Hopfl, 1991). This has a Luther tract of 1523, *On Secular Authority* (*Von Weltlicher Oberkeit*), and the chapter on civil government from Calvin's *Institutes* (IV 20), translated from the Latin 1559 edition. I have also quoted from the translation of the complete *Institutes* by F L Battles (London: SCM Press, 1960).

In Cicero, the quotations are from the *Tusculan Disputations*, *De Re Publica*, and *De Legibus*. The allusion to Cicero's idea that universal consensus shows something to be innate is to *De Natura Deorum* I, 17. 'ST' in quotations from Aquinas refers to his *Summa Theologiae*. The main block of this on law is questions 90–97 of the first half of the second part (*prima secundae*, abbreviated as '1a2ae.'). These questions can be found in Volume 28 of the Blackfriars edition of the *Summa Theologiae*, edited by Thomas Gilby, 1966 (with Latin text and facing English translation). There is an earlier *Selected Political Writings* of Aquinas, also with Latin text and facing English, which reprints some of this, edited by A P D'Entreves (Oxford: Blackwell, 1948).

The parliamentary acts quoted can be found in G R Elton (ed.), *The Tudor Constitution*, which is a collection of documents (Cambridge: Cambridge University Press, 1960). The *Exhortation Concerning Good Order, and Obedience to Rulers and Magistrates* is usually thought to have been written by Cranmer, and is part of the official *Homilies* of the Church of England (declared to contain 'godly and wholesome doctrine' in Article 35 of the Anglican *Articles of Religion*).

The translation of Montaigne's *Essays* used is that of E J Trechmann (Oxford: Oxford University Press, 1935) and that of Charron is the early seventeenth-century translation by Samson Lennard.

Obviously this chapter contains a rapid, rather impressionistic sketch of some of what was going on before my main players enter the stage. Reader wanting a fuller (and much more authoritative) account should consult the two-volume work, *The Foundations of Modern Political Thought* by Quentin Skinner (Cambridge: Cambridge University Press,

1978). Volume 2 of this ('The Age of Reformation') is about Luther, Cavin, and the resistance theories developed by both their followers and their Catholic rivals.

Chapters 2–4 (Hobbes)

The writing and titles of Hobbes's main works are explained in the chapter. The editions I quote from and use, my abbreviations, and my reference systems are as follows:

['*Elements*']   *The Elements of law Natural and Politic*, edited with an introduction by J C A Gaskin (Oxford: Oxford University Press, 1994). This is cited by chapter and section number.

['*De Cive*']   *Elementa Philosophica de Cive*. A critical edition by Howard Warrender, Oxford: Oxford University Press, 1983. This is the Latin text used, cited by chapter and section number. For the English translation, I have used *On the Citizen*, edited and translated by Richard Tuck and Michael Silverthorne (Cambridge: Cambridge University Press, 1998).

['*Lev*']   I have used two editions of *Leviathan*, that edited by Richard Tuck (Cambridge: Cambridge University Press, 1991) and that edited by Edwin Curley (Indianapolis: Hackett, 1994). Tuck reproduces what he takes to be his best guess at the original (working with various first editions). Curley notes the principal changes in the Latin Leviathan, and translates additional material (such as the appendices) from the Latin Leviathan. Like Curley, I have modernised the capitalisation and punctuation, but otherwise I do not think that these two versions differ in anything I quote here. The new Oxford edition of Hobbes has not yet (2002) reached *Leviathan*; when it does, there will be a full, modern, variorum edition. The Latin text of this late (1668) work by Hobbes can be found in Volume 3 of the nineteenth-century edition of Hobbes's Latin works, edited by W Molesworth. Unfortunately, Hobbes does not use the chapter and section system of reference in *Leviathan* he uses elsewhere, which permits easy cross-reference between various editions. So I have used a double-reference system, which should aid cross-reference. I refer to it in the form [12.1, p. 52], where the first reference is chapter.section, except that the section numbers are not in the original, nor therefore in most editions [they are in Curley]. The page number reference is to the Head first edition of 1651, since it is sometimes given in modern editions (for example, by Tuck, and less precisely by Curley).

Some of the background to these three central works of Hobbes's political theory is in other works he wrote. His early translation of Thucydides has been republished as *Hobbes's Thucydides*, edited by Richard Schlatter (New Brunswick, NJ: Rutgers University Press, 1975). In 1642, shortly after his flight to France, Hobbes wrote a lengthy Latin criticism of a contemporary work that contains a first account of his scientific interests. This has now been translated from the MSS in Paris, first into French and then English (*Thomas White's De Mundo Examined*, Bradford: Bradford University Press, 1976). The final treatment, *De Corpore* has not, I think, been fully translated into English; some of it is in Thomas Hobbes, *Metaphysical Writings* (LaSalle, IL: Open Court, 1905; 1989) and some in the J C A Gaskin edition of the *Elements*, described earlier. *De Homine* is translated in Thomas Hobbes, *Man and Citizen*, edited and introduced by Bernard Gert (New York: Doubleday, 1972). As the title suggests, this also contains the seventeenth-century translation of *De Cive*, which was thought until recently to be by Hobbes himself; it was therefore also the one used by Oxford in its *Collected Works* volume (as *De Cive English Version*, edited by H Warrender, 1983). As I said earlier, I have preferred to use the recent Cambridge translation.

The original Latin of Hobbes's triple account of body, man, and citizen can be found in the Nineteenth Century *Latin Works*, Vols. 1 and 2. As well as this five-volume Latin Works (London: Longman, 1839–45), Sir W Molesworth also edited an eleven-volume *English Works*. Both contain extensive material on geometry and optics. The *English Works* also reprints a controversy about free will that Hobbes engaged in with Bramhall in the 1650s. Some of this has been recently reprinted as *Hobbes and Bramhall on Liberty and Necessity*, edited by Vere Chappell (Cambridge: Cambridge University Press, 1999).

Of the later work that Hobbes was not allowed to publish in his lifetime, his history of the civil war, *Behemoth*, was edited in the late

nineteenth century by Tonnies, and this edition has been republished with an introduction by Stephen Holmes (Chicago: University
of Chicago Press, 1990). His *Dialogue Between a Philosopher and a Student
of the Common Laws of England* has also been produced by the University of Chicago Press (edited and introduced by Joseph Cropsey,
1971). There is a magisterial edition of Hobbes's complete correspondence, edited by Noel Malcolm, as part of the new Oxford *Collected
Works* (Oxford: Oxford University Press, 1994). (Although this pro-
jected new 'collected works' has now been referred to twice, in fact no
works beyond these this and *De Cive* were collected by the end of the
twentieth century.).

I refer in the main text to contemporary criticism of Hobbes. Four
contemporary responses (Filmer, Lawson, Bramhall, Clarendon) have
been republished as *Leviathan, Contemporary Responses to the Political
Philosophy of Thomas Hobbes*, edited and introduced by G A J Rogers
(Bristol: Thoemmes Press, 1995).

There is, as might be expected, an enormous quantity of secondary
literature. I have used and been influenced by the writings of Richard
Tuck. He has introductions to the recent Cambridge texts (1991, 1998,
Leviathan, De Cive) and a short Past Masters treatment, *Hobbes* (Oxford:
Oxford University Press, 1989). However, there is more about Hobbes,
in the context of Grotius and others, in his *Philosophy and Government 1572–1651* (Cambridge: Cambridge University Press, 1993). A. P.
Martinich's *The Two Gods of Leviathan* (Cambridge: Cambridge University Press, 1992) argues for the importance of God in Hobbes's thought,
and, as such, renovates what used to be called the Taylor-Warrender
thesis – namely, that Hobbes had a traditional conception of natural
law upheld by God. Warrender's case can be found in *The political philosophy of Thomas Hobbes* (Oxford: Oxford University Press, 1957). Useful
aspects of this old dispute, and other leading papers of that time, can be
found in K. C. Brown, editor, *Hobbes Studies* (Oxford: Blackwell, 1965).
A more recent collection, with full awareness of history, is *Perspectives
on Thomas Hobbes*, edited by G A J Rogers and Alan Ryan (Oxford:
Oxford University Press, 1988). The Cambridge *Companion* to Hobbes,
edited by Tom Sorrell (Cambridge: Cambridge University Press, 1996)
has Tuck on the moral philosophy and Alan Ryan on the political

philosophy. It has a 'summary biography' by Noel Malcolm, and A P
Martinich has written a recent book-length biography, *Hobbes, A Biography* (Cambridge: Cambridge University Press, 1999); for biography,
Malcolm's notes to the *Correspondence* are also helpful.

The transformation of Hobbes' thought into modern games theory
was started by David Gauthier in *The Logic of Leviathan* (Oxford: Oxford
University Press, 1969) and then developed by Gregory Kavka in *Hobbesian Moral and Political Philosophy* (Princeton: Princeton University
Press, 1986) and, especially, Jean Hampton in *Hobbes and the Social Contract tradition* (Cambridge: Cambridge University Press, 1986), which
models aspects of the thought as various kinds of games. Hobbes is
also discussed extensively (including the 'foole') in David Gauthier's
analogous attempt to found ethics on games theory, *Morals by Agreement* (Oxford: Oxford University Press, 1986), although this does not
discuss politics. Other treatments of the thought are A P Martinich,
Thomas Hobbes (New York: Macmillan, 1997), Tom Sorrell *Hobbes* (New
York: Routledge, 1986), D D Raphael, *Hobbes* (London: George Allen
and Unwin, 1977), and (of a quite different character) Leo Strauss, *The
Political Philosophy of Thomas Hobbes* (Chicago: University of Chicago
Press, 1952). The Marxist treatment of Hobbes (and Locke) in C B
McPherson, *The Political Philosophy of Possessive Individualism* (Oxford:
Oxford University Press, 1962) has been so often and so thoroughly
refuted that I suppose it may now be considered to have departed from
the intellectual map. Quentin Skinner's *Reason and Rhetoric in the Philosophy of Hobbes* (Cambridge: Cambridge University Press, 1996), situates
Hobbes's thought in the history of rhetoric for the period, and argues
for much greater differences between the content of Hobbes's different books, arising from their different styles and languages, than I
assume in my treatment.

Chapter 5 (Grotius and Pufendorf)

Grotius and Pufendorf texts
Many of these works, in both original and translation, are in the series
Classics in International Law produced by Oxford University Press in
the 1920s. *De Jure Belli ac Pacis* is translated in this series by Francis
W Kelsey, and this translation appeared in 1925.

For Pufendorf in this series, we have: *Elementorum Jurisprudentiae Universalis*, translation here by W A Oldfather, 1931; *De Jure Naturae et Gentium*, translation by C H and W A Oldfather, 1934; *De Officio Hominis et Civis juxta Legem Naturalem*, translation by Frank Gardner Moore, 1927.

Outside this series, there is an edition of Grotius's *Mare Liberum* with Latin text and facing English translation by Ralph van Deman Magoffin (New York: Oxford University Press, 1916). There is also a useful edition of a paper, 'De Statu Hominum Naturali' (*On the Natural State of Men*), which Pufendorf wrote in defence of his views, with Latin text, translation, and introduction by Michael Seidler (Edwin Mellen Press, Lampeter, 1990).

Of other translations, or more accessible editions, the eighteenth-century translations of both Grotius and Pufendorf by Basil Kennet read much better than any twentieth-century version and (at least for the large works) may well be as accessible as the 1920s versions. There is also a nineteenth-century edition of Grotius's DJBP with full Latin text and abbreviated translation at the foot of the page by William Whewell (Cambridge, 1853; he does not translate Grotius's copious quotations from other works). More recently, the *Prolegomena* to Grotius' DJBP (in the Kelsey translation) is a separate paperback in the Bobbs-Merrill *Library of Liberal Arts*, Indianapolis (1957); *The Political Writings of Samuel Pufendorf* (Oxford: Oxford University Press, 1994), which contains an abbreviated translation of EJU as well as a highly abbreviated translation of DJNG; and *Of the Duty of Man and Citizen* (Cambridge: Cambridge University Press, edited by James Tully and translated by Michael Silverthorne, 1991), which is a full translation of Pufendorf's DO.

Chapters 6–8 (Locke)

The main text is the *Two Treatises of Government*, and the standard edition of this is that of P. Laslett (Cambridge: Cambridge University Press, 1967). Quotations are from this, using all Locke's words but modernising capitalisation, emphasis, and punctuation. The works on toleration as a whole (that is, with the *Second Letter for Toleration* and the *Third Letter*) can only be found in the eighteenth- or nineteenth-century *Works*, where they form Volume 6. However, there is a convenient modern edition of the main letter, with critical articles, in *John Locke: A Letter Concerning Toleration in Focus*, edited by J Horton and S. Mendus (London: Routledge, 1991). Similarly, the *Reasonableness of Christianity*, with its *Vindication* and *Second Vindication*, is to be found in Volume 7 of the *Works*. My page references are to the 1823 edition, but the pagination seems to be the same as in the 1794 edition, which has recently been produced in a facsimile edition by Thoemmes Press, Bristol (1997). Locke's early *Essays on the Law of Nature*, together with two early *Tracts on Government* and many entries from his notebooks relating to political philosophy, ethics, and toleration, are collected together in Mark Goldie, editor, *Political Essays* (Cambridge: Cambridge University Press 1997). [An earlier edition of the *Essays on the Law of Nature*, edited by W. Von Leyden, with Latin text and facing English translation is Oxford: Oxford University Press, 1954.] Filmer's works (the target of Locke's criticism) can be found in Johann Sommerville, editor, *Patriarcha and Other Writings* (Cambridge: Cambridge University Press, 1991).

On the secondary material, Hume's essay, 'Of the Original Contract' originally appeared in his *Three Essays, Moral and Political* in 1748, and is here quoted from David Hume, *Essays Moral, Political, and Literary*, edited by Eugene Miller (an edition with variant readings (Indianapolis: Liberty Classics, 1987). Of more modern secondary material, the study by John Dunn, *The Political Thought of John Locke* (Cambridge: Cambridge University Press, 1969) has worn well. In particular, the importance of Locke's religious thought for his political theory is coming back again, and can be seen in such recent commentary as John Marshall, *John Locke: Resistance, Religion and Responsibility* (Cambridge: Cambridge University Press 1994). The political background and Locke's own seditious activities are described in Richard Ashcraft *Revolutionary Politics and Locke's Two Treatises of Government* (Princeton: Princeton University Press 1986). Ashcraft also has a more textual study, *Locke's Two Treatises of Government* (London: Allen and Unwin, 1987). There is a good first account of the *Second Treatise* in D. Lloyd Thomas, *Locke on Government* (London: Routledge, 1995). On property, a main work is James Tully *A Discourse on Property* (Cambridge:

Cambridge University Press, 1980), which is, however, firmly criticised in Jeremy Waldron *The Right to Private Property* (Oxford: Oxford University Press, 1988). Tully also has a more recent collection, *An Approach to Political Philosophy: Locke in Contexts* (Cambridge: Cambridge University Press, 1993), which contains some reply, and is also interesting on the American aspects of Locke's thought, for which there was no space in my text. The best current studies of both this and other aspects of Locke's thought are the two books by A. John Simmons, *On the Edge of Anarchy* (Princeton: Princeton University Press 1993), which is on consent and political obligation, and *The Lockean Theory of Rights* (Princeton: Princeton University Press 1992).

Chapter 9

Butler's note is to the first of his *Fifteen Sermons Preached in the Rolls Chapel*, first printed in 1726. The quotation given in the text is from it as reprinted in D.D. Raphael, editor, *British Moralists 1650–1800* (Oxford: Oxford University Press, 1969). The reference given is to the Raphael volume and page number. Raphael also reprints selections from Richard Cumberland, *De Legibus Naturae*, in the original Latin with a facing English translation by Raphael himself. Quotations here are from this edition (although with reference to Cumberland's chapter and section numbers). Another translation of selections from Cumberland can be found in J B Schneewind, editor, *Moral Philosophy from Montaigne to Kant*, Vol. I (Cambridge: Cambridge University Press, 1990). This uses a 1727 English translation (Cumberland was translated into both English and French in this century; earlier, Pufendorf used him as well as Hobbes in his expositions of natural law). The quotation from Nietzsche is the initial twelfth maxim in the *Twilight of the Idols* (here as translated by R.J. Hollingdale (London: *Penguin Books*, 1968); the reference to Mill's 'offensive clarity' is on p. 67 of the Hollingdale translation. Adam Smith's *The Theory of Moral Sentiments* is in an authoritative edition edited by D D Raphael and A L Macfie (Oxford: Oxford University Press, 1976).

Index

["Hobbes" and "Locke" are indexed only by key topics; the Book Notes are not indexed]

277

Lightning Source UK Ltd.
Milton Keynes UK
UKOW04f0908031217
313777UK00001B/24/P